# Southern West Cameroon Revisited
## Volume Two
## North-South West Nexus 1858-1972

## Anthony Ndi

*Langaa Research & Publishing CIG*
*Mankon, Bamenda*

*Publisher:*
*Langaa* RPCIG
Langaa Research & Publishing Common Initiative Group
P.O. Box 902 Mankon
Bamenda
North West Region
Cameroon
Langaagrp@gmail.com
www.langaa-rpcig.net

Distributed in and outside N. America by African Books Collective
orders@africanbookscollective.com
www.africanbookcollective.com

*ISBN: 9956-791-32-6*

© Anthony Ndi 2014

DISCLAIMER
All views expressed in this publication are those of the author and do not necessarily reflect the views of Langaa RPCIG.

*To the unsung patriots and heroes, whose names are enshrined in these pages, that the eternal ideals for which they burnt out their lives may remain radiant beacons for Cameroon posterity.*

# About this Book

This book argues that Southern Cameroons up to the late 1960s had extensively developed an evolved mature, political culture. It was amazingly led by a range of: simple, visionary, austere, honest, peace-loving and realistic leaders, almost without exception; vintage products of their epoch. Distinguished by good governance; throughout it organized frequent free, fair and transparent elections, peaceful handover of power and enjoyed free primary and adult education. It was further crowned with an ideal, efficient civil service, literally, corruption free. In fact, the period, 1955-1968 in the history of Southern Cameroons qualifies as a "Golden Age" for that nostalgic state, whose citizens were repeatedly referred to as "nice, peace loving, loyal, good and hospitable people" by administrators, missionaries, visitors and those who got to know them closely. The most remarkable observation however, was that finally made by Malcolm Milne, the greatest critic, who noted that during his last couple of years in the Southern Cameroons administration, he dealt with: "People of high intelligence who knew exactly what they wanted." Of the civil servants, he maintains that they had greatly enriched his time in the colonial service; "There was something very special about that corps; their service was their watch word." This superlative description by Malcolm Milne was being made of a combination of the people of the present North and South West Regions, whom he saw as a socio-cultural, economic and political unit. It is therefore obvious that from 1955 - 1968, Southern West Cameroon came close towards becoming an ideal state.

# Praise for this Book

"In his new work, Anthony Ndi bombards us with exciting new revelations about the events leading up to the reunification of Cameroon and beyond. What counts for many still today as a tragic historical memory, is given substance and cause in his careful analysis of the sources available, now reinforced by new materials released since 2012 from the archives of the UK Foreign Commonwealth Office. Ndi's focus on the personalities of the major players leading to the breaking of the promise made by the British to support independence for Southern Cameroons and the subsequent plebiscite decision to re-join La République du Cameroun, enriches our understanding of the mixture of shrewd tactics by and naive blunders of the many that actually shaped events. As a case study in the realities of how decisions were made and later regretted in a period of quite shameful indiscretion, we are given a salutary account of how a history that hitherto had been written from the standpoint of the victor, needed to be and here is rewritten from that of the vanquished."

**Michael Rowlands, Emeritus Professor of Anthropology and Material Culture, University College London**

"A monumental treatise with startling revelation on Cameroons' national history, written with superb confidence suitable in the circumstance of celebrations marking the Golden Jubilee of Southern Cameroons independence- mature times enough for the inescapable traps of its history to be unveiled and unleashed for posterity."

**Professor Tafah Edokat Oki Edward, Vice Chancellor, University of Bamenda**

"Writing a foreword to a book written by a luminous historiographer like Anthony Ndi can be exciting and challenging. Exciting because it gives on the opportunity to discover new facts and appreciate new techniques in the state of the art of historiography. In the same instance, presenting a foreword to a study of this calibre is challenging.

Challenging because the historical plot espoused by the author resides in a setting of controversies where the tension between the force of argument and the argument of force seem to be conspicuously evident and where rhetoric and reality stand astride"

**Mathew Basung Gwanfogbe, PhD, Associate Professor of History, University of Bamenda.**

"This book by Anthony Ndi argues forcefully and convincingly that Ahidjo's 'bad faith' and determination to introduce a centralized personal authoritarian rule largely explains the failure of the Federal Republic of Cameroon… without a fair trial period"

**Professor Tazoacha Asonganyi, University of Yaounde I**

## About the Author

**Anthony Ndi** pursued Bed(Hons) History at the University of Ibadan, Nigeria, and proceeded to the School of Oriental and African Studies (SOAS), University of London for the MA and PhD in African History, He was the Registrar and Head of the History Department at the Bamenda University of Science and Technology (BUST) for eight years and currently is the Deputy Vice Chancellor for Research and Cooperation and Head of the History Department in the Catholic University of Cameroon (CATUC), Bamenda. He is Visiting Lecturer at the Universities of Buea and Bamenda. Anthony Ndi is Associate Professor of History and has published numerous articles and books. He belongs to several professional history and related associations and currently is Associate Editor of *Pan-Tikar Journal of History* of the University of Bamenda. He has a passion for historical research.

# Table of Contents

Preface..................................................................................ix
Acknowledgements...............................................................xi
Lists of Photographs, Maps & Illustrations......................xiii
Abbreviations......................................................................xv

## Chapter 1: Independence and Reunification: An Analysis of Basic Issues    1
A Historical Panorama............................................................1
Double British Standards........................................................4
The Paradox...........................................................................8
Southern Cameroons refused independence.........................9
Nature, Reason and shape of Reaction................................12
Milne's Revelations Revolutionize Cameroon History........15

## Chapter 2: Grassland, Forest and Coast........................25
"Switzerland of Africa"..........................................................25
Friends and Neighbours........................................................29
Endeley and Foncha: Grassland and Forest.........................32
Evidence on Record: Building Bridges.................................36
The Reality: Undiluted loyalty to Endeley...........................38
German Legacy: Quest for Robust 'Native Labour'..............46
Bali-German Hegemony and Brutality................................51
Incredible savagery: Depopulation of vassal villages..........52
Haemorrhage and Demographic imbalance.......................56
Of Public Apologies: J.N. Foncha and S.T. Muna...............58
Open Tribute to Founders and Donors................................61

## Chapter 3: North and South West: Factors in Reunification......................................................................66
A Case of Identity.................................................................66
Charles Assale: Painful Truth and Arrogance......................70
Suppressed Rebellion and the Federal National Assembly, 1972....................................................................73
Return to Legality, Reason and Hope..................................74

Durable Tangible and Intangible Bonds............................ 76
The World: A Global Village........................................... 78
The Kingdom of Belgium and Others............................... 79
Anglophones could not have voted for Self-Annihilation.......... 81
Evolution of Southern Cameroons: Basic Mile Posts.............. 82
Partition of German Kamerun....................................... 83
Condominium League of Nation Mandates....................... 83
UN Trusteeship Period: 1946-60/61................................ 87
The Rise of Nationalism.............................................. 88
Role of Native Authorities............................................ 90
French Policy of Assimilation........................................ 91
Policies: Socio-Economic and Political............................ 93
Seeding Reunification................................................. 94
Southern Cameroonian Roots: Victoria Colony (1858-1886)...... 95
Alfred Saker's Hinterland Vision..................................... 101
A broad Conclusion................................................... 103

**Chapter Four: Southern Cameroons: Political Maturity...... 105**
An Evolved Political Crisis........................................... 105
Qualifications and Political Leadership............................ 108
Distinct Southern Cameroons Political Culture.................... 115
Peaceful, Harmonious Transfer of Power in 1959................. 116
The Sagacity of Traditional Rulers................................. 117
High Calibre Political Leaders: Products of their Time............ 118
"Maquizzards," Rebels, Nationalists, or Freedom Fighters........ 122
"Jocular" Not Bloody fights......................................... 126
Political Leaders: Past, Present and Global........................ 127
Visionary Leaders: Simple, Austere, Honest and Realistic.......... 130
Malcolm Milne pays glowing tribute to Foncha Cabinet........... 131
A unique Southern Cameroons Civil Service....................... 132
Cameroonisation..................................................... 134

**Chapter 5: President Ahidjo: Alpha and Omega............... 139**
A larger than life French Creation................................... 139
Ahidjo: Solid steps towards a Federal Constitution................ 142
Work of joint Federal Constitution Committee..................... 144
Geopolitical Contradictions: Federal Inspectorates................ 147

Emergency Laws: Opposition Leaders Jailed........................ 153
The Ebolowa UC Congress, 1962...................................... 156
Deceit, Falsehood and Terror............................................157
The Unitary State Already Envisaged in 1964!..................... 159
Subverting the KNDP, "Unitary Group" Partner....................161
Attempted Reformers within the UC-KNDP Unity Group........ 163
The CUC................................................................... 165
Formation of the Cameroon National Union (CNU)............... 168
Proof: CUC First to Fuse with UC..................................... 173
Inexplicable Absence of the "Ahidjo Factor"........................ 175
Malcolm Milne and President Ahidjo.................................. 177
Conclusion.................................................................178

**Postscript**............................................................... **181**
**Historiography**.........................................................**189**
**Epilogue**................................................................ **195**
**Appendices (I-VI)**.................................................... **212**
**Bibliography**........................................................... **243**
**Index**....................................................................**245**

# Preface

## Historiography and Truth

As I read in the post script of this work "Isolated facts in history make no sense. They must be seen in the context of place, time and circumstance." I understand from this that there is a certain unity in history or that all history constitutes a whole. This brings to mind an important statement of the Second Vatican Council on the subject. The Council stated:

> "The accelerated pace of history is such that one can scarcely keep abreast of it. The destiny of the human race is viewed as a complete whole, no longer, as it were, in the particular histories of various peoples: now it merges into a complete whole." (Vatican II, GaudiumetSpes, no. 5)

It becomes imperative for me to ask after the underlying element that makes for the unity in history or for the wholeness of history. It is obvious that beneath all that changes there is much that is unchanging. Apparently, I do not have to go far to find what makes for the wholeness or unifying factor in history as I read in the same post script: "It is for this reason that anything classified as history or as historical should of necessity be credible, a reference point for posterity, clarifying doubts and placing people and events in their correct and proper perspectives." Our historiographer is therefore saying that what is classified as history or historical must be what is true. It is the truth that is that unifying factor in history or that makes for wholeness in history. Ultimately, there can be only one Truth. Whatever is true in any other context including the historical is a participation in that one Truth.

In this sense, the historiographer does not make or create history when he/she writes. This is in the direct sense but his work could become history especially when it comes into consideration eventually by others. The historiographer presents, analyses, interprets the history that is already there. The historiographer must therefore consider his task, even when he seeks to communicate knowledge as essentially the communication of truth. In this way the task of the historiographer is fundamentally transformed into a unique participation in communicating and witnessing to the truth. He must guide is readers beyond his mere words to the heart of total Truth. This is certainly delicate but it can and has been done. In my humble reckoning this is what Dr. Anthony NDI has attempted to do in this historiographical work. Far from being a historiographer (in the strict sense of the term) myself though with some familiarity in the theology of history, his effort is certainly one to be recommended.

Let me conclude these few lines by referring to an appreciation of the dignity of the human intellect and truth by the Second Vatican Council. In many ways, this suggests how the historiographer could carry out his delicate task:

> "Man, as sharing in the light of the divine mind, rightly affirms that by his intellect he surpasses the world of mere things. By diligent use of his talents through the ages he has indeed made progress in the empirical sciences, in technology, and in the liberal arts. In our time his attempts to search out the secrets of the material universe and to bring it under his control have been extremely successful. Yet he has always looked for, and found, truths of a higher order. For his intellect is not confined to the range of what can be observed by the senses. It can, with genuine certainty, reach to realities known only to the mind, even though, as a result of sin, its vision has been clouded and its powers weakened." (Vatican II, GaudiumetSpes, no. 15).

As a scientific study, therefore, historiography leads to the immediately perceivable truth and ultimately to the Truth that is God himself.

**Father Anthony YILAKA (PhD)**
**Associate Professor,**
**Catholic University of Cameroon, (CATUC) Bamenda**

# Acknowledgments

This book has been realized with noteworthy contributions from several institutions and individuals. Among these, are public archives including: the Buea National Archives, (NAB) the Bamenda Regional Archives (BRA) and the St. Thomas Aquinas Major Seminary (STAMS), Bambui, library and archives. Further to these, I was privileged to be granted access to rare private archives of families and individuals such as those of the Foncha Family, Mr. Nicholas Ade Ngwa's scrap book, and the personal papers of Messrs. Francis Nkwatoh, John Mofor Ndi (Late), Mr. Chris Choves Loh, Hon Joseph Kwi, Mr. Nelson Ngayinkfu and, a priceless collection of papers from Professor Verkijika Fanso. In addition to these contributions, I also had in-depth discussions with many of these people and dozens of others acknowledged in the text. Mr. Primus Forgwe and his assistants went to great lengths in rendering me inestimable assistance at the National Archives in Buea. I have taken the liberty to exclude persons whose names are already cited in the book.

Most of all, this work has been enriched by the individual and collective, open, critical observations and discussions with the entire faculty of the History Department of the Higher Teachers' Training College, (HTTC) University of Bamenda (UBa) from among whom mention may be made of Doctors Nixon Takor, Michael Lang, Kingsly Ollong and Professors Mathew Basung Gwanfogbe and Canute Ngwa,. In a special way, I recognize my colleagues; Professors Charles Alobwed'Epie and Rev. Anthony Yilaka of the Catholic University of Cameroon (CATUC), Bamenda. They did an x-ray of the manuscript, while Professor Tozoacha Asonganyi of the University of Yaoundé I has significantly enhanced the argument by his insightful contribution in the postscript. Once again, I emphasize the crucial contribution made by the *Summit Magazine* Interview with Professor Victor J Ngoh in shaping the presentation in this volume.

Doctors Emmanuel Sobseh and Michael Lang of UBa besides repeatedly, critically reading through the manuscript were part of the production process, while, Dr. Walter Nkwi of the University of Buea shadowed me throughout the process from conception to realization.

Generally, a dutiful spouse, over this exercise, Patience Ndi further distinguished her talents as a keen and critical proof reader. Research assistance and Secretarial processing was amply provided by a diligent team variously comprising: Mado Kichuisi, Henry Yombo, Marina Titu Nfor, Lilian Biih and Manuela Kamga.

I cannot find appropriate words to express my profound indebtedness to these dedicated and selfless folks without whose individual and collective contributions this book would hardly have seen the light of day. However, finally, alone, I take full responsibility for all the defects and conclusions reached.

# Lists of Photographs & Maps

**Photographs**

| | |
|---|---|
| President Paul Biya, and Ni John Fru Ndi | xvii |
| Golden Jubilee Logo | xviii |
| Christian Cardinal Tumi | 11 |
| Johnson O. Field | 16 |
| Sir Sydney Phillipson | 22 |
| Eugen Zintgraff | 43 |
| Galega I, Fon of Bali | 48 |
| Gustav Conrau | 50 |
| Jesko von Puttkammer | 51 |
| JN Foncha and ST Muna | 58 |
| Sir Abubakar Tafawa Balewa | 62 |
| Prof Bernard Nsokika Fonlon | 72 |
| Foncha and UN Visiting Mission in Nkambe | 85 |
| UN Visiting Mission and Youth in Mamfe | 86 |
| Some Native Authorities (Fons) in Bamenda | 90 |
| Alfred Saker | 99 |
| Victoria Centenary Monument | 102 |
| Endeley's Executive Government | 109 |
| Peter Ndembo Motomby Woleta | 110 |
| Dr. & Mrs. Endeley congratulate JN Foncha | 113 |
| Fon Achirimbi II of Bafut | 115 |
| Individual UPC Leaders | 122 |
| UPC Group picture | 124 |
| Muamar Ghadaffi | 129 |
| Foncha's KNDP government | 130 |
| Omer B.B. Sendze | 134 |
| President Alhadji Ahmadou Ahidjo | 140 |
| Jean Claude Ngoh | 151 |
| Simon Ngeh Tamfu | 155 |
| Malcom Milne receives President Ahidjo | 171 |
| Ambassador C.E. King delivers Queen's Speech | 173 |

## Maps
Federal Republic of Cameroon..................................................23
Southern Cameroons Ethnic groups..................................27
Southern Cameroons divisions......................................... 64
Neu Kamerun....................................................................... 80

# Abbreviations

| | |
|---|---|
| ANLK | Armée Liberation National Kamerun (Military wing of UPC) |
| CAM | Cameroon Anglophone Movement |
| CNF | Cameroon National Federation CNU Cameroon National Union |
| CUC | Cameroons United Congress |
| CO | Colonial Office |
| CPDM | Cameroon People's Democratic Movement |
| CPNC | Cameroons Peoples National Congress CWA Catholic Women's Association |
| CWU | Cameroon Welfare Union |
| CYL | Cameroon Youth League |
| DO | Divisional Officer |
| EO | Executive Officer |
| FASAF | Father Samson's Foundation for Underprivileged Children |
| FRC | Federal Republic of Cameroon |
| GCE | General Certificate of Education |
| GCEB | General Certificate of Education, Board |
| KNDP | Kamerun National Democratic Party |
| KNC | Kamerun National Congress |
| KPP | Kamerun People's Party |
| KUC | Kamerun United Congress |
| KUNC | Kamerun United National Congress |
| LGB | Leader of Government Business |
| NA | Native Administration / Native Authority |
| NAB | National Archives, Buea |
| NCBWA | National Congress of British West Africa |
| NCNC | National Council of Nigeria and Cameroons |
| NYL | Nigerian Youth League |
| OK | One Kamerun (party) |
| PRO | Public Records Office |
| PT | Pupil Teacher / Probationary Teacher |

| | |
|---|---|
| RC | Republic of Cameroun |
| SCHA | Southern Cameroons House of Assembly |
| SDF | Social Democratic Front |
| SDO | Senior Divisional Officer |
| STAMS | Saint Thomas Aquinas Major Seminary (Bambui |
| UC | *Union Camerounaise* |
| UNTC | United Nations Trusteeship Council |
| UNVM | United Nations Visiting Mission |
| UPC | *Unions des Populations du Cameroun* USSR |
| | Union of Soviet Socialist Republics |
| UNTC | United Nations Trusteeship Council |
| WWI | First World War |

President Paul Biya, Head of State (Right) and Ni John Fru Ndi (Left) Leader of the SDF Opposition

President Paul Biya: through the 1990 Liberty Laws, reintroduced Multiparty Politics and authorised Celebrations marking the Golden Jubilee or the Fiftieth Anniversary of Southern Cameroons Independence and Reunification

Logo: Golden Jubilee Celebrations 1961 - 2011

Note the National Monument in the Background

# Chapter 1

# Independence and Reunification: An Analysis of Basic Issues

**A Historical Panorama**

**Introduction**
*Southern West Cameroon Revisited,* is a series comprising two volumes with a central theme hinged on its historical, geographical, socio-economic, cultural and political evolution, re-examined in commemoration of the Golden Jubilee or Fiftieth Anniversary celebrations. However, while Volume One tackles generic questions on the subject matter of Southern Cameroons Reunification and Independence within the larger framework of the Federal Republic of Cameroon up to 1972, Volume Two specifically examines issues that mutually affect the two former Provinces (North and Southwest) that constituted the "State of Southern Cameroons" and, later "West Cameroon", hence the appellation "Southern West Cameroon". This is examined from its genesis in 1858 to the demise of the "Federal Republic of Cameroon" in 1972. For maximal benefit, it is advisable to first browse through the *Summit Magazine* Interview in the Epilogue and the declassified British Secret Papers in the Appendix.

In any case, both volumes remain complementary and dependent on each other. Volume Two like Volume One is the product of a triple mandate triggered by a presentation the author made at the Regional Symposium held in the Bamenda Congress Hall on 17 May 2011 and concluded at another conference organised by the Minister of Arts and Culture in Yaoundé on 28 June 2011 in connection with celebrations marking the Golden Jubilee of the "Independence and Reunification of Southern Cameroons". It was in this context that the author took up the assignment to immortalize this unique occasion by critically re-examining some of the crucial issues in the history of Southern Cameroons. Coincidentally, these meetings happened at about the same time that the Summit Magazine in its issue of 6 April-May 2010 granted a classic interview to Dr. Victor Julius Ngoh, Professor of

History and Deputy Vice-Chancellor in Charge of Research, University of Buea.[1]

By all counts it was a remarkable interview of epic proportions as it turned out to be wide ranging and all – embracing: challenging and raising several controversial issues of historical interest, many of which had already been expressed in his earlier historical publications that need re-examination. As a result, the interview generated comments among all categories of the public including; the man in the street, politicians, lawyers and above all, intellectuals, serious political analysts and historians.

Since then other reputable journals have either spontaneously on their own, tackled this subject or taken the cue from the *Summit Magazine,* generally, greatly enriching and enhancing the historical debate. However, it is in part as a rejoinder to the interview and, as,part of the enduring debate on the issue of the "Golden Jubilee Celebrations" marking the independence and reunification of Southern Cameroons and the Republic of Cameroon, that this modest contribution is being made and, strictly, from a historical and intellectual perspective. As far as possible, the entire account focuses exclusively on principles; while individuals are only referred to where they impinge on the historical nexus. Finally, as a matter of course and principle in historiography, every generation faces the eternal challenge to rewrite its own history in the light of: new interpretations of its past; or, the emergence of new information; new inventions and discoveries that question lopsided prevailing concepts; new evidence erupting from research and archaeological findings, as well as fresh technologies for translating existing historical knowledge. In this light, the Golden Jubilee approximates close to two generations, thus qualifying for a tall critical retrospective look at Cameroon History in all its ramifications. This is possible using the penetrating rear mirror of history with the advantage of time, the unfailing catalyst; which allows the dust of controversies to settle, permitting sober reflections to supervene over hasty emotional and temperamental conclusions of the past to mellow in favour of more impartial, mature judgment.

---

[1]For further details on the issue of publication, see the Epilogue

The research resulting in this book was largely, but not exclusively generated by the vital questions raised in the *Summit Magazine* interview: even more, it was prompted by a broad spectrum of other historical considerations. Positively, in the first place, however, the interview provided fresh historical information to the public but, because of the miasmic nature of the issues raised, at the same time it exposed substantial areas of commission, omission or of default that this piece of work seeks to redress. Thus, despite the fact that the British left indelible, nostalgic Anglo-Saxon legacies and footprints worthy of emulation in the areas of: good governance, human rights, quality education, self-actualization and ethics, there were as well lamentable lapses of profound nature that totally elude rationalization. These lapses were glaring in the spheres of economic development and, above all in the political culture of graciously letting go of Southern Cameroons with the approach of independence. This defect gravely undermined the objective of British tutelage throughout the Mandate and Trusteeship periods in the Territory from 1922-1961.

Thus, critical in any balanced account of the History of Cameroon since Reunification is the primeval role played by "Southern Cameroons," which alone underwent the birth pangs that begot the "Federal Republic of Cameroon": the reunion with "equal status" of the former United Nations Trust Territories of, "French Cameroun" and "British Southern Cameroons". It took the two to unite but the rigours undertaken towards the plebiscite applied only to the latter. Much earlier, Britain had arbitrarily by an Order in Council carved out "British Northern Cameroons" on 26 June 1923, when it was still a Mandated Territory of the League of Nations. This initially created as a matter of administrative convenience for them finally established the reality of "British Southern Cameroons and British Northern Cameroons" not originally previewed in the League of Nations Mandate, which had formally divided the former German Kamerun colony between Britain and France on 20 July 1919. Originating provisionally as "Provinces" within their Nigerian Colony for easy administration, they calcified and became *de facto* distinctive political entities as carefully designed by Great Britain. With intensified British machinations the gulf between them greatly widened such that as independence approached in 1961, one section voted for integration with Nigeria, while the other, which resisted British pressure chose reunification with the Republic of Cameroon. For this recalcitrance the British sought inestimable vengeance through setting up inescapable traps for them.

**Double British Standards**

These clandestine manoeuvres were brought out to the surface with the publication of the declassified British secret papers in which it was openly stated that as far as British interests were concerned, compared with Northern Cameroons; "Southern Cameroons was expendable." Throughout the Trusteeship period, everything was done to ensure that the "radicalism" inherent in the latter did not infect the former. Consequently, when it came to the plebiscites, which were largely concocted through British intrigues, the provisional split of British Cameroons in 1923 was concretized and they were henceforth recognized and treated as two separate, political entities to all intents and purposes. In fact, as a result of this scheme over time, they became widely different in several ways; such that, describing Southern Cameroons as suffering from "benign neglect" under British rule, the situation of Northern Cameroons was dismal. It was so socio-politically and economically stagnated that the first indigenous political party there, the "Northern Cameroons Democratic Party" (NKDP), literally an extension of the KNDP in Southern Cameroons was only created in 1959. Understandably, it was highly critical of the British Colonial Administration and campaigned either for an independent sovereign status or a reunified state with Southern Cameroons and eventual unification with Republic of Cameroon. Obviously just like with the KNDP, these options were anathema to British policy. The other political parties there such as: the Fulani dominated Northern People's Congress (NPC) and the Northern Elements Progressive Union (NEPU) were entirely Nigerian based. These were disagreed on the way forward though broadlyfavouring integration with Nigeria.

To ensure that the results of the impending plebiscites reflected the British aspirations of integration with Nigeria, they proposed to the United Nations Trusteeship Council that: the Northern Cameroons plebiscite should take place simultaneously with that in Southern

Cameroons; the electors asked the same questions, but strangely, that the votes should be counted separately, as well as the declaration of results. To further confound issues for an already confused electorate, the Northern Cameroons was made to participate in the Nigerian Federal Elections. In fact, two plebiscites were conducted there; the first in November 1959 in which the people advocated for continued Trusteeship under Britain, which was easily interpreted as a vote against integration with Nigeria.

However, since the direction of the wind had been made clear after that first plebiscite, Britain working with the Nigerian based political parties did everything to turn the tables before 11 February1961. As expected, integration with Nigeria in the second plebiscite won by a wide margin of 146.296 to 97.659 votes. However, had provision been allowed for tallying the votes of both British Northern and Southern Cameroons, reunification would have won handsomely since combining the votes would have amounted to Southern Cameroons' 233.571 votes being added to those of Northern Cameroons' 97.659 making a total of 332.230 votes; while integration with Nigeria for Southern Cameroons with:97.659 votes added to those of Northern Cameroons': 146.296 would have totalled 244.037 votes leaving reunification (331.230 –244.037)with a distinct victory margin of87.193 votes.[2]

**Southern Cameroons for Reunification**

The entire history of 'British' Southern Cameroons is exceptionally, the unfolding of the process that ended up in its reunification with the Republic of Cameroun on 1 October 1961. In French Cameroun, the "Kamerun Idea" fossilized in the hands of the *Unions des Populations du Cameroun* (UPC) in 1948.[3] It was so glaring that during the presentations before the United Nations Visiting Mission (UNVM) in

---

[2]*Cameroon Tribune, Hors Serie Octobre* 2011. pp. 74-76., Kimeng Hilton, "Unease with Northern Cameroons Results."

[3]Their own demand like that of the One Kamerun (OK) party which replaced them after they were banned by the Endeley Government for their radical communist sympathies and a predilection for violence in 1957 was for immediate "independence and reunification". It is also insinuated that their inclination towards an alliance with the KNDP posed a threat to Endeley's KNC.

1958, they ruled out the need for any referendum in the case of French Cameroon as was the situation in British Southern Cameroons. The course and form of that union might have been different but the ultimate objective of reunification never really wavered on either side of the Mungo. While the antecedents of that event for British Southern Cameroons stretched as far back as to the 1940s, when the idea was first mooted, the process acquired an unprecedented momentum and dimension of its own during the decisive years running from 1958 - 1961.

This is largely the period dealt with in the interview as well as the substance of this exposition.[4] After achieving independence on 1 October 1961, Southern Cameroons metamorphosed into 'West Cameroon', an appellation by which it was known until 24 July 1972, when a Presidential Decree set up seven Provinces to replace West and East Cameroon as a unitary state.[5] This was atransient existence of barely a decade, and a period[6] far too short for it to have proven itself either as a success or a failure, when juxtaposed with nations that have survived for centuries and even millennia and are still evolving.[7] This was essentially the scheming of President Ahmadou Ahidjo, ironically the one individual whose responsibility it was to secure its invincibility.

However, broadly talking about "Southern Cameroons Fifty Years After Reunification," could take more than one perception; as, it could arguably mean the entire period covering 1961-2011, when it was politically and "geographically" transformed8through the stages of the Federal Republic, 1961-1972; the Unitary State, 1972-84 and, finally,

---

[4] Ngoh's, *the Untold History of Cameroon Reunification* published after the *Summit Magazine* interview equally covers this period.

[5] Read Victor LeVine, "Political Integration and the United Republic of Cameroon", p. 279, in David Smock and Kwamena Bentsi-Enchill, eds., *The Search for National integration in Africa,* London, Free Press, Collier, Macmillan Publishers, 1976.

[6] There are current debates as to whether what took place as the "Peaceful Revolution" of 1972 could qualify for a valid referendum comparable to the 1961 plebiscite in Southern Cameroons conducted by the UN; more especially as it violated Article 47(1) of the constitution of the Federal Republic of Cameroon.

[7] Britain is presently undergoing throes of devolution with Ireland, Scotland and Wales seeking autonomy after centuries of centralized administration from London.

simply subsumed into the "Republic of Cameroon,"⁸February 1984 – date.⁹ Throughout this period the erstwhile Southern Cameroons however, has maintained its basic essence and therefore within the context implied in this book; revisiting "Southern Cameroons 50 Years after Reunification" implies more or less, a re-examination of the events affecting the inhabitants encapsulated in this geographical circumscription.

As a matter of course, the persistent arguments and complaints by North and South-Westerners as exemplified in the interview over issues such as: "bad faith," "marginalization," "assimilation," "annexation," "absorption", second class citizenship and the like are symptoms that unlike "independence," which was a single, finite "act" – actually, an event that took place precisely at midnight on 1 October 1961, "reunification" on the other hand is an ongoing, multi-dimensional and emotionally charged process. This is best expressed by the Cameroon Anglophone Movement (CAM) in their memorandum to the Head of State on constitutional reform with reference to the political unrest that gripped the nation in the early 1990s. In it, referring to the Anglophones, they reiterated:

> The frustration born of oppression, subjugation, marginalization and neglect finally led some Anglophones in desperation to organize political dissent in May 1990, to which the Cameroon Government responded by shooting dead six persons in Bamenda and telling Anglophones to go elsewhere. But Anglophones do not want to go anywhere else; their demand is for a return to the legality of the 1961 constitution of the Federal Republic of Cameroon.¹⁰

---

⁸Examples abound, Britain alone has had to review the Acts of Union with Ireland, Scotland and Wales dating back to the 18th Century in favour of dialogue, peaceful coexistence, devolution and even independence.

⁹Law No 80.001, abolishing the United Republic of Cameroon and resuscitating in its place the Republic of Cameroon which at independence on 1 January 1960 became a member of the United Nations with defined internationally recognized boundaries. See, Albert W Mukong ed., USA, *The Case for Southern Cameroons*, 1990, p.21.

¹⁰See, "Cameroon Anglophone Movement: a socio-cultural association", Douala 5 December 1991. Chief Dr. HNA Enonchong was chairman; also, the Epilogue in

The coming together of the two former UN Trust Territories torn apart by the vagaries of colonial intrigues for forty years was much like a marital union calling for a genuine conversion and bonding of hearts, minds, wills, thoughts and actions of the parties and not merely a matter of legality, lip service and form.

In fact, this dismal situation is more pungently expressed in Foncha's words in his Letter of Resignation from the CPDM in 1990; as the one man who had fought for reunification and won by a landslide majority of 233. 971 votes (70.49%), to 97.471 (29.51%) votes for integration. After enumerating the ravages that Southern Cameroons had gone through economically, socially and politically since reunification, he wept over the plight of his people noting:

> The Anglophone Cameroonians whom 1 brought into the union have been ridiculed and referred to as *"Les Biafrais", "Les Enemies Dans La Maison" "les traitres"* etc. and the constitutional provisions which protected this Anglophone minority have been suppressed , their voices drowned, while the rule of the gun has replaced the dialogue which the Anglophones cherish very much.... The national media has been used by the government through people who never voted for unification to misinform the citizens about Bamenda..[11]

Of course, this is the machinery that has deliberately but subtly been put in place to drive wedges between peoples of the two Regions for easy manipulation.

## The Paradox

When historically contextualized today with the North and South West Regions simply reduced to two of the ten Regions (former Provinces) that constitute the Republic of Cameroon, the product is something of a freak, a contradiction in terms. This, essentially, because prior to reunification in 1961, Southern Cameroons had

---

Ndi, *Mill Hill Missionaries in South-West Cameroon*, (Pauline's Press Nairobi, 2006). My emphasis

[11] Foncha's Letter of Resignation fromthe CPDM, 9 June 1990.

already attained and enjoyed all the attributes and privileges of statehood stretching to as far back as 26 October 1954, when as a State with a Quasi Federal status within Nigeria, it had an Executive Council led by Dr. EML Endeley as Leader of Government Business. The state was adequately defined with a specific geographical circumscription, a permanent demographic population with its own Legislative Assembly, independent judiciary and executive paraphernalia, which qualified it for internal self-government. However, in matters of defence and international relations it depended on Great Britain, the administering authority. In essence, it had all that it took to be identified as a state on the basis of possessing: executive, legislative and judicial arms of government with its own territory and nationality laws.

**Southern Cameroons Refused Independence**

This status was further, vastly extended in the Southern Cameroons Order- in-Council or indeed, the Constitution, which went operational on 1 October 1960, before the plebiscite and one whole year before independence. By it, the House of Assembly was significantly enlarged and comprised three ex-officio members, 26 elected Members of Parliament, an Executive Council headed by a Premier, who could appoint up to seven Ministers and three Parliamentary Secretaries with the Commissioner of Southern Cameroons playing the role of Her Majesty the Queen's Governor.[12] There was a High Court with a Judge, Financial autonomy and a Public Service Commission with a Chairman. Finally, a House of Chiefs, a sort of Upper House or Senate (House of Lords) was granted.

So far advanced, the Trust Territory was just one short step away from the final goal of total sovereignty or independence, the obstacles to which as will abundantly be demonstrated in this thesis, inexplicably were mounted and masterminded by Great Britain to which it was Trustee. Great Britain had solemnly, conventionally and legally by Article 76 (b) of the Charter of the United Nations in 1946 undertaken

---

[12]The 1961 elections to the enlarged parliament were massively won by the KNDP, which swept 29 of the 34 seats leaving the CPNC with barely five seats thus confirming the political landscape earlier shaped by the hotly contested plebiscite. Later, these were reduced to a rump of two; Endeley and Mbile.

to guide Southern Cameroons towards that grand objective. In fact, the atrocious manner in which Britain failed to do this constitutes the most important missing component in the *Summit Magazine* interview which consequently, an extensive portion of this treatise sets to redress.

This attitude by Great Britain clearly amounted to an act of a grave betrayal of trust. Above all, it largely continues to account for the bulk of the woes and misgivings that "Southern Cameroonians" face and complain about till today.[13] The other paradox is that having evolved so far and finally, actually become an ideal 'state' savouring the flavours of internal autonomy for close to twenty years: 1954-1972, it was systematically demoted first, to the status of simply being relinquished to one of the seven Provinces of the United Republic of Cameroon: 1972-1984 and, finally, inexplicably split into two, namely, the North and South West Provinces, July 1984 - date of the Republic of Cameroon. Put in proper perspective this has been a traumatizing experience, tantamount to the loss of self-identity; in short, to anonymity and obscurity having first acquired formal statehood within the Federal Republic of Nigeria (1954 -1961) and then within the Federal Republic ofCameroon (FRC) 1961-1972.

This, for a people who since the 1940s had been craving for a corporate individuality and identity becomes paradoxical. It should equally be recalled that had Southern Cameroons opted by the Plebiscite in 1961 for integration with Nigeria, it would have been accorded the status of a full autonomous Region equal in every way to that enjoyed by the other Regions (States) in the Federation of Nigeria. This conundrum is examined in all its ramifications within the context of the "Ahidjo Factor" as well as under the compatibility of the North and South West Regions[14].Taking a more detached and mature but penetrating observation of the situation, the popular, outspoken, erudite and fearless, prelate,Christian Cardinal Tumi observes that, "The Anglo-Saxon Minority Needs Protection". Going further he points out that:

---

[13]See the Legal Criteria for Statehood as defined by the 1932 Montevideo "Convention on Rights and Duties of States"; Article 1(a, b, c & d).
[14]For details see Chapter 3

The formal agreement of 1961 in Foumban foresaw neither the assimilation, nor the dilution, nor the complete disappearance of the personality of the English- speaking part of the country. It is obvious that Ahmadou Ahidjo, making absolute use of the absolute and exceptional powers the president had, did away with his Anglophone partners in Foumban by imposing on them a gradual and political change and development which was completely different and opposed to their own political ambitions.[15]

*Christian Cardinal Tumi*
**A Popular, Outspoken and Fearless Prelate**

He identifies fully with the political analyst, Shanda Touré, who argues that the so–called Peaceful Revolution of 1972 organized at a time, when the country was ruled with a rod of iron; citizens had no freedom of speech; they had no right to vote nor the right to be citizens in the real sense of the term; the 20th May can only have an unhappy significance. Tumi concludes with Shanda: "We have no right whatsoever to attribute to a people the results of a Referendum that

---

[15] 15 Christian Cardinal Tumi, *My Faith: a Cameroon to Be Renewed*, (Les Editions Veritas, Douala, 2011), p. 38.

was organized by a bloody dictator".¹⁶ Referring to the English - speaking Cameroonians, Cardinal Tumi, who is best placed and knows intimately about his people, minces no words when he literally propounds:

> These fellow countrymen and women, whether they occupy important or unimportant places in the social and political hierarchy, make known in private, their deep sentiments of disgust, of deception and of repulsion. All of them are convinced that they are oppressed, marginalized and deceived in many ways.¹⁷

For the solution, quoting Professor Bernard Fonlon, he proposes three things; including, the basic principles of the culture, which should undergo a thorough objective and scientific examination, followed by a logical and decisive choice that is not passionate and finally, the modalities of choice that should be judiciously and energetically put into practice.¹⁸

## Nature, Reason and shape of Reaction

Initially, after reading the *Summit Magazine* interview on this sensitive, emotive and rather thorny topic, I was minded to react in much the same way as those who did so spontaneously over the airwaves and in the press.¹⁹ However, on further reflection of the fact that Professor Ngoh was selected by virtue of the fact that he is a seasoned historian, writer and university professor, I decided to tackle the response from a purely historical perspective, the proper medium for intellectual discourse. This way, the points made could be seen holistically in their broader, less distorted historical context instead of selectively picking up each of the myriad of indictments pitched in the interview against John Ngu Foncha as an individual, the Kamerun

---

¹⁶Shanda Touré, article in *Le Messager* No. 2133 of 24/05/06 quoted in Tumi; *My Faith: A Cameroon to Be Renewed*, pp. 38-9.
¹⁷Ibid.
¹⁸Ibid., p.40.
¹⁹There were hot exchanges between Profs. Victor Julius Ngoh vs. Verkijika Fanso and Jonny Nfonyam, which were carried in e.g., The Post Newspaper and other publications.

National Democratic Party (KNDP), its leadership, and the Southern Cameroons political elite and people as a whole.

For yet another reason, this form of the response could come in handy for those who might not have read the particular issue of the *Summit Magazine* that carried the classic interview[20] and could therefore serve as a historical document for further debate and future reference. The most important reason however is that Dr. John Ngu Foncha, specifically targeted in the interview bears little resemblance to the man l knew personally in practical life or from literature and ubiquitous public opinion about him and, already undertaken substantial research towards writing his biography. Much of what resonates in the interview is a nauseating repetition of the conspiracy theories that for years have been peddled about the man. It is time long enough for the records to be straightened on this, as on similar issues.

Having said that, it should quickly be added that putting together this account has been a traumatizing experience; given that it did not evolve as an original, spontaneous option, but sprouted in reaction to an external agenda consisting of the litany of indictments mounted in the interview on widely disparate subjects. An attempt has been made to reclassify these into themes or chapters that carry a sense of cohesion. Consequently; the approach unavoidably leans heavily towards rectification of the mostly skewed information that abounds in the journal and other literature on this topic. Therefore, it is advisable to browse through the *Summit Magazine* interview which is reproduced in its entirety in the epilogue, where necessary to stay focused.

The presentation was flawed in several ways and historically by the sketchy or near total absence of reference to the "declassified British secret papers" made public as far back as 1998. These were further confirmed and consolidated by Malcolm Milne's denunciation of the entire British Colonial Policy in the Trust Territory. Taken together; the disclosures emanating from these sources have literally revolutionized political thought and trends in Southern Cameroons History in particular and Cameroon History as a whole. In these, the intrigues organized by the Colonial Office and faithfully executed by Messrs Johnson O Field and Malcolm Milne, the Commissioner and

---

[20] For the sake of clarity and easy cross-referencing the interview is reproduced in its entirety as the "Epilogue".

Deputy Commissioner of Southern Cameroons respectively, and CE King, the British Ambassador to Yaoundé[21], Cameroon are exposed. Their total omission on a topic in which they were the fundamental executors can hardly be justified.

The other yawning chasm is the near absence or sparse reference to the odious role played by President Ahmadou Ahidjo, whose insatiable craving for power was matched as much by his "absolute" cynicism with reference to federalism and democracy. Unfortunately, this was not as obvious to his contemporaries as it has become presently with hindsight. Coincidentally, like what the declassified British secret papers and Malcolm Milne ended up doing, so also are the disclosures of how Ahidjo was contemptuous and sceptical over the idea of reunification and federalism. Consequently, in re-examining the facts available, "Fifty years after Southern Cameroons Independence," it is obvious that nobody and nothing could have stopped his determination to dismantle the Federal Republic of Cameroon for which absolutely he had no regard and in which he had no faith *ab initio*.

Intellectually, no historian can disclaim or ignore what is now so widely available; information emanating from the declassified British secret papers as well as that on President Ahmadou Ahidjo; reasons that have occasioned my response through this exposition. Historians owe it as a duty to posterity just like the medical corps do in the "Hippocratic Oath," to reconstruct the past authentically and to render the truth and nothing but the truth within their competence to the public in a sort of 'Herodotic' oath.[22] Absolute truth as such may not be possible; since the humanities and the social sciences to which history belongs are approximate sciences. Nevertheless, the public should be afforded what it takes to make informed opinion, distinguishing between fact and opinion and an author's views and historical facts on any given issue, aware that in matters of history as in all academic pursuits subject to continuing research, no one has ever put a finite conclusion on any topic. This is most applicable to History, which by its very definition refers to: "enquiry" and first hand,

---

[21] Ibid., PRO CO 554/2254 XC 4478.12
[22] Herodotus is the Greek Father of History. See Chapter 10 Section on Methodology in this volume.23

uncorrupted report; all of which point at continuous, relentless research and investigation. History above all else, is dynamic as each generation is challenged to rewrite the history of its past in the light of unfolding information and techniques of research, reconstructing the past in the perpetual search for authentic truth or, as EH Carr better puts it: "History is the continuous process of interaction between the historian and his facts, an unending dialogue between the present and the past."[23]

## Milne's Revelations Revolutionize Cameroon History

A personage whose conversion and revelations have done much to uncover, revolutionize and radicalize the history of Southern Cameroons is Malcolm Milne, the Deputy Commissioner of Southern Cameroons, who amazingly featured prominently in many accounts as the *administrator par excellence*. But, for yet another reason not so obvious in the interview is the fact that he and his boss, Johnson Field, the Commissioner of Southern Cameroons were the central actors, in effect architects and executors of British colonial policy in the Trust Territory of British Southern Cameroons especially during the critical period of 1958-1961. However, Malcolm Milne further distinguishes himself as one person, who has elaborately documented most of what transpired during this period in his autobiography.[24] In this respect, writing in 1998, he profusely regretted:

> [What] I had not come to terms with the conviction myself – was that we were doing the Cameroons a wrong. We should have struggled harder to continue our trusteeship for several years longer. But the forces against us were too strong and I judge now that had I, as Commissioner of the Cameroons taken this line in

---

[23] EH Carr, *What Is History?*, ( London; Palgrave , 2001).
[24] 24 Ibid., Milne, *No Telephone to Heaven*: This, to say the least marks one of the lowest points in British colonial history. Malcolm Milne attempts to throw further light on why he had been so grossly misled.

1959 – 61, I should merely have made a great nuisance of myself and achieved nothing.²⁵

Consequently, he is attributed a substantial section in this work in fact a chapter, and so are: the plebiscite, President Ahmadou Ahidjo, John Ngu Foncha, the Foumban Constitutional Conference, the North /Southwest Regions, Cameroon West of the Mungo" or "Anglophone Cameroon". The sections on Ahidjo and the Foumban Constitutional Conference are further enriched with recent accounts by first hand reporters revealing inconceivable snares that were carefully hatched to lure the Anglophone delegates at the Foumban Constitutional Conference intocomplacency and impotency.

**Johnson O Field**

**Commissioner of Southern Cameroons and Malcolm Milne's Boss**

Malcolm Milne's views after his rather theatrical and mysterious conversion are powerfully corroborated by those of his compatriot, John Percival, who came out to Southern Cameroons on a United

---

²⁵Ibid., p. 395; see also NAB, Vb /b/ 1962)*2 Press Release No.1498*"Southern Cameroons discussed in British Parliament". My emphasis

Nations ticket as one of the twenty-five Plebiscite Officers, recruited by the British Government and seconded to the UN. Thus his background and even temperament were totally different from those of his countryman. However, it is amazing that though these two gentlemen approached the question of British Colonial Administration in Southern Cameroons from two vastly dissimilar; literally opposite experiences they arrived with mathematical precision at the conclusion that the British made an awful mess of their mandate in the Trust Territory. Equally, they conclude that they (the British) ought to right the wrongs done to these nice trusting, loyal people. Actually, Percival, a liberal and critic of sorts, after a careful study of the situation was totally disenchanted and took the radical view that the British Government had neglected its responsibilities forcing the people to make a difficult decision with far reaching consequences having failed in the first place to adequately prepare them economically and politically for selfhood. He categorically took note that:

> Many Southern Cameroonians continued to plead for the colonial administration to be prolonged for a little longer, to give them a chance to make informed decision about the future, but both the UN and the colonial authorities had refused to countenance this option. … with Ian Macleod as colonial secretary, the British Government of the day was only too eager to wash its hands off the Cameroons… as quickly and painlessly as possible.[26]

Consequently, Percival rejected the tinted view of the deplorable British Administration in Southern Cameroons and argued fervently in favour of independence. In fact, in many ways, though an Englishman engaged in the service of the United Nations, he was more drastic in his castigation of both establishments; Britain and the UN, than Malcolm Milne. After six months in the country and intensely engaged in all the processes leading to the plebiscite, he declared: "The experience awoke me to the consequences of colonial rule. I still believe that Britain should do its best to ensure the lasting welfare of

---

[26]John Percival, *The Southern Cameroons Plebiscite, Choice or Betrayal (Langaa Research & Publishing CIG, Mankon, Bamenda), Pp.77-78. In other* words, the KNDP stand for extended trusteeship fairly represented the wishes of the people.My emphasis

territories it once ruled." Far away in Wum, where he was posted, Percival was shocked to discover that:

> People who lived only a morning's walk from the DO ... had spent the best part of a life time under British rule without setting eyes on a white man. And now that they were setting eyes on one it was the closing days before independence.[27]

This is a brutal indictment and speaks volumes of British neglect of Southern Cameroons and further elaborates their attitude to the people and their leadership as independence approached. To Percival, even then, the people were well informed and knew exactly what they wanted. And, of the plebiscite, he made the cryptic observation:

> It was quickly made clear to me that they wanted no part of it and that they saw the whole thing as a sham, a cosmetic exercise in democracy. The only decision they were allowed to make was to choose whether to throw in their lot with Nigeria or French Cameroon, and they wanted neither of them. All the other decisions had been taken thousands of miles away by officials who thought they knew what they needed better than the people themselves.[28]

Many of the people wanted the white man to stay at least for the time being, and were hurt and angry to think that the British were going to abandon them forcing them to choose between the Nigerians whom they considered "cannibals" and "Frenchy people" whom they saw as robbers. The real choice of "independence" was denied them.[29] It is also amazing and a lot more than a mere coincidence that these two men; Malcolm Milne and John Percival, like numerous other administrators, missionaries, casual visitors and tourists commonly arrived at the conclusion that Southern Cameroonians were exceptionally hospitable, kind and trustworthy. Consequently, of these "wonderful people," Percival like Malcolm Milne concluded as recently

---

[27] Ibid., p. 33ff. My emphasis
[28] Ibid., p. xiii.
[29] Ibid., p.32.

as 2008, when he passed away: "I still retain to this day, a powerful affection and respect of the Bamenda Grasslands and the beautiful country where they live".[30]

It is in this connection and, with this knowledge that one can hardly resist the endorsement of the compelling penultimate concluding statement in the editorial of the *Eden Xtra Magazine No. 001 of October 2011*, in which the editor in his wisdom predicts: "We may yet fall back on the relevance of history to correct today's wrongs and fashion the tomorrow that we desperately hope to attain."[31] This statement encapsulates the expositions in that timeless edition of the paper especially, when juxtaposed with the "prophesy" by Malcolm Milne that the British would not only regret for their misdeeds but would be held accountable for them some day. Possibly, this is where law would capitalize on the excavations of history to redress and re-kindle the blighted aspirations of a suppressed promising nation that once was. This after all may not be too farfetched taking the cue from the redress presently being awarded by the very British Government to the victims of the "Mau Mau" independence movement in Kenya in the 1950s, to the extent of undertaking to construct a monument in their honour.[32] In a nutshell, challenged by the plethora of issues and questions raised in the *Summit Magazine* interview, an endeavour has been made in this work to identify the sources, context and nature of the woes that have bedevilled Southern Cameroonians since "Reunification and Independence", fifty years ago. These can roughly be placed in the hands of an odd triad comprising: in the first instance, Britain, the administering power of the Southern Cameroons Trusteeship;[33] secondly, the southern Cameroons political leadership and thirdly, the regime of President Ahmadou Ahidjo.

Of these three, the *Summit Magazine* interview focused exclusively on the defects of the Southern Cameroonian political leadership

---

[30]Ibid., p. 103

[31]Eden Xtra Magazine No. 001 October 2011, p. 5.

[32]In the 1950s, towards Kenyan independence: a secret nationalist Kenyan organization set up in 1952 with the objective of forcing European settlers from the land and ending British rule in Kenya. As recently as November 2013, the British Government announced their readiness to construct a monument to the MauMau rebels (nationalists) in addition to paying reparations.

[33]Secondly, the Southern Cameroons political leadership itself.

literally to the exclusion of the British Colonial Administration, the most powerful prop of the tripod followed by President Ahidjo.[34] Massive evidence that the British covertly and overtly obstructed all attempts at secession from Nigeria, extended Trusteeship or much worse, "independence for Southern Cameroons" led by the Foncha Administration, lay buried in the archives until this masquerade was unmasked with the publication of the declassified British secret papers in the late 1990s. Further missing links and lingering doubts were at last, abundantly divulged in the unnerving confessions paradoxically by Malcolm Milne himself, the erstwhile Deputy Commissioner of Southern Cameroons, and practically one of the hatchet men who executed the colonial atrocious plots against that Trust Territory.

Ultimately, he came clean and took revenge against a system that had used him as tissue paper, against the people of Southern Cameroons and their political leadership. Most amazingly, at the end of the day, though reluctantly, Malcolm Milne graciously conceded that these political leaders were the best breed of people he had had the occasion to work with throughout his long career in the colonial service spanning from Eden and the Gold Coast to Nigeria. He played the role of advocate for the people of Southern Cameroons whom he thought had been gravely wronged by the heartless British Administration operating from Whitehall.

The Foumban Constitutional Conference and the Federal Constitution resulting from it with all possible shortcomings was nevertheless the best thing that could have happened to Southern Cameroons in the prevailing circumstances. This is precisely what it failed to become in the hands of President Ahidjo, who as pointed out was innately antidemocratic and could not contemplate sharing power with anybody. The eventual result was the decimation of the ten year old budding democratic State of West Cameroon, which had enjoyed Self-Government since 1954 with its own legislature; House of Assembly and House of Chiefs an Executive arm and Judiciary, each of which by Westminster parliamentary democraticprinciples and procedures was thoroughly conscious and jealous of its rights,

---

[34] Even when referring to President Ahidjo, this is done with a slanting rather reverential, benign approach. Interestingly, existing historical evidence and simple logic bear heavily on them.

privileges and prerogatives. There was a distinct separation of powers and exercise of checks and balances among them. It could be said that the blossoming Federal Republic of Cameroon within which it existed was blighted at birth and, with it, the dreams, aspirations, visions and expectations of the citizens leaving behind a dazed community in total disbelief. Herein lay the source of most of the woes, frustrations and problems that erupted and continue to fester in a fluid state of affairs without a clear vision of the way forward or an appropriate means of expression and dialogue by the aggrieved party.

In a sort of conspiracy of circumstances arising from the lack of understanding of the historical backdrop of these issues; sheer prejudice or culpable ignorance and condescension, Foncha and his administration who, in a proper analysis of the manifest historical data available should rightly be regarded as "victims" crushed in between these imponderable forces, have instead been made to appear as culprits placed in the dock at whom accusing fingers are relentlessly directed being made to answer for transgressions externally inflicted on them as individuals and on the country at large. This is the paradox of Southern Cameroons history but as Malcolm Milne concludes, the British would have to right these wrongs one day. Within this logic, it is just possible that law and equity could tango with history and logic to right the wrongs done to the 'nice trusting, little people of Southern Cameroons manhandled in the first place by a mindless colonial machine remote controlled from Whitehall in London on the one hand, and then thrust into the claws of an insatiable, supposedly 'fraternal' and benign Ahidjo Regime on the other. That is precisely what this exposition seeks to examine in both Volumes One and Two of this series.

Sir Sydney Phillipson: Constitutional and Economic Expert engaged with the assistance of Malcolm Milne. His slanted reports to the UN influenced the exclusion of "Independence" as an option during the 11 February 1961Plebiscite

Map: Federal Republic of Cameroon 1 October 1961 - 2 June 1972

# Chapter 2

## Natural Blend: Grassland, Forest and Coast

### Southern Cameroons "Switzerland of Africa"

Southern Cameroonian roots are firm both adventurous, spreading far and wide, as well as, radical, penetrating deep down to the rocks. Thus, the geographical blending of grassland, forest and coast like in the principle of the "Repulsion of like charges" inextricably complement each other - bonding them not necessarily because they are similar, but because like acouple in a marriage they attract and need each other. These, over the past century were further amplified and strengthened as will be seen, by Socio-economic, political and cultural factors. Consequently, they have evolved an unshakeable ethos of their own which exceed political decrees and fiats, and cannot simply be wished away. Seen in this light, Southern Cameroons came to be regarded as "Africa in miniature", the Switzerland of Africa and the tourist destination of choice, while its inhabitants have variously came to be described as: nice, gentle, peace loving, hospitable, loyal and simple people.

In the *Summit Magazine* interview with Professor Julius Ngoh, great play is made of the incompatibility of the North and South West Regions of Cameroon. This largely overlooks the solid historical, socio-economic, cultural and geographical complementary features, which had distinguished their uniqueness for nearly half a century of harmonious and uninterrupted political co-existence. For one thing, the type of unity in uniformity, not unity in diversity advocated in the interview is illusory and unattainable in Cameroon or anywhere else. The discussion painted a picture of these Regions as being monolithic and mutually exclusive polities, incapable of unity with "sad experiences of a raw deal" in the past by the South Westerners under the administrations of Foncha, Jua and Muna.

Nowhere can progress and unity be attained in any community by celebrating and emphasising its differences. The general practice is to highlight and harp on the positive values that unite to move the society forward as demonstrated in the evolution of Southern Cameroons itself, struggling to forge an identity from the formation of the Cameroons Youth League in the 1940s to the creation of the KNC and KPP as full-fledged "national" political parties in 1953, the stark differences among Endeley, Kale, Mbile and Dibongue notwithstanding. On the other hand, there is an undue emphasis on the differences between Foncha and Endeley further given an ethno-regional twist.

The manner of presentation in the *Summit Magazine* interview smacked strongly of the 'VIKUMA' [i.e. Victoria, Kumba and Mamfe] diatribes of the Walter Wilson Mbong and Wilfred Nkwenti fame.[35] However, in another interview with the *Time Scape Magazine*, Ngoh went even further and declared without equivocation:

> There is absolutely no way that the present day North West and South West Regions would accept to form one state. Let us be frank, go to the villages and ask in a free, fair and open election, would you want the North West and South West to form one state? From my findings, the answer would be no.[36]

---

[35] These gentlemen led mudslinging tirades over the two Provinces at the time playing on the negative feelings of some politicians much like happened during the early 1990s. There are a few politicians and some elite who stand to benefit from such a division. Nkwenti maintains that he was basically reacting to unprovoked and unreasonable attacks by Walter Wilson Mbong. Though attacking North Westerners, he worked in close collaboration with Mr. Simon Angafor, Proprietor of Nacho Comprehensive College, Mankon, Bamenda, whilehis school was largely staffed by North Westerners. Nkwenti interviewed in February 2013, later Professor Elias Nwana April 2013.His school was largely staffed by North Westerners

[36] Ibid., Time Scape Magazine

# Map Southern Cameroons Ethnic Groups 1950 -1961
(Southern Cameroons had some 200 ethnic groups)

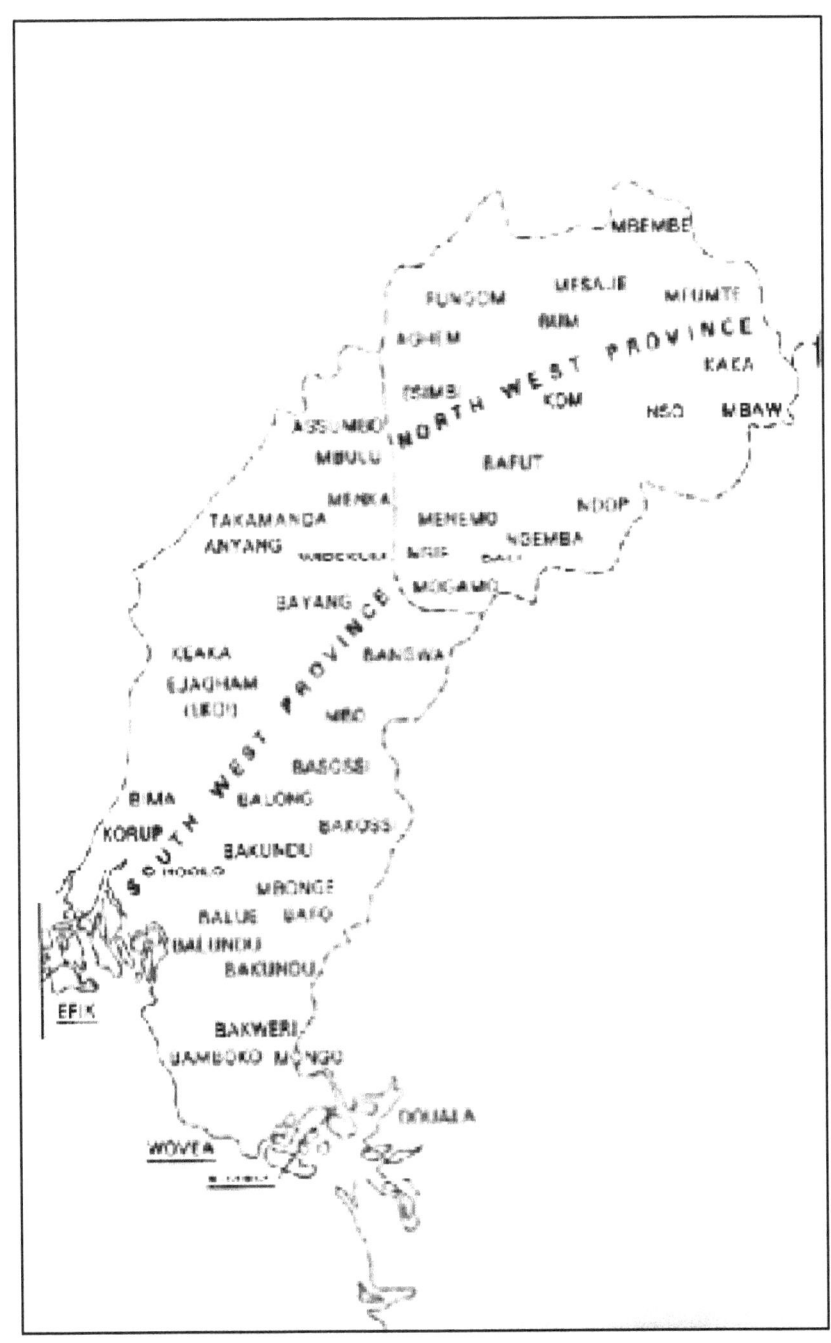

Of course, this remains Professor Ngoh's view, which should be respected as such but it is fresh in many memories that the people of these Regions were never remotely informed or much less consulted when they had to be causelessly split, while the rest of Cameroon remained intact until 1984. In fact, were such an opportunity to be given to *bona fide* Southern Cameroonians of both Regions to prove themselves over a situation that was imposed on them, there already exist track records. In the first place, it would not merely be a repeat performance of what took place during the plebiscite of 11 February 1961 rather, after the experience of the litany of woes over these years, at the hands of the majority Francophone administrations; it would be a clean sweep of the board as explained further on in this chapter. Of course, as massively demonstrated at the AACI in 1993, it would be a case of returning to the historical State for which the masses of Southern Cameroonians valiantly clamoured from 1950-1961; really a "Golden Age" that continues to conjure vivid nostalgic memories.[37] This unanimity and determination was demonstrated at great cost in their struggle for an Anglo-Saxon type University and the Cameroon General Certificate of Education (GCE) Board as the repository of that culture.

Strangely, again, the allegations made are not borne by any statistically demonstrable or solidly documented evidence of the time, as can easily be established from the account of their origins (i.e. Northwest and Southwest), from pre-colonial through colonial times to independence and post-independence as a political entity naturally bonded; physically, demographically and economically in the first instance. Politically, this was concretely demonstrated in the voting patterns, ministerial appointments, both intra- and inter-party from 1951 to 1966. Under the administrations of Endeley, 1954-1959; Foncha, 1959-65; Jua, 1965-1968 and Muna, 1968-1972, there were usually conventional attempts to balance up the ministerial appointments in government as well as in top parastatal positions between the regions.[38]

---

[37]Ndi, *The Golden Age*
[38]Ibid., Kale, Political History of Southern Cameroons,

## Friends and Neighbours

These issues are examined at length and deep down to their roots with ample illustrations later on in this chapter. However, logically speaking and by the theory of "radicalism," the perpetrators and advocates of the North- South- West divide, would sooner rather than later realise that with the removal of the "North-West bogey" many more ethnic hydras would surface to invade the evacuated terrain. Southern Cameroons with all its flaws was known territory compared to no other and standing together as of old is definitely more beneficial than with these regions going their separate ways were such an option a possibility.

As will lavishly be demonstrated, even without any formal political bonding ties; the socio-economic, cultural, educational and religious ties between these Regions continue to flourish freely especially with improving road network and communications as never before, the political hurdles notwithstanding. The policies chosen by the leaders of the time sought always to appeal to the collective electorate and not to mere geographical, sectional, cultural or ethnic affinities, which in any case were a given. It will be amply demonstrated without any hint of triumphalism, that the Southern Cameroons electorate was far and away more politically advanced than their counterparts elsewhere along the West African coast or within the Central African region. The initial divisions between them were surreptitiously sown and encouraged by the Ahidjo Regime, which did not favour a strong and united Southern Cameroons especially under Foncha and Jua for fear that they would cultivate stronger ties of unity and identity that could advance secessionist tendencies.

This was part of the policy "to divide so as to better control", which was finally accomplished with the institution of the Unitary State on 20 May 1972. For that matter, Ahidjo was furious and sent a strong message to the leaders of the CPNC and the KNDP in 1965, when it became clear that they were about to forge a union of both parties prior to the formation of the CNU, warning them that the move was against national unity. All he desired was a weakened and divided Southern Cameroons, which he could manipulate. The confirmed discovery of appreciable oil reserves at Bakassi in 1969 by *Elf Serepca*, which reversed the stigma of insolvency with which the State of West Cameroon was identifiedto that of a breadbasket and breadwinner for the Federal Republic of Cameroon only worsened things; strengthening fears of secession.

Ahidjo's solution was typical; hard and swift, the abolition of the FRC and division of West Cameroon.[39] A methodical and constructive study of this subject is handled by George Ngwane, a Socio-Political analyst.[40] Dealing with what he termed 'self-examination' typifying the north and south westerners, he illustrated this with Etekele Endeley who had remarked:

> Like it or not, the North Westerner will always be "hot blooded", wary of making concessions when he thinks he is right; a born fighter and uncompromising radical while the South Westerner will always be a gentleman, even when he knows the other party is wrong. In short, he is a dedicated moderate. We all want national unity, but we need union with ourselves first.[41]

This is apparent, given the fact that people everywhere are a product of their environment: geographical, historical, cultural and social. Like the union between husband and wife, true harmonious family life begins with the couple understanding and respecting each other's peculiarities, strengths and weaknesses. So, if the inhabitants of these Regions know themselves as described above, then it is the best means of defusing any tensions. And in reality, despite the verbiage, there are no recorded feuds with bloodletting in the history of their relations as is evident among the ethnic groups within the regions. Furthermore, discounting these two Regions which can at least look back to a near century long of peaceful co-existence, no other examples can be cited elsewhere in Cameroon.

---

[39]These assertions have been examined in earlier chapters and are dealt with further on in this chapter

[40]George Ngwane, *The Anglophone File (Or, The Story of The Gulf Between The "Coastal "and "Graffi" in Anglophone Cameroon)*. Serialised in the Messenger and published in 1994. P.20

[41]Ibid., The Anglophone File.

Using the quotation above, typology as such is a weak instrument of classification especially in the case of the North and South West Regions, which are inhabited by vastly heterogeneous ethnic groups. It should always be borne in mind that the existing boundaries were German colonial impositions inherited and consolidated by the British Colonial Administration and, finally adopted by the national administrations. One of the first acts of the Organisation of African Unity (OAU) in 1963 was to accept as inviolable, the existing colonial boundaries. The intra-ethnic differences that exist within these Regions are as significant as the inter-Regional ones between them.Relations at all levels are basically governed by mutual interests and relative advantage. We may choose our friends but we cannot choose our neighbours.

In the case of the North West Region it is easy to point out to the long standing, often bloody land- based feuds between villages such as: Bali Nyonga-Bawock; Bali Nyonga –Ngyenmbo; Balikumbat- Bafanji; Balikumbat-Bambalang; Oku-Mbessa; Bambili-Bambui; Bambili-Babanki, Bambui; Nkwen-Bambili and several others.[42] These are no less neighbouring villages because of their differences but they continue to cohabit, learning to accommodate each other. The two Regions for that matter have no such conflicts and **above** all, are both friends and neighbours.

As well, this largely goes to explain the explosion from this thickly populated Region to the coast even long after the departure of the Germans. Organised labour recruitment drives in "Bamenda" for the coastal plantations such as PAMOL, SOCAPALM, CDC, Mukete Farms became common especially after the exodus of Ibos at independence. Earlier in 1927, a census of the labourers on the CDC plantations revealed that of 10.582 workers, only 732 were indigenous to the area with the balance of 9.810 being mostly strangers from the grasslands. This created a situation in which the indigenous people felt like minorities at home and, threatened with this large stranger

---

[42]Nug Eliana Fonsah, "The Ngyenmbo – Bali Nyonga Land Conflict: 1905-2003, MA Dissertation, Dept. of History, University of Yaoundé I, 2005, p.52. Other villages which took up suits against Bali Nyonga included: Mankon, Chomba, Mbu, Mbatu, Tuanyang, and Kurawan.

population naturally developed negative attitudes towards them.[43] Were it ever to be possible to extract the grasslanders from the coast, (South West) there would be intensified feuding between and among the existing ethnic groups. This is best captured by Willard Johnson and Edwin Ardener, who have carried out extensive studies on the area. Drawing from pertinent earlier studies by Murdock, Chilver and Edwin Ardener; Johnson concludes:

> In reality, the unity of the "forest" occasionally exhibited in the politics of West Cameroon, especially when this area is in conflict with the "grassfields "is really precarious even fallacious unity. The forest peoples, by the very nature of their traditional structures, are a fragmented collection of small clans. It is the height of folly to speak of the "forest peoples" as if they constituted a cultural community...[44]

This observation is the result of serious studies by renowned scholars over several years and not an individual's fertile imagination.

## Endeley and Foncha: Grassland and Forest

The *Summit Magazine* interview dwelt at length on the two political leaders of the time; Endeley and Foncha, who represented the Grasslanders of the North-West and the Foresters of the South–West Region. Coincidentally, these are taken care of in an analytical article by Francis Wache entitled: "The Plebiscite: Thirty Years After, The Choice between Fire and Deep Water".Drawing from a close study of the two leaders who were engaged in the political struggle for Southern Cameroons, he makes pertinent comparisons, recalling that: "Endeley returned to Southern Cameroons from Nigeria in 1947, a towering figure, who prided himself as being; the only other Cameroonian with a university degree. He tended to be brash, scornful and downright

---

[43] Henry Kam Kah, 'The Anglophone Problem in Cameroon: The Northwest/Southwest Dichotomy from 1961-1996, in the Cameroon Journal on Democracy and Human Rights. CJDHR Vol.6 No. 1 – June 2012,'p.76.
[44] Johnson, pp. 46-47.

contemptuous of other politicians." He habitually considered his political rivals as mere minions and the villagers as outright natives. Stories of his disdain are legion and apocryphal. Wache cites just three examples. Drawing from Willard Johnson's observations on Endeley's tribalism and arrogance, after his resounding victory in the 1953 election, he noted: "On the other hand, Endeley's tribal loyalties were strong; sometimes combined with his own personal pride to generate hostility among other groups". He notes how:

> Once on a visit to the Mamfe area he boasted to the people there, that whatever they did, they could never achieve the intellectual brilliance and prowess of the Bakweris, epitomised of course, by him, Endeley. This hurt. And the electorate remembered.[45]

Endeley himself a prince and heir apparent is reported to have treated the highly aristocratic Fon of Bali, Galega I, with levity. "One version holds that on a trip to London, after alighting from the plane, he peremptorily asked the Fon to carry his bag. The Fon never thereafter forgot nor forgave."[46] Another relates how Endeley told a rally that; "If the people did not vote, then the stones and trees of Fako Mountain were sure to vote for him". Of John Ngu Foncha: Wache notes:

> On the contrary was a dapper former headmaster, although in most areas in Cameroon at the time the headmaster (HM) represented the acme of academic achievement. Foncha's position *vis a vis* Endeley – was that of subordinate and senior. But Foncha was endowed with other endearing qualities; he was unassuming, unobtrusive and down to earth. Foncha was, in fact, a people's

---

[45] He was the renowned editor of the Cameroon Post, a leading paper
[46] The issue of "bag carrying" was first disclosed by Professor Ngoh as a historical truth. However, he later denied it. Apparently such a thing never happened. During the 1957 London Conference, Fon Galega II, who was there as a representative of the KNC, rejected Endeley's option of integration and when Endeley wanted to push him to support the ideology of the KNC that chose him to attend the conference, Galega II made an idiomatic expression saying that Endeley wanted him to "carry his bag"; Additional clarification by Dr, Michael Lang.

politician; a grassroots politician. He would perch on his bicycle and furiously peddle into the nooks and crannies of his constituency. Or, where the roads were 'unbicycleable', he would trudge for miles just to meet the people.⁴⁷

Again, Wache, contrasting the pair noted: "While Endeley was inclined to scoff at any one who showed signs of slow-wittedness", Foncha, with a pedagogue's patience, took pains to explain and convince." He adds that above all, Foncha exploited his intuitive understanding of the whims of the Fons, and was scrupulously reverential and deferential towards traditional rulers. He concluded: "Thus, while Endeley thrived, or, rather, waned, through arrogance which was to turn out as his political nemesis, Foncha cultivated and nurtured homeliness, humility and tolerance."⁴⁸ In other words, the differences between the two men and impact on their political achievements went far beyond simple sectional and ethnic explanations. There was a world of difference in their attitudes to the populace (electorate). This had little or nothing to do with North and South West but rested on their individual characters.

An external but ardent and disinterested contemporary observer, John Percival, one of the UN Plebiscite Officers, who dealt with the two personalities closely at the most critical moment in their political life and that of Southern Cameroons as a whole, noted with a certain degree of precision:

> Foncha had a strong following in the grasslands and many people evidently felt greater affinity for their cousins on the Francophone side than they had for Nigerians. 'Ibophobia' was widespread and the KNDP took full advantage of it. Dr. Endeley's CPNC on the other hand, seemed to take little interest in the campaign, perhaps assuming that the violent upheavals in Cameroun would win the case for Nigeria.⁴⁹

---

⁴⁷Ibid., Cameroon Life pp. 6-8
⁴⁸Ibid., Cameroon Life.
⁴⁹Ibid., See, John Percival, The 1961 Plebiscite, pp. 77-78.

Nevertheless, Ngwane critically believes that we should build bridges and not walls. Who really stands to benefit from the division between these Regions? It is by recognising, accepting and analysing our differences that the way forward can be constructed wary of mistakes and pitfalls of the past. He analyses this 'divide' factor from a psycho-historical perspective. To Ngwane:

> The North/South West divide is built in the psychology of the people; it is one that has left scars in the minds of the old. It is indeed the bitter memories of a fratricidal conflict, provoked by personality clashes, escalated by behavioural attempts and exploited by bread and butter politicians. It is a case of a breach of trust and a crisis of confidence between two brothers who are nonetheless bound to share a common vision if they must avoid an imminent cultural holocaust.[50]

Other influential advocates of a return to the two state Federation like Professor Kale admonish the admission of errors of the past, sinking differences, defending cherished cultural values in the face of Francophone aggression, while, Lawyer Nico Halle castigates hatred, mudslinging, resentment and fragmentation which impede Anglophone unity and holds that these should be replaced with love.[51] However, finally, when placed squarely in the Cameroon context; examining all the alternatives, it clearly emerges that the Southern-West Cameroon unlike all the other Regions has a track record of having existed as a political entity comparatively with the most minimal disagreements, the exaggeration of differences notwithstanding. Their being split was the personal decision of President Ahidjo in violation of the Federal Constitution. Besides, it took a UN organised referendum to establish the Federated State but a Presidential Decision to split the State into provinces. Far too much was taken for granted and all of these mark out a flurry of grave irregularities.

---

[50] Ngwane, Anglophone File, p 20. However, questions about who he was, what qualified his being quoted and in what context he made his statement are another issue.
[51] Ibid., Henry Kah.

### Evidence on Record: Building Bridges

Interestingly, allegations about the incompatibility of these sister regions are not backed by any documented evidence of the time, as can be demonstrated from the tracts of their historical origins from pre-colonial through colonial times to independence and post-independence. This is obvious in the voting patterns, ministerial appointments, both intra- and inter- party from 1951-1966. Under the administrations of Endeley, 1954-1959, Foncha, 1959-65; Jua, 1965-68 and Muna, 1968-72, there were usually recognized conventional attempts to balance up the ministerial appointments in government as well as in other top positions between the regions.[52] In fact, Endeley had more North Westerners than South Westerners in his cabinets while, Foncha and Jua had more South-Westerners than North-Westerners in their cabinets. Southern Cameroons was not extra-terrestrial but a state of mortals with all human weaknesses. However, they did better than similar nations. This emphasizes the factor of the political options chosen by the leaders and their appeal to the electorate and not merely to geographical, regional or ethnic affinities. In Chapter Four it is amply demonstrated that the Southern Cameroons electorate was politically more mature than their counterparts elsewhere.

Furthermore, statistically using the February 1961 plebiscite as the most credible benchmark, Endeley's own Victoria Constituency voted only 25% for integration with Nigeria, and a whopping 75% for reunification with Republic of Cameroun, while Nkambe in the extreme North West grasslands, voted 66% for integration with Nigeria (Endeley) and a meagrely 24% for reunification withRepublic of Cameroon (Foncha). Nor was this an isolated case, rather it was the typical example of a pattern that had been consistent since the introduction of democratic elections in the territory in 1951. It is easily pointed out as evidence of the depth of these divisions that a pro-

---

[52]Ibid., Kale, Political History of Southern Cameroons; Emmanuel Aka, The British Southern Cameroons 1922-1961; A Study in Colonialism And Underdevelopment; (Madison: Nkemnji Global Tech, Platteville), 2002 p.254.

CPDM South West Elite Association (SWELA) and the South West Conference of Chiefs advocated a ten- state federation for fear of Northwest hegemony. This is countered by the strong argument that what is required are genuine leaders not self-styled individuals, who think their education and wealth make them leaders. The argument continues: "Anglophones should desist from using others as stepping stones to rise to top positions or using them as pawns in the political chess game".[53] However, it should also be noted that no recent census or study has been conducted to establish the fact that the differences between these Regions have widened.

However, without any studies, but just by systematic observation, it is obvious that the factors that divide these Regions are by far weaker than the ones that bond them. Rumourswerefloated at one time suggesting the merger of the South-West Region with Littoral as well the North West with the Western Region, so as to dilute and neutralize their identity. It will be recalled that these feelers received very hostile reaction from the Anglophones and were quietly shelved. Even then, up to 1990, the Military Commands for the South West and North West Regions were deliberately situated at Douala and Bafoussam, capitals of the Littoral and Western Regions respectively.[54] And in any case, finally it must be stressed that nowhere, whether in Cameroon or in any other nation is the type of compatibility envisaged in the interview between and among political units possible.[55] In fact, any such 'global' study is likely to indicate that if anything, in Cameroon, the Anglophones of the two Regions are those with the least divergences and likely to stay and work together as they have done and still do even without any political ties.

Logically, taken a step further, the two Regions in many ways possess ideal composite: geographical, human and natural resources which, when blended, complement, enrich and strengthen each other like mortar in a concrete structure. That is why as Southern-West Cameroon, the territory was appropriately depicted as 'the Switzerland of Africa, 'an island of peace and a perfect tourist destination of choice. It cannot be for nothing that this territory earned the

---

[53]Ibid., Kah p.91
[54]See, the case for Southern Cameroons, p.42.
[55]It would be wonderful to have any such example given

description of 'the nice little' or 'gentle', hospitable people of Southern Cameroons' under British Administration.[56] It cannot be over emphasised that generally, it is a matter of minimizing differences while maximizing the factors that blend to foster unity, coupled with the benefits accruing from such relationships that bring diverse groups of people together. As a result, this makes for unity in diversity rather than unity in uniformity. Any sort of unity forged out for the purpose of uniformity such as that intimated in the interview without elbow room for flexibility and liberty is likely to be brittle and to shatter under stress. This is a basic principle in drawing up any Fundamental Law of the Land, which like the American constitution is expected to endure. There can be no durable unity without liberty.

Consequently, for any thought of the two Regions coming back together as a political unit the capital question would be the nature of such a union. Significant changes have taken place over the years and so careful thought would have to be given to it so that any lessons learnt from experience and history are heeded to as the way forward towards fruitful unity. This can only make for a better future. Neither should it be forgotten that the two Provinces, which on 11 February 1961 had voted for reunification were not even remotely consulted before their separation, nor reasons advanced before, or after the decision was taken and implemented. As has been demonstrated, the most significant change that took place transforming the Federal Republic of Cameroon into the Unitary State was the splitting up of the State of West Cameroon into two, while the rest of former East Cameroon stayed intact until 1984. The explanation may not be found in records but abounds in the logic of events.

**The Reality: Undiluted Loyalty to Endeley**

With references to the past, loyalties to the early leaders, Endeley and Foncha from the populace were never so widely ethnically or regionally based as commonly portrayed, a factor which becomes clearer given the population imbalance between the two regions. In making any comparisons this fact must always be borne in mind and

---

[56]Ibid., Malcolm Milne p.434, also Golden Age of Southern-West Cameroon, etc.

the politicians of the time were always conscious of this inequality when drawing up their political strategies or making important appointments. Nevertheless, one indisputable point deserves to be made from the start: that from 1951 till 1955, Endeley enjoyed the total and unqualified support of all the North West (grassland) MPs, Chiefs and populace, with Foncha as one of his staunchest and most loyal supporters. As Secretary General of the KNC, Foncha worked harmoniously and faithfully with Endeley and the KNC party until March 1955, when deepening differences between them over reunification led Foncha to create his own party.[57]

His stand behind Endeley was clear and unshakable.[58] Originally, opposition to Endeley rather came from Mbile and his KPP and from his own cousin, PM Kale, who maintained that although they were very close, when it came to politics, they never agreed. He points out how much he deeply appreciated the faith and confidence Dr. EML Endeley had in him on "matters pertaining to the Cameroons, historically and otherwise". He further points out to the fact that they lived together in Lagos for seven difficult, unbroken years "as seekers of adventure ... trying to find a means of carving a niche for Cameroons in the history of the world".[59] However, he concludes:

> Paradoxically, Dr. Endeley and I have never seen eye to eye in politics over the years. We have always had ideological clashes. But in writing this book as the first one, he has been most enthusiastic and vocal in urging me to reproduce my experiences in book form.[60]

It should equally be noted that other than PM Kale, Endeley had grave differences with Dibongue and Mbile both of them from the coastal region. Hardly at any point in their political exploits did PM Kale in any meaningful way join forces with Endeley, preferring either to work

---

[57]Dan Lantum ed., Foreword by ET Egbe, "Tribute to Dr. John Ngu Foncha 1916-1999." This was amply demonstrated in his reply to PM Kale when requested to detach himself from the Benevolent Neutrality Bloc of Endeley to join the Mbile camp.

[58]Ibid., Robert Louis Stevenson.

[59]Ibid., Preface to Political Evolution in the Cameroons, PM Kale.

[60]Ibid., PM Kale.

with Mbile, alone, or finally as it turned out with Foncha and the KNDP.[61] In other words, with this particular example neither consanguinity nor tribal or regional affinity could be used exclusively to explain support for either Endeley or Foncha. In substance it took a lot more than that to draw the massive support of the population.

By the same token there are no significant differences of any kind recorded between Endeley and either Foncha or Jua from the grasslands before the schism of 1955. The split resulted eventually from ideological and not regional or ethnic differences. During the heat of the plebiscite wrangling, JO Field the Commissioner observed with consternation in one of his reports to the Colonial Office that the disparities between and among the KNC/KPP alliance leadership were demonstrably worse than those they had with their KNDP opponents.

In fact, Foncha's overall support for Endeley was clearly established in his unshakable stand behind Endeley's 'Benevolent Neutrality Bloc'. This is best expressed in his letter to PM Kale of 6 May 1953 appealing for solidarity. In other words, Foncha, the 'grasslander' (grassfields person) was pleading with Kale, Endeley's cousin to join him and the other Cameroonians in support of Endeley's ideology on disentanglement from Nigerian affairs. In the letter Foncha declared without prevarication:

> I stand by the policy of Benevolent Neutrality (Endeley) not because our support of the NCNC was not beneficial but because I feel that Cameroons should begin to manage its own affairs without undue outside influence. I feel that the NCNC and the others have 'shown the light' and Cameroonians must 'find the way'.[62]

This brief extract is significant in more than one way. It clearly demonstrates that Foncha's stand in 1953 was precisely what he stood for during the elections in 1959 and the reason why he and Jua had parted ways with Endeley's KNC to form the KNDP in 1955. Throughout, he had remained faithful and consistent on secession

---

[61] However, Kale was a member of the KNC/KPP Alliance from 1957-1959 but he did not hold any significant post.
[62] Ibid., Kale., p. 41.

from Nigeria and eventual independence for Southern Cameroons. With regard to his letter to Kale, having stressed his stand on Southern Cameroons seceding from Nigeria and managing its own affairs, a policy he never deviated from to the very end, Foncha declared without evasion:

> Any Cameroonian who will stand by any Nigerian political party in order to be led to find his way is false to his own conscience and to the Cameroons at large. I am calling upon you to assist our effort. ... We don't trust the imperialists. Therefore stand with those for the policy of neutrality (Endeley) and help the nine who stand by it. We do not consider whatever took place in Lagos but we merely believe in the ideology involved. It gives the Cameroonians a wider field to exploit opinions ... for the benefit of the Cameroons National move for separation with all its parts appended to Nigeria.[63]

In the first place, anyone accusing Foncha (and Muna) of low educational qualifications would certainly re-think the accusation after critically reading this letter. Foncha's support for Endeley's stand on secession from Nigeria was total, a position he continued to hold and which led him to create the KNDP in 1955, when Endeley wavered. It was precisely the reason why he wanted Kale on board. However, for inauspicious reasons, Kale preferred to back Mbile against Endeley.

Throughout the entire political existence of Southern-West Cameroon as a political entity, Victoria from which Endeley came remained a KNDP stronghold, while Nkambe and Kumba after the KNC/KPP alliance because of Mbile, became loyal to Endeley and the CPNC. Yet, geographically, Nkambe was in the extreme north of the Bamenda Grasslands, while Victoria was at the heel of the Coastal Forest Region. Nor should any false impression be given that the inhabitants of either Region were monolithic and unwaveringly belonged together. Emmanuel Aka converts this analysis into simple statistical form for better understanding. He even demonstrates this comparatively and internationally:

---

[63]Ibid., Kale pp. 41-41.

In fact, unlike Nigeria and French Cameroon, the main political parties in Southern Cameroons were national rather than tribal and regional until after independence. In the 1957 elections, for example, the KNC got only 38% of the votes in Victoria; 42% in Kumba; 39% in Mamfe and 51% in the grassfields region, while the rest of the votes were given to the KNDP. Indeed, many of Endeley's staunch supporters were from the grassfields region and many of Foncha's strong supporters were from the coastal districts.[64]

These are indubitable facts of history. Indeed in matters of policy, Foncha's primordial attachment to the development of the Limbe Deep Sea Port and the security of the CDC and Marketing Board against the predatory ambitions of the Francophone administrations till his dying day were unrivalled and irrefutable.[65] The intriguing questions good for research should be why and how Endeley came to lose this initial ubiquitous support, popularity and adulation which he enjoyed throughout Southern Cameroons up to 1957.

---

[64]See Emmanuel Aka, *British Southern Cameroons* p.195; also, Ndifontah B Nyamndi, the Bali Chamba of Cameroon: a Political History. (Paris: Editions Cape), 1988.

[65]Ibid., Foncha's Letter of Resignation.

Eugen Zintgraff, German Explorer in Bamenda 1889-1892
Seeds of Discord: Migratory Lessons in History

We live in a rapidly shrinking and changing world governed by irrepressible technological, socio-economic and political forces that are forever creating new forms of conurbation. Consequently, reference to North Westerners settled in the South West should be understood in their proper historical context such that; the "Come no go", "Sons of the soil", settler syndrome as became prevalent during the political turmoil of the 1990s can be put to rest as regrettable, insensitive and unfortunate utterances ensuing from culpable ignorance, prejudice and self-gratification by a few "underachievers" and self-seekers. When appropriately analysed, they deserve to be classified under, "crimes against national integration and national unity".

For most residents of the South West of North West extraction unlike their compatriots from other parts of Cameroon, their origins there must seriously be taken into account. Some have ancestry there dating back to over a century, so reference here is being made to third generation Cameroonian citizens, whose grand and great-grandparents were drafted, literally "press-ganged" at gun point to work as labourers on the German plantations at the coast which were subsequently transformed to present day CDC property. With Zintgraff's explorations in the Bamenda grasslands from 1889-1892 and the discovery of large reserves of robust manpower there, the German Administration was determined to harness them to replace the foreigners who currently supplied the labour needs for the plantations at immense socio-economic costs to the German plantation owners.[66] This is to say, these grasslanders did not go to the coast on safari. For proponents of division, "It's an ill wind that blows nobody any good". This only emphasizes the point that right from German times, Bamenda Grasslands and the Coast were seen and treated as a complementing socio-political and economic unit.

Nowhere in Cameroon or in Africa as a whole for that matter, can communities be found that are wholly homogenous and sedentary, claiming to be indigenous settlers of the areas which they presently occupy. Taking a bird's eye view of the continent: the Fulani with origins in the Futa Jalon Mountains in Senegal are spread throughout the breadth of West to Central Africa; the Yoruba are found all over Western Nigeria and overflow into Benin and even Togo, while the Ibos who even claim Israeli ancestry are found everywhere in Africa and beyond. The history of much of Africa therefore is characterized by migrations, caused by great movements such as the "*Mfecane*" (or Shaka Wars) in Southern Africa, which after clashes with the Afrikaners (Great Trek) affected not only that region but several modern day states as far away as: Mozambique, Tanzania, Malawi, Zambia and Zimbabwe. On the other hand, Bantu origins largely resulted from population explosions which are traced to the Central African Region with Southern Cameroon specifically identified as the base extending to the Congo Basin. It is generally described as an "ethnic shatter zone." In short, the history of Africa is a flux of migration, integration and disintegration and few, if any ethnic groups can logically claim sole heritage to the land they presently occupy to the point of excluding others.

Willard Johnson, one person who carried out an in-depth study of patterns of identity in the indigenous cultures of Southern Cameroons

---

[66] EM Chilver, Ministry of Primary and Social Welfare and West Cameroon Antiquities Commission, (Government P3r9inter, Buea, 1966), pp. 30-33.

(citing Edwin Ardener in the Kamerun Idea, on the issue of affinity between British and French Cameroon), firmly reiterates:

> If all irredentist theories were allowed full rein, the Southern Cameroons would be destined to be torn asunder by its neighbours, or conversely, it would assimilate vast tracks of these neighbour's own territory.[67]

This quotation demonstrates the superficial, impractical and ridiculous context of the 1990 hate slogans. In fact, in this analysis, Ardener in: Coastal Bantu of the Cameroons elaborately demonstrates the extent to which the coastal ethnic groups are a series of "discontinuities" with the Bakolle, Bamboko and Bakweri; all being offshoots of the Douala.[68] On the other hand, as regards the claims of coastal-forest unity, Johnson vividly dismisses this as a misleading notion. He maintains that the unity of the "forest" occasionally exhibited in the politics of West Cameroon habitually erupts only "when this area is in conflict with the Grass Fields". At the cost of repetition, he considers it "a precarious, even fallacious unity" maintaining that:

> The forest peoples by the very nature of their traditional structures are a fragmented collection of small clans. It is the height of folly to speak of the 'forest people as if they constituted a cultural community, except perhaps in terms of the anthropologist's general categories.[69]

Within the same breadth, turning to the Wedikum, of the North West Region as if anticipating the profile that follows, Willard further posits that: "The unity of the Wedikum Clans tends to crumble when there is no anti-Bali issue".[70] In the South West Region, the scattered settlements of the Kpe-Mboko Group comprising over 104 villages in the mid-1950s were self-evident. This situation was made more

---

[67] 34Ibid., Johnson, P.42.
[68] Edwin Ardener, Coastal Bantu of the Cameroons, (London International African institute), 1956.
[69] Ibid., Johnson. p. 47.
[70] Ibid., Johnson

complex by the German colonial policy which focused at economic exploitation of the natural and human resources of Kamerun pure and simple, countenanced no opposition and used all means at their disposal to attain this objective without compunction.[71] After acquisition of vast stretches of the fertile volcanic land along the coast and opening up large plantations, throughout their rule, they never found adequate labour, till their expulsion in 1915. This led to the desperate search for labour from as far afield as: Liberia, the Gold Coast, Togo, Lagos and the Congo. German replacement by the French, who introduced their own colonial policy of 'Assimilation' in French Cameroon with the *indigenat* (or *corvee*), similar to the German version of forced labour, led to waves of refugees migrating to the plantations from varied ethnic backgrounds including: the Ewondo, Bassa and Bamileke. These found solace in the coastal plantation towns of Victoria, Tiko, Muyuka and even in Kumba, but generally, throughout Southern Cameroons.

## German legacy: Quest for Robust "Native Labour"

However, the German labour recruitment policy as applied in the North West is a case apart and deserves more than just a passing comment. The extent to which the German plantation labour policy was extreme and led to the depopulation of Bali and its vassal villages is best illustrated in its impact on the Moghamo Clan.[72] One of the main purposes of opening up the Cameroon interior was to create and maintain a steady supply of labour to the German plantations in the south and as a steady source of income to the Colonial Government treasury in the form of taxes.

The Germans were convinced that they could not do this all by themselves and so co-opted some indigenous rulers into a new ruling class to act on their behalf in the recruitment of labour and the collection of taxes.[73] Between 1898 and 1901, the WAPV and other

---

[71] Ibid., Bob O'Neil, p. 142.
[72] 39 In fact, this is a fertile area for investigation, good enough for a PhD dissertation in: History, or other work on Conflict Resolution: a failed nightmarish example.
[73] Ibid., Ndi, p. 108.

German plantation interests were encouraged and motivated by the supply of labourers from Bali to the coast. From earlier on they had realized that the profitable exploitation of the Cameroons plantation resources depended on ample local labour supply. Comprehensively citing original sources on the difficulties of acquiring local labour, the cost of externally imported labour as well as the high cost in human life from Bamenda, Bob O'Neil, who carried out extensive research on the topic lucidly reports:

> This question of labour supply had been a critical problem at the coast. The point was that the coastal peoples refused to work on plantations and the practice of contracting for foreign labour from Cape Verde to the Congo, especially for Wey, Bassa, and Krumen from Liberia, could not be continued. It was thought that workers from the Grass Fields, being acquainted with agricultural practices more than coastal and forest peoples, were better suited to plantation work. Unfortunately, malaria as well as cocoa did well on the slopes of Cameroon Mountain and many sent from Bali died. One report sent in 1901 reported that between 25 and 50% never returned after their contracts were up.[74]

Reliance on foreign labour from these distant places was difficult to sustain, expensive to maintain, retain and became economically untenable. Eugen Zintgraff, who entered German Government service in 1886, first reached Bali in January 1889, precisely to seek their replacement with sturdy natives from the interior. Thus, in 1890 during his second visit, Zintgraff arrived in Bamenda on an important mission set to:

> Cement the friendly relations with the chiefs, to maintain peace and order in the hinterland; to use all efforts to open undisturbed and secure caravan routes to the coast; and to channel the trade of the hinterland along these routes to the Kamerun coast.[75]

---

[74]Ibid., Bob O'Neil, p. 114.
[75]Ibid., Ndi, p. 97.

### Picture Galega I Fon of Bali

### Got into Blood Pact with Zintgraff

Fon Galega I of Bali; an eminent ruler of a large Kingdom in an area that was "divided into several tribes with chiefs of little authority over them", easily stuck out as the most prominent ruler in the Grasslands who met the German prescriptions of a collaborating ruler. Immediately, Zintgraff was determined for his purpose, in the interest of the German Government to increase the power of Galega I, with Bali becoming a full - fledged German station and even capital of the Bamenda Grasslands. With attractive propositions, Galega offered him an exceptional mutual blood brotherhood pact, usually contracted under very serious circumstances between most intimate friends.(43)?By this the Fon undertook to send several hundred men annually to the coast for each of whom he received a head tax. In this policy Zintgraff was assisted by other Germans, Franz Hutter, who ran the Baliburg Station and Conrau, the WAPV Labour officer, who was active in Bali until his death, while on a recruitment drive at Fontem in 1899.[76]

Gustav Conrau, the German commercial agent got to Azi, the Fontem capital in February 1898 in search of commodities such as: rubber, ivory, and artworks but especially labourers for the plantations at the coast. During the first trip he took with him porters for the merchandise he had acquired to the coast but returned without them and without any plausible explanation. The following year he had the audacity to ask for yet more labourers, whereupon he was tactfully held hostage until he could account for the men. Realizing the perilous situation he was in, among many plans, he is alleged to have shot himself to avoid capture and torture. When news reached the Coast of Conrau's death the Germans reacted excessively; not only was German rule precipitated in Azi and Lebang, but as well in the rest of Bangwa country. Yet by German standards of brutality, this was not enough:

> In typical colonial German punitive tradition, the recriminations were harsh and severe. Houses were burnt and the palace at Azi suffered serious damage. Asonganyi escaped to a hideout but eventually surrendered, if only to halt the pain being inflicted on his people. The king of Lebang was exiled to Garoua in 1911 … The surrender, capture and exile of Fontem Asonganyi emerge as the logical consequence of a defeat in battle but retrospectively, the outcome for the Nweh people went beyond mere capitulation, capture and exile.[77]

---

[76] Ibid., Ndifontah, p.99.
[77] Ibid. Chilver, Zintgraff p.VIII.

**Gustav Conrau: Served in Kamerun 1892-99**

In 1900, Captain Ramsay, who had become the General Agent for the geschelelshaftnordwestkamerum (GNK) North West Cameroon Company, joined the fray for trade and labour concessions. The first to benefit from this deal was the *West-Afrikanische Pflanzsellschaft* Victoria (WAPV) who received the Bali recruits in June 1897. Following this by 1900 the (GNK) challenged WAPV monopoly seeking for a share in the deal as well. However, instead of sharing the labour supply between them, the quotas were instead simply increased to meet the new demands.

Galega and Fonyonga who succeeded him resorted to mass recruitment launching indiscriminate, reckless and inhuman raids throughout the Bali Empire. By 1904 alone, Fonyonga supplied 1.700 able bodied men to the plantations and in 1912 the entire Bali Empire was vastly depleted with no more than 4.000 men, down from 20.000 at its peak in 1900. With such mind boggling numbers, it becomes heartless and insensitive to regard people whose forebears were victims of such barbaric German labour policy to be regarded simply as

"Come no go". By the same logic these immigrants should respect the traditional values of their host country as it was customary grassland tradition as well.

Jesko von Puttkammer, Governor 1855 - 1917

## Bali - German Hegemony and Brutality

In retrospect, Captain Adametz was led with uncommon candidness to observe that: "The flower of the Bali nation lies on the Cameroon Mountain".[78] Not content with the Fons's hegemony so far, on 13 January 1903, Governor Puttkammer issued a release placing

---

[78] See, Michael Ndobengang and Fiona Bowie, "Azi Since Conrau", in, For Shirley G Ardener - Iya Efosi, p, 101.

Fonyonga II, who had succeeded Galega I, "full protection of the Imperial Government". They would stop at nothing to empower the Fon in supplying labour. For this purpose, on 15 June 1905 before an assembly of 47 Grassland Chiefs, his paramountcy over 31 villages of "his empire" was formally declared under the watch of Captain Hans Glauning. In fact, eleven Wedikum villages were physically and savagely detached, and resettled in Bali, which alone increased its population again to 20.000 in 1907. The Germans had calculated that by recognizing Fonyonga's position and boosting his ego, they would ascertain his loyalty to their cause and increase his potential and effectiveness as an agent in recruiting labour and collecting taxes.[79] German plantation labour demands were insatiable and their brutality as well knew no bounds.

## Incredible Savagery: Depopulation of Vassal Villages

The WAPV investments were so precarious that they were not too concerned with the extreme forms of viciousness used by the recruiters. Fon Galega was given a free hand in his recruitment methods and allowed his well-armed 'basoge' traditional troops – actually labour raiding bands of warriors, who numbered some 6,000 free rein. They were well trained and equipped to the hilt with M-71 riffles under Captain Franz Hutter. The development and brutality of these German supported raiders (Bali-Troop) from 1891 to 1893 turned even "Old Moghamo trade friends" against Bali Nyonga. Their inhuman tactics resulted in the depletion of Moghamo village manpower and by the same measure gravely undermined the socio-political and economic authority of the village leadership.Bali-German hegemony was felt as far afield as: Baforchu, Pinyin and Nkombu. But eventually, plantation labour supply came from every nook and cranny in the North West Region.

In fact, the story is still told of Fon Acha of Batibo, who at the summit of the aggressive recruitment refused to send any more of his people to Fonyonga of Bali but instead sent him a stone. This was considered intolerable insolence by the Fon and the Germans.

---

[79] 46Ibid. p.98.

Consequently, Fon Acha was arrested and banished to Banyo. On being released, he still had to pay homage as well as tribute of elephant tusks to the Fon of Bali.

Furthermore, the Bali soldiers under Captain Hans Glauning burnt and ransacked Ngyenmbo in 1905.[80] Whole areas between Ambo Village and Batibo together with a strip along the escarpment ridge along Lower Ashong were depopulated.[81] By 1902, the opening of Bamenda Station in addition to the WAPV and the GNK made its own extra demands for messengers, labour for road building and porters for expeditions. It was soon discovered that the Bali irregulars had degenerated into armed raiding bands whose influence went beyond Moghamo to as far south as Kumba, where they extracted ivory and revived slavery, capturing some of the labour recruits intended for the plantations. They were becoming rivals to the Germans in the control of the trade routes to the south. Better put:

> Increased labour recruiting for plantations, road-building, work at the Bamenda Station, carriers for food, maintenance of area paths and Rest Houses, and claims for tribute and workers at Bali, became intolerable and led to open rebellion. Anong, Batibo, Enyoh, Bunji, and Ambo were among the villages that were part of the uprising in 1906.[82]

However, the rebellious villages were energetically punished and had to submit to forced labour, the delivery of ivory and livestock once their tenacious resistance was broken. It was something of a scorched earth policy especially as the Batibo people in particular were in Bob O'Neil's words:

> .... plundered of their most valuable resource - much of their able bodied population – excluded from former trade agreements and from sources of wealth on main trade routes of former days – slaves, ivory and other products – harassed by armed Bali irregulars

---

[80]Ibid., Ndifontah p. 109.
[81]Ibid.,Nug Eliana Fonsah, "The Ngyenmbu – Bali Nyonga Land Conflict: 1905-2003," MA Dissertation, Dept. of History, University of Yaoundé I, 2005, p. 49
[82]Ibid., Bob O'Neil, pp. 95-97.45

village authority in Moghamo had little choice but to unite their meagreresources to resist further demands of recruiters...[83]

So far, fairness, justice and compunction were not part of the game, but after the killing of Glauning in March 1908, it became apparent that the Moghamo villages had been thoroughly exhausted and deserved to be allowed to rest and recuperate. It was also discovered that native farms were neglected, family life shattered and it was necessary for the few people left behind to be controlled so as to provide portage for local produce. When in 1984, Bob O'Neil was carrying out research in the area; passions were still aroused over the boundaries set between Moghamo and Bali Nyonga. The memories of nineteenth century Bali-German raiding bands, seizure of their land and depopulation with enduring lamentable consequences were still fresh.

The Bali-Ngyenmbo neighbours who suffered the same fate revolted repeatedly against Bali Nyonga hegemony in: 1906, 1907 and 1914, after their chiefs had been humiliated and flogged in public to little avail. Consequently, they abandoned their compounds and sought refuge in the nearby villages of Mankon, Kobinyang and Baforchu leaving empty depopulated areas by as much as 85% behind. This was followed by litigation which was ongoing as recently as 2012, when the research was being carried out.[84] All told, the Germans disappeared from the Cameroon scene after 1915, a century ago, after irreparable demographic damage had been inflicted both on the Cameroonians at the coast and in portions of the grasslands, with accusing fingers continuously pointed at the Bamenda–Grasslanders. These are indelible facts of local and national history that deserve further investigation about the Bali and their neighbours under the Germans.

These people as clearly identified were if anything, themselves mortal victims of the German colonial policy of insatiable labour recruitment for their plantations at the coast. One socio-economic and cultural corollary not immediately visible has to do with the depopulation especially of Moghamo area and the physical relocation and resettlement of eleven villages in Bali Nyonga. Equally, it is

---

[83] .50Ibid., Bob O'Neil, p. 125.
[84] Ibid. Bob O'Neil. p. 129.

established that 25-50% of the able bodied manhood from Bali and the vassal Moghamo villages, who were forced to the plantations at the coast never came back. The question of what happened to the forlorn wives, widows and female population left behind in the fluid circumstances, where there was a general reversion to slavery and slave labour in Bali under the Germans could well be conjectured. The answer logically may partially be found in the embedded Bali Nyonga tradition of polygamy and concubinage.

The Bali Nyonga of Chamba extraction, are often cited as a typical example of a homogenous Fondom especially when compared to the fractious Tikars and Wedikum ethnic groups. However, there exists an intricate social mechanism in the Fondom for absorbing and integrating immigrants into its social fabric. This process was greatly enhanced during the devastating German Labour recruitment practices which added 31 smaller fondoms to the Bali Empire and flooded the polity with an influx of Moghamo and Baforchu male but mostly female folk.

A lucid anecdotal example is given by Mr. John Fomuso who recounts that his father, an immigrant from Baleng in Bagangte, West Province was most cordially received and given ample land, which still exists, where he built a large compound of 48 houses each of which accommodated between one and three women. This was far from being an isolated case but a hospitable trait of the Fondom by which numerous immigrants were incorporated for as long as they paid allegiance to the Fon and respected its traditions. This explains the fast expansion of the Fondom. In other words, the visible external solidity resulted from a carefully constructed internal machinery fashioned to integrate foreigners in the Fondom. In the case of the Fomuso family they were large enough requiring their own Based Mission Church, which all the women and children especially were compelled to attend on Sundays. Arising from this practice a significant number of the sons became pastors and presently serve throughout the national territory with the PCC and other protestant denominations.

# Haemorrhage and Demographic Imbalance

This premise is further reinforced by the fact that women generally were regarded as chattel and a ready source of farm labour especially with the introduction of coffee as a cash crop in the region. While there was a superfluity of the female population in Bali and the vassal villages, the exact opposite obtained in the plantation towns at the coast. In fact, the situation arising out of the influx of women was such that traditional titled personalities had to be appointed to handle the new situation. These held the ranks of 'Gwan' or special advisers to the Fon as Privy Councillors in the hierarchy; one of whom received and accounted for the new group of immigrants, especially women coming into the Fondom and the other who ensured that they were properly appropriated among those privileged to be given a share of these women who invariably became wives, house maids or concubines. This practice may not wholly explain the origin of polygamy in Bali Nyonga but certainly enhanced it to the point where it has become an intractable culture in the Fondom[85]. Here reference is being made to hundreds of women. So far it has been established that a vast number of the pioneer labourers drafted from the grasslands, who could not weather the storms of malaria and other tropical, coastal diseases succumbed and paid with their lives.[86] Most of the survivors settled at

---

[85] Ibid., Nug Eliana Fonsah, "The Ngyenmbu – Bali Nyonga Land Conflict: 1905-2003", MA Dissertation, Dept. of History, University of Yaoundé I, 2005, p. 52. Other villages which took up suits against Bali Included: Mankon, Chomba, Mbu, Mbatu, Tuanyang, and Kurawan.

[86] They were known as "Gwan'fogbe" ,and "Gwan' Mesia" respectively. "Gwan'fogbe", literally translated as "the noble at the entrance", was responsible for receiving and incorporating 'strangers' into the clan. Of course, the vast majority of these were the female folk. Responsibility for the distribution of the women was that of Gwan' Mesia. Some of the nobility possessed as many as thirty wives besides concubines, a practice that was considered legitimate. Professor Mathew "Gwan'fogbe's" grandfather, likely the first holder of that title, was modest and married only 27 women, while, Mrs. Elizabeth Gwanyama's grandfather who had as many as thirty wives was no exception: Discussions with Professor Elias Nwana, March 2013, CATUC, Bamenda; and further discussions with Ba'Nkom, Dr. Thomas Tatah Fofung, a title holder in the Bali Nyonga Fondom as well as with Professor Mathew Gwan'fogbe, University of Bamenda and Mrs. Elizabeth Gwanyama in June 2013 Mr. John Fomuso is a retired " Commissaire Principal". The author is married to Patience Luma Ndi, daughter of Ba'Nkom Mukong Gwanyama who was married

the coast in the plantation towns and account for a sizeable population of the "grasslanders" in the region.

To call these compatriots on whose sweat and lives the economy and development of the region has not largely been built, such derogatory names as was the case in the 1990s is certainly insensitive; nor does Cameroon Land Law discriminate against South Westerners of North West origin and vice versa. It is worth noting that there is no comparable aversion for South-Westerners anywhere in the Northwest Region[87] possibly because their numbers even in Bamenda, the NW Regional capital are hardly significant.

Giving the impression of such incompatibility between people who were administered as a single political entity under the Germans but more significantly under the British with Buea as their capital, 1916-1972 negates historical evidence and fans unnecessary flames of discord at a time when the call is for national unity. This in no way condones the arrogance frequently ascribed to South Westerners of North West extraction, who traditionally should behave as worthy guests or immigrants to their coastal hosts. This does not reflect the assumed grassland traditional respect paid to hosts, strangers and elders

Referring to those sowing seeds of discord, Foncha thoughtfully enumerated and analysed the adversities which Anglophones have suffered since 1961 reaching a peak in the early1990s and the extent of the division between North and South West Regions as well as Francophones and Anglophones as a whole. He declared that it was deliberate, veiled government policy under Ahidjo. He categorically disclosed this in his Letter of resignation in 1999 noting the fact that:

> The national media has been used by the Government through people who never voted for unification to attempt to isolate the Anglophone Cameroonians who voted for unification and subject

---

to three wives. These examples can be replicated effortlessly to dozens if not scores of other such families. For further details see, Anthony Ndi, "Relations between the Catholic and Basel Mission in Bali" in, *Fifty Years of Selfhood of the Basel Mission.*

[87] Ibid., Ndifontah B Nyamndi, *The Bali Chamba of Cameroon: a Political History.* (Paris: editions cape, 1988).

them to hatred and more discrimination and harassment from other Cameroonians.[88]

**Foncha and Muna; Timeworn Friendship**

Foncha simply highlights the fact that the over played differences between the North and South West Regions are remote controlled and fanned by government agents of destabilisation. This was a matter of policy by the Ahidjo Administration.

## Of Public Apologies: JN Foncha and ST Muna

Commenting on the apologies made by Dr. JN Foncha and ST Muna at the All Anglophone Conference (ACCI) at Mount Mary, Buea in 1993, in the *Summit Magazine* interview, Professor Ngoh noted the "sad part" and that:

> It was an opportunity that the Fonchas and Munas wanted to polish up the mistakes that they made in 1959, 1960, 1961. Surprisingly in that hall in Buea, there were politicians as well as civil servants and civil society members who knew exactly what the situation was in 1959 and 1960s... when they were told that they

---

[88] This is another challenging area good for research.

had a poor deal with Ahidjo because they did not have lawyers, none of them raised a finger.[89]

However, the more significant point should really be the fact that AACI was one of those occasions which plainly demonstrated the decisive solidarity among Anglophone, Southern Cameroonians when critical issues had to be discussed, that touched their hearts. The same unanimity had happened when clamouring for the creation of the University of Buea as an Anglo-Saxon type institution and the GCE Board to conserve their British cultural heritage. Attendance at the Buea Conference cut across all ethnic, geographical, political, age and religious divides. The prayer said by Rev. Pastor Ayuk on that occasion continues to resonate in many hearts. They acted in unison and spoke with one voice. By all descriptions, definitions and critical analysis, AACI remains a great historical Anglophone land mark, a story of success, the hostile political climate of the time notwithstanding.[90] However, a report of the same occasion by a veteran journalist is rendered here. It reads differently:

> Pa Foncha had an opportunity to explain himself and apologize to his people during the All Anglophone Conference in Buea in 1993. With superb courage, sincerity and humility, an ageing Foncha drew some tears when he said: 'We tried our best at the time … but we made our mistakes and pleaded for forgiveness.'[91]

This is the version the rest of 'us' heard.[92] Among the over 5.000 strong population not only were tears shed, it was one of those very rare occasions, when the participants spontaneously rose to their feet

---

[89] Ibid., Foncha's Letter of Resignation.
[90] *Summit Magazine*, Epilogue.
[91] Turning back to the question, Professor Ngoh himself was there among the more than 5.000 participants and did not raise his own 'finger'. What again went wrong with this throng, were they hypnotized or just plain stupid? Honestly speaking, how were these octogenarians in 1993, expected to polish the mistakes of 1959-60? Bring back the arms of the clock?
[92] Ibid., Tribute.

and gave the ageing statesmen Pa Foncha and Pa Muna a passionate, hair raising, standing ovation just as described by the journalist above.[93] Certainly they were not mesmerized to behave this way. It was the Anglophone ethos that moved them.

The apology by Dr. Foncha (as well as that by Mr. Muna) at the AACP' meeting in Buea in 1993, was not because he failed at Foumban or anywhere else but rather because he thought that his administration would have done better if they had the qualified personnel and lawyers (Messrs Egbe, Dinka, Engo and others were still studying in London) at their disposal at the time. Indeed, it was a genuine expression that came from the heart and was received with equal vehemence by the crowds that thronged Mount Mary. It is interesting how simple statements can be interpreted out of context. Put in proper perspective, it is enigmatic to have expected Foncha to apologize for the Foumban Constitutional Conference which, when well understood then and until today remains such a huge success as demonstrated earlier.Besides, full thought should be given to the happenings at the Buea Tripartite Conference.

Dr. JN Foncha was prolific at the art of seeking forgiveness and that he apologized on that occasion was only one of the countless times he had done so privately and publicly during his political career. For all there is in the character of great leaders known in history, the first quality generally is humility and the realization of human frailty. It is this virtue which leads them to apologize, a sign not of weakness and failure but of fortitude, courage and strength. This effuses from a feeling of continuous self-evaluation, magnanimity, prowess and above all the desire to do better.

The other pertinent take-home message from the All Anglophone Conference holding at Mount Mary, Buea in 1993 was the sagacious answer Mr. ST Muna gave to a question, when asked why he had stuck with Ahidjo for so long despite his anti-Anglophone policies. Mr. Muna's response was memorable. He said he had been hopeful and expected positive change, which unfortunately was not forthcoming and that was when he resigned. To illustrate this he gave the pertinent

---

[93]Perhaps, Dr. Foncha (and Mr. Muna) were supposed to be condemned and sentenced to some lengthy terms of incarceration for daring to "confess" that they did so much and could have done better given the means.

proverb: "When crossing a deep river with a fast current you plod with a long stick and when you find that the current is too powerful and would sweep you away, it is prudent to reverse." This explanation like the Foncha apology drew deafening, thunderous applause. Those who are self-centred, conceited, arrogant, insensitive (to the plight of the masses) never even get to know what is wrong or right because they are full of themselves. This of course, is the stuff dictators and masochists are made of.

In recent times, we have been witnesses to public apologies made by renowned world leaders like: Popes John Paul II and Benedict XVI, Tony Blair, Presidents Barrack Obama and George Bush and the Archbishop of Canterbury, Ronan Williams. Still of great momentous classic proportions is the case in South Africa with the apologies made by Frederic W de Klerk, Nelson Mandela and Archbishop Desmond Tutu, which have seeded the now famous 'Truth and Reconciliation Commission' phenomenon used in Sierra Leone, Liberia and currently underway in Ivory Coast and still spreading.

## Open Tribute to Funders and Donors

Foncha is said to have written "secret letters" to French Cameroonian billionaire businessman, Soppo Priso 'begging' for funds to run the KNDP. Elsewhere and at other times, he would have used such wealth to line his pockets! But to Foncha and his colleagues across the political divide in Southern Cameroons, such was hardly ever the case. The money was put at the service of the public or exclusively for party use. The "gigantic" KNDP secretariat (at the time) in Buea which became state property after 1966 is evidence in itself. Further to this, Foncha, rather than act secretively and covertly as depicted in the interview, publicly and openly paid glowing tribute to those who had rendered such noble service or assistance to enable the success of his party including President Ahmadou Ahidjo. (See appendix 5) However, all the political parties needed funding especially during the hectic plebiscite campaigns.

**Picture Sir Abubakar Tafawa Balewa.**

Prime Minister of Nigeria, Assassinated in the 1966 Nigerian Coup d'état

Thus the CPNC sought and received heavy funding and assistance from Nigeria. For example, writing back from Lagos, where he had gone to solicit assistance for the KNC/KPP alliance campaigns for the plebiscite from the Nigerian Government, Mr. RJK Dibongue disclosed that he had frank and cordial talks with Chief Festus Ekotie-Eboh, Federal Minister of Finance," in which he touched on all aspects of the political problems facing the party in Southern Cameroons. In Dibongue's words:

> Chief Festus was kindness itself and gave assurance that Nigerian political leaders were willing to render financial, propaganda material as lay in their power and all that was required was for the party to indicate their requirements upon which Dibongue enumerated: propaganda vehicles, funds and a team of propaganda experts to reinforce our own propagandists ... I

pointed out that our political opponents, the KNDP, have had similar assistance from political leaders in what is now the Cameroon Republic.[94]

In all, as requested the assistance totalled 12 land rovers or trucks, 10.000 pounds for a start, and propagandists for the six Divisions. Chief Festus considered these demands modest and all that was required was the assurance that the party would campaign fervently for integration with Nigeria. Eventually, a lot more than this was delivered as even the Prime Minister of Nigeria, Sir Abubakar Tafawa Balewa personally flew into Victoria and campaigned for the CPNC party.[95] This of course was normal. The point however is that in the interview, Foncha is isolated and negatively depicted as a beggar. This is a solid point that should have been made contextually and comparatively to illustrate the manner in which the political parties raised funds for their campaigns during the plebiscite and possibly how this enabled one side to elbow the other. This bias trend is patent throughout the interview; a factor which undermines the historical value of the important issues raised.

So far, it is obvious that several irreversible trends have taken place profoundly affecting the lives of the people of the former Southern Cameroons. These constitute the fact that having been administered as a political unit first by the Germans till 1915, followed by the British for over forty years from 1922-1961, and, finally as part of the FRC from 1961-1972, there are indelible traitsingrained in the psyches of the people of these regions that forever will identify them as "Anglophones". To these should be added the geographical, socio-cultural and economic factors that tangibly and intangibly will continue to bond them. At the human level, the reality of the Grass-landers forcibly settled and integrated in the coastal areas of Southern Cameroons as a deliberate consequence of German colonial plantation labour policy is equally a given. These are facts and lessons of history

---

[94]Why this apology drew tears from the masses but almost 'jeers' from Professor Ngoh is paradoxical; the same occasion widely positively reported in most papers.

[95]Ibid., Mbile, Cameroon Political Story-Memories of an Authentic Eyewitness, (Presbyterian Printing Press, Limbe), 1999, p.135.

63Ibid. p. 141.

that we have to live with wholly independent of our individual whims and caprices likes and dislikes.

## Southern Cameroons: Divisions 1948 – 1961

There were two Provinces: North West with the Capital at Bamenda and South West with Buea as the Provincial and State Capital

In context, it is established that the majority South Westerners of North West origin did not go there on their on their own volition. It was a result of brutal colonial German plantation labour policy and they paid dearly for it. The adverse effects of this policy in the North West Region are still hurting in relations between the Balis and their neighbours. These facts should be known in proper context to avoid insensitivity and to cultivate greater tolerance and understanding between both Regions. Without becoming partisan, history is the single most appropriate discipline that is positively and deliberately used by Governments to instil national integration and national unity. Lessons can be learnt from all our former colonial masters: Germany, Britain and especially France which pursued the policy of assimilation.

# Chapter 3

## North and South West: Factors in Reunification

### A Case of Identity

The strength of the nation at large depends on the coherence of the individual families, ethnic groups and larger units that constitute it. And, since much of the art of nation building from disparate polities is done by using the rear mirror of history to chart the way forward, the examples of the rise and decline of old nations and states is usually taken as models. For Cameroonians, the example of Germany its erstwhile colonial master is most instructive. Theirs was a conscious and deliberate option in which they took off with 300 principalities or states in 1648; coalesced into 39 at the Treaty of Paris in 1815, then again in 1849 and finally in 1871 unified as the German Empire under the hegemony of Prussia with Count von Bismarck as Chancellor and Frederick William I as Emperor. This was a clear case of unity in diversity and not unity in uniformity with states like Hannover, Bavaria and Prussia itself retaining their identities within a Germany, whose political, commercial, industrial, naval, military and imperial might became globally overwhelming and even threatening. Therefore, it is illogical and impractical to conceive of a solid unity of the whole (Cameroon) without considering that of the parts that embrace it.

Thus, to place the North and South West Regions that until 1972 constituted the State of Southern and later West Cameroon, as anything less is clearly being oblivious of the historical hallmarks, lessons and milestones through which the present Regions passed, conscious that people are products of their past. It would also be tantamount to dismissing the bases on which anyone can talk of an "Anglophone problem" or their marginalization within the larger Cameroon unit. With the passage of time, political intrusions and even some disguised English-speaking Cameroonians by word and deed have distorted the historical concept of the 'State' of Southern/West Cameroon. This is extensively and rapidly being eroded and fading into the textures of; a "minority group", section, or even being attributed tribal connotations and equations. Much worse, there are those who regard the Anglophones as nothing more than insatiable trouble makers and rabble rousers, who deserve no undue attention. It is such culpable ignorance that this work sets out to redress.

Such of course is oblivious of the historical origins of the North and South West Regions and far removed from the point of departure on 1 October 1961, the significance and invincibility of which was engraved in Article 47(1) of the Federal Constitution. Reunification and independence on which it was mounted historically remains a political decision, the dissolution of which paradoxically was predicated on unsubstantiated economic excuses. However, the socio-cultural, economic and ethical traits are indelibly ingrained in the consciousness of the people. Historically, Cameroon comprises Anglophones Francophones distinguished by culture, language and geography. Without reference to this foundation, there can be neither reason nor basis for talking of an Anglophone problem. This is the basis for corporate feeling, identity and the platform from which to declare such distinctiveness and be recognized as such.

By the way, it was Southern Cameroonians (NW and SW) who sought for and fought for reunification at a time when French Cameroonian political leaders were still dabbling with ideas of fusion into France as an extension of the French Overseas Community. This was one major reason which Endeley claimed led him to turn his back on "reunification" even with Dibongue the leader of the French Cameroon Welfare Union. The logical excuse was that Southern Cameroons could not be contemplating reunification with French Cameroon which was toying with becoming an overseas territory of France.[96]

The real tragedy is that since the parting of ways of the influential troika comprising Mr: Ekontang Elad and Doctors Carlson Anyangwe and Simon Munzu, who like the magi in Bethlehem ably galvanised the Anglophones and infused in them a sense of identity, focus and purpose, the Anglophone cause has since become a spent force. Presently, with so many discordant factions with voices contradicting

---

[96] In the recent past, especially during the political campaigns in the 1990s, there was fervid talk of *Sawa* connections galvanising South Westerners against the North West but this pretty soon vaporized.

each other's values and demands, there is an endemic crisis of leadership. Were the powers that be ready to address the so-called 'Anglophone problem' in any radical, meaningful manner there would hardly be any agreeable leadership to speak for all of them. Here Professor Tazoacha Asonganyi interposes with a terse philosophical view that connects firmly with the vision of this paper, on the continuity and dynamism of history. He makes the succinct philosophical comment that:

> Time has eventually done what it does best. It has eaten into the foundation of the United Cameroon and revealed it to be frivolous. It is difficult to accept that over 50 years later, the Anglophones from a sovereign, democratic Southern Cameroons that had seen democratic change of government in 1959, chose unification with Francophone Cameroon in order to support the moral and political contradictions, and one –man show so prevalent in our society today, Cameroon seems to be trapped in the throes of the French, and yet the only person who can save Cameroon from the confusion generated by that is the Anglophone.[97]

In fact, he makes the unassailable point that Southern Cameroons is an indispensable equation in the solution of national unity in Cameroon. In a genuine democratic setting, it is understood that; while the majority may have their way, the minority have their say. Their needs are listened to and met. And, for that matter former Southern/ West Cameroon comprising the 'Anglophones' was not merely a minority but a solid political unit, a State, which as 'West Cameroon was co-equal with 'East Cameroon' (Republic of Cameroun) as a bilingual, bi-cultural Federation at reunification on 1 October 1961. There was no question of size such as subsequently crept in. This is a fact of history, a rock on which the Cameroon nation will stand or fall. It stands to reason that for any enduring peace, sanity and stability for the Republic of Cameroon a solution wherever from, is required as a matter of necessity. However, while Malcolm Milne apologized on behalf of

---

[97] Ibid., *Eden Xtra.*, p. 54. As analysed in the Foncha Resignation Letter, the divisions could be part of government design as a means of divide to better control.

British misdeeds and asked for amends, Charles Assale the staunchest Ahidjo henchman was adamant and non-committal, when a similar question was put to him.

## Charles Assale: Painful Truth and Arrogance

Charles Assale, the first Prime Minister of the Federated State of East Cameroon, together with President Ahmadou Ahidjo signed draft Federal constitutions and other documents with the Foncha Government. His 'voiced opinion' in a public interview was quoted in *'Le Temoin', Le Patriote* and the Cameroon Radio and Television Corporation (CRTV). He rightly but rather arrogantly, provocatively and with incredible insensitivity declared that reunification was essentially an Anglophone affair. To this effect he pointed out that:

> Ahmadou Ahidjo was never interested in reunification... French Cameroon became independent without reunification and assumed sovereignty on 1 January 1960 to become Republic of Cameroon .... The 1961 United Nations plebiscite, which resulted in the Cameroon union, did not involve the Republic of Cameroon. Of their own accord, Anglophones unilaterally opted to achieve independence by joining the Cameroon Republic. Reunification was not an imposition from Francophones.[98]

Of course, it is not true that reunification was absolutely unilateral. Assale accompanied Ahidjo during his maiden visit to Southern Cameroons and was certainly party to his pronouncements at: Tiko International Airport, Buea and above all at Victoria on 17 July 1961 on the openness of Republic of Cameroun to receive Southern Cameroons, the terms of such a union and the declaration that unification was a debt both Trust Territories owed to their ancestors.

---

[98] Nicodemus Fru Awasom, "The Reunification Question in Cameroon History: Was The Bride An Enthusiastic or Reluctant O6n3e?" in, *Africa Today*, Volume 47. No. 2. Generally, the Francophone political elite in particular and the public at large are not versed with the historical roots of the Anglophone woes or even the basic facts of reunification. This largely affects their unsympathetic attitude towards the Anglophones whom they regard simply as minorities and trouble makers.

Logically, taken another step further, if the Anglophones on their own opted unilaterally for reunification, they should by the same token be free to make other options. However, as a matter of fact, Assale says nothing new but painfully pours salt into the gaping wounds wrought by his master, President Ahmadou Ahidjo, who operated with his assistance and connivance. It should be recalled that he served as Ahidjo's greatest prop and together with him and Foncha co-signed, two broadly Federal constitutions on record, neither of which featured at the Foumban Constitutional Conference; while hell was let loose about Foncha keeping back a copy of Ahidjo's own highly centralized Federal Constitution. This confirms and imputes the fact that from 1 October1961 to 2 June 1972, he was only playing for time to dissolve the FRC.

Assale's remarks would confirm Foncha's observation in his Letter of Resignation that:

> The people of Southern Cameroons never participated in the elaboration and adoption of the supposed federal constitution of 1961, which was adopted by the National Assembly of la Republique du Cameroun and promulgated by the President of la Republique du Cameroun on 1 September 1961 that is to say one month before the birth of the Federal Republic of Cameroon. These same people never participated in drawing up the unitary constitution of 1972, which was imposed upon them in a nationwide referendum.[99]

For Assale to have turned round to boast of such dastardly deeds done to the people of Southern Cameroons is a mark of supreme arrogance, insincerity and insensitivity. Foncha further declared logically and categorically: "I can state here and now that the people of Southern Cameroons would never have voted in favour of unification if it had not been for the assurances given that the resulting union would take the form of a federation".[100]

---

[99] Ibid.
[100] Ibid., Dr. Foncha's Speech during the Constitutional Consultative Committee in December in 1994.

**Professor Bernard Nsokika Fonlon [1924 -1986]**
**Frist Cameroon Ph.D. Graduate, Minister in Ahidjo Government**

Assale's stance contradicts that of his boss, Ahidjo, who, when addressing the National Assembly of la Republique du Cameroun in August 1961 on the subject of unification explained to the representatives of his people that:

> The different colonial experiences towhich ourtwoterritories have been subjected had left an indelible mark on our political and administrative habits , on our methods of work and on our ways of life; that it would be futile, and a sign of serious lack of understanding to this, and that it was out of the question that la Republique du Cameroun would want to impose its system of thought, its way of life and particularly its manner of conducting public affairs that had been differently brought up in these matters.[101]

When on 6 May 1972, the same President Ahidjo singlehandedly announced to the Federal National Assembly his unilateral decision to

---

[101]Idem.

abolish the Federation and replaced it with a Unitary State nothing practically had changed from the situation that obtained in 1961. The Unitary State was therefore no more justified in 1972 than it had been in 1961. Consequently, with hindsight, it was now obvious to Foncha that:

> The process of annexation of Southern Cameroons by la Republique du Cameroun had begun almost as soon as unification had been achieved and against which many individual and collective voices were raised among the leaders and people of Southern Cameroons including myself and the KNDP.[102]

Among the many paradoxes of Southern Cameroons history is the fact that both the British Administration and the Ahidjo Regime considered it an economic liability, reason why it was jettisoned by Britain and reluctantly accepted for fostering by the Ahidjo's Regime. However, the discovering of oil reserves in 1969 became the reason for strapping it firmly to the apron strings of the Republic of Cameroon.

**Suppressed Rebellion Federal National Assembly, 1972**

It was generally known but highly concealed in the dictatorial climate of the time that after President Ahidjo unilaterally announced the dissolution of the East and West Cameroon Houses of Assembly and House of Chiefs; and declared the referendum of 20 May 1972, there was a groundswell of opposition throughout the territory. At the highest level, there was a threatened rebellion, which like many things has remained muted. This was when all the ten West Cameroon Members of the Federal House of Assembly walked out together with Dr. Foncha and gathered in Dr. Fonlon's residence leaving the forty Francophone Members of Parliament in the House. Tension built up rapidly as Ahidjo ordered armed troops to surround the premises, meanwhile negotiations were going on.

After deep reflection, Fonlon cautioned that as he saw it, further resistance would spark the beginning of a civil war that would be futile

---

[102] Idem.

as they were simply going to be crushed without any consequence. He then counselled that they should return to the Assembly and "leave the war to be fought by their forebears".[103] These facts of history should rekindle minds and spirits making this generation wiser, more mature and better informed than their ancestors. This is the liberating value of history, which in matters of wisdom is comparable only to the bible; however, unlike the bible, 'history does not forgive those who fail to learn the lessons of history'. With these facts it is difficult to pretend that nothing awful happened as we cannot disown what we have lived and experienced not only for ourselves but for posterity. Sweeping and hiding the dirt under the carpet does not solve any problem. It only postpones the day of reckoning.

## Return to Legality, Reason and Hope

In this light, Awasom points out that the Southern Cameroons National Council (SCNC) an umbrella Anglophone pressure group together with the Diasporas, stand for the restoration of the federal status, arguing that Francophone politicians have betrayed the basis of reunification which they initiated. They stress that: "The former British Southern Cameroons was neither conquered; captured nor annexed by the Republic of Cameroon." In view of the fact that Anglophones alone participated in the 1961 plebiscite that resulted in reunification, a view negatively affirmed by Charles Assale, an Ahidjo's apologist, they point out that:

> Today no group of people who freely join a political union would want to be treated as a captive people. In 1961, the people of Southern Cameroons, through a United Nations plebiscite, decided to enter a political union with la République du Cameroun, whom they considered as their brothers and fellow countrymen. They did so by grace of God, freely and without involvement or participation of the people of la République du Cameroun.[104]

---

[103]Discussion with Hon. Joseph K Kwi, at CATUC, Bamenda, 11/05/13. As a qualified Labour Officer, he was a significant intellectual actor in the Southern Cameroons drama.

[104]"The All Anglophone Conference" quoted in Awasom.

Like many broadminded, forward looking, compatriots and nationalists, Ngwane, who has given serious thought and researched on the idea of federalism, is an optimist and a visionary, who should be taken seriously. To him, the future holds bright prospects for the federated state of West Cameroon in particular and the Federal Republic in general, a spirit which he thinks should be kept burning. Here he shares the views of Professor Asonganyi and concludes poetically:

> It rings a bell that the democratization process in Cameroon can only be delayed, it can never be denied. It rings a bell that though we all climbed the Mount Mary mountain top together; some of us some time descend the valley of despair and still grope in the wilderness of mutual suspicion. But even though we are weary and our minds worried, our eyes have seen the promised land of federalism and we shall get there sooner than later.[105]

And to say the least, these 'Anglophones' at Mount Mary, Buea for want of a better name, camefrom within and without the country in their numbers at great cost, inconvenienceand sacrifice. To minimize the significance of that event is to play the ostrich or as they say: 'to have learnt nothing and forgotten nothing'. It equally makes the point that Anglophone unity is not a matter limited to the North and South West Regions. Any reference to unity between them that ignores the Diaspora is myopic and unrealistic.[106] Further contextualizing the issue, the *Eden Xtra* editorial reminds readers that Southern Cameroons took the lead in initiating and furthering reunification and has become the only country in post-colonial Africa except Eritrea and Southern Sudan, both of which have become independent, to have known internal colonization after having been fully prepared for self-

---

[105]Ibid.,Ngwane Anglophone File,p. 31. See also "The All Anglophone Conference, The Bamenda Declaration,"April 29th - May 1st.1994.
[106]The concept of "nation" transcends geopolitical boundaries; the Jews maintained their unique existence for centuries until 1948. The Southern Cameroons diaspora is increasingly being infiltrated and becoming polarized as well.

government and been freed from the shackles of European colonization.[107]

## Durable Tangible and Intangible Bonds

The political factor apart, there have been by far, other stronger tangible and intangible bonds developed over the years between these two complementary regions which no wishful thinking can dismiss. These ties are based on linguistic, socio-economic, cultural, historical, religio-pastoral and above all, geographical and demographic which go far beyond any administrative or legislative statute. The flames of division are mostly fanned by a handful of self-seeking, self- appointed politicians and elite, who arrogate to themselves the authority and privilege to speak on behalf of the voiceless masses. While, no census or study has been undertaken to support the assumptions on the incompatibility of the two Regions the educational, cultural, spiritual, economic, social and fraternal ties grow steadily from strength to strength. Following these natural trends and with improvement in socio-economic, cultural and communication links, these imperceptible bonds would in time create a solid polity on their own accord.

Bonds established through intermarriage, economic, educational, cultural and spiritual interaction are imperceptible but are real, profound and far stronger than meets the eye. One only has to listen to the news or announcements over the radio, read the papers and visit the transport agencies to take a pulse of what transmits between these historic sister- regions. Rev. Fr. Arthur McCormack an early principal of St. Joseph's College Sasse, visiting West Cameroon sixteen years later as an expert on population matters in the early 1960s was amazed at the socio-economic and educational progress that had been made. In admiration of what he had seen he clearly announced:

> I would have liked statesmen of developing countries which have racial or nationalistic troubles to have seen how in friendship and partnership, peoples of different nations and races are working together for development in Cameroon- the same friendliness and

---

[107] Ibid., Eden *Xtra* editorial.

courtesy, the same welcome to the stranger were in evidence, the same fine people of a beautiful country with leaders more concerned with the progress of their country than personal position or power.[108]

It is remarkable that these unique, admirable qualities are not appreciated, treasured and emphasized by some citizens of these highly endowed Regions but, who rather seek needles in haystacks to highlight their differences. The flawless communities sought for exist nowhere save in fantasy. If anything, relations in the Christian Churches are continuously being reinforced despite the push and pull factors. Generally the various Christian denominations set out positively and deliberately as a matter of principle to promote fraternal and national unity. This can be observed at the level of the North and South West Regions in the pastoral structures and utterances of the Bamenda Ecclesiastical Province (BAPEC) for the Catholics; the Presbyterian Church in Cameroon (PCC) and the Cameroon Baptist Convention (CBC) for the Baptists. Besides and even more pungently, a casual cross-checking of the records of attendance, admissions, transfers and graduations in secondary, technical, commercial, grammar and increasingly in tertiary institutions would reveal an amazing transformation that is naturally taking place largely between the two regions and cross-culturally between the Anglophone and Francophone Regions. Any talk of national integration in Cameroon has much to copy from the examples being practically demonstrated by these mainline religious denominations. These clearly are unstoppable trends.

For emphasis, this bonding came out forcefully as indicated, during AACI, which held at Mount Mary, Buea in 1993 and the resolutions taken there, especially with regard to a federal constitution, despite political restraints[109]. With the completion of the ongoing road construction and other communications network following the Green Tree Accord, connections within the Southwest Region and between the two Regions deliberately left to atrophy since reunification would naturally be strengthened. And by the way, even if these regions never

---

[108] The Editorial, *Catholic Information Bulletin*, 24 March 1964.
[109] This could constitute a challenging area for research.

return to any form of political union in the short run, improved relations between them as neighbours and friends would continue to benefit national unity and national integration. It is an acknowledged fact that unity of the whole is strengthened by that of the parts that constitute it.

**The World: A Global Village**

Historically, the world daily contracts in the face of the fast advancing technology and all the nations including our former colonial masters are groaning under the throes of "devolution," a syndrome that is affecting even France, one of the most highly centralized nations. However, Great Britain and Belgium make better case studies in relation to Southern Cameroons. Britain which once possessed a vast Empire over which it was boasted "the sun never set", brutally, suppressed nationalist aspirations in Northern Ireland and, from 1600 with mild alterations in 1832, and in 1918 fought endless brutal wars to frustrate Irish aspirations for autonomy. Welsh nationalism censored since 1534 had by 1979, some five hundred years later, begun enjoying a measure of autonomy; while Scotland savagely scorched like Northern Ireland and forced in submission to unite with Britain in 1701, now has its own parliament, with options to declare full independence outside Great Britain. This is history in its true essence, dynamic, whose wheels are unstoppable, forever in motion. It also affirms the fact that what Britain did to Southern Cameroons though anachronistic was not an isolated case.

## The Kingdom of Belgium and Others

Belgium is a case apart. King Leopold II, ruler of that tiny Kingdom colonized, personalized and ruthlessly exploited the vast Belgian Congo severaldozen times its size from 1884-1908, when the territory was taken over by the Belgian State. Nevertheless, the plunder of the resources and subjects continued, a legacy bequeathed to the neo-colonialist regimes at and after independence in 1960. It is instructive that Belgium itself finally became a federation only in 1970 after one and half centuries. Presently, it is being threatened with further balkanization in three or four different directions: Flemish, Walloon, French and German. Placed in this context Cameroon is still in an embryonic state. Equally, we lived the experience of the mighty Union of Soviet Socialist Republics (USSR) which shattered like sheets of paper in a blast of wind in the 1990s at the same time as East and West Germany reunited pointedly as a "Federation"!

Among former Third World colonial states, India once the "Pearl of the British Empire" 'begot' Pakistan and Bangladesh. Coming closer home to Africa, there are numerous examples of states and nations that have evolved from the ashes of others such as: the former Central African Federation known as Rhodesia and Nyasaland, which today comprise three full blown states: Zimbabwe, Zambia and Malawi. There are as well premature failures like the Senegambia (an attempted union of Senegal and Gambia); and the transient Ghana, Guinea, Mali Union; from which lots of lessons can be learnt. Other examples include the Somalis: British, French and Italian. The celebrations marking the founding of Southern Sudan as the newest African sovereign state are a heartening example but that came at a high prize, after a bloody struggle with millions of lives lost and property destroyed over several decades. The other startling lesson is that in none of these examples have states that enjoyed autonomy been subjected into any centralized system; always it has been unitary states breaking up into autonomous components. The other example involving a former German Colony is that of Tanganyika and Zanzibar which federated into Tanzania.

Map: Neu Kamerun
Apogee of German Kamerun 4 November 1911 - 4 March 1916

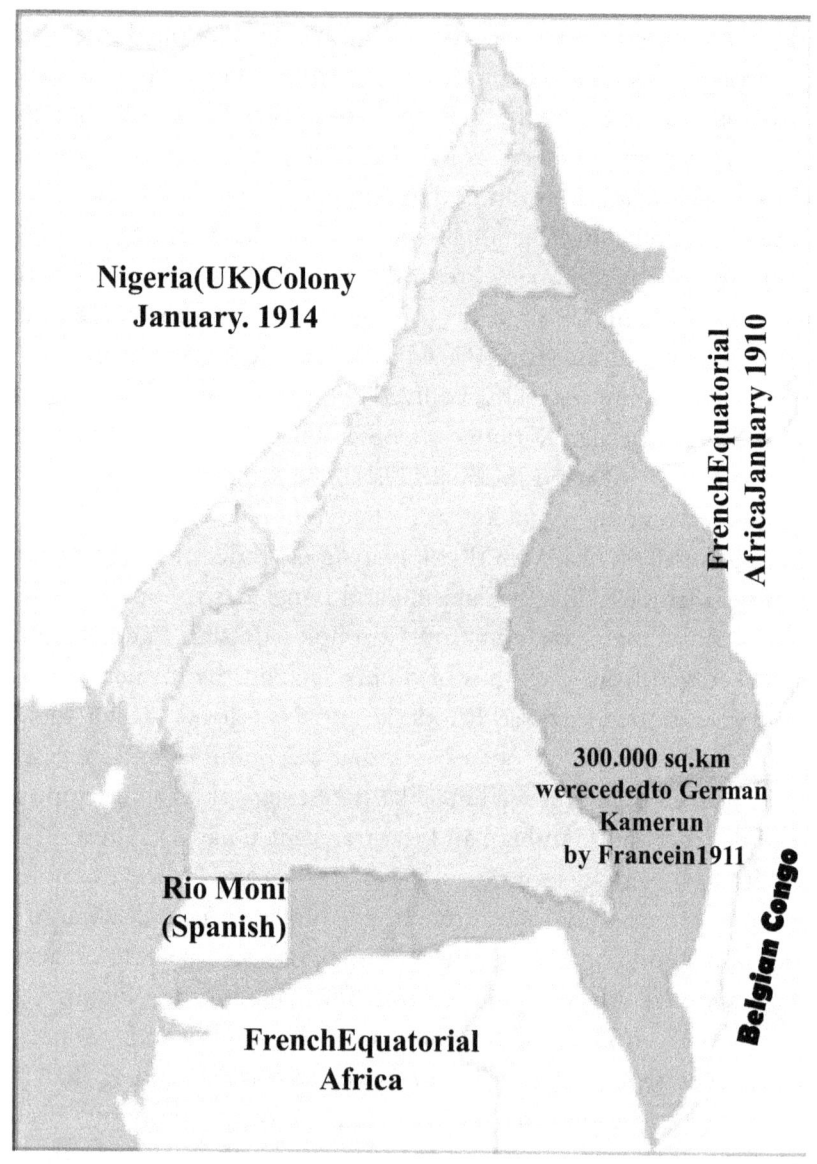

Adapted from en, wikipedia.org/wikiNeukamerun.

## Anglophones Could Not Have Voted for Self-Annihilation

Lessons here using the British example amply demonstrate the fact that state formation could be an extremely slow, lengthy and arduous process which could take hundreds of years. For as long as there are unheeded and ignored nationalist murmurs with people ready to take up the cause and pay the required prize, there is always hope. From the example especially of Britain, the adage that: "Those who suppress evolution make revolution inevitable" comes to mind. Taking the cue from what is taking place in old states and nations like Great Britain, Germany, Belgium and elsewhere in Europe, as well as in India, Pakistan, Bangladesh and Sudan, all that can be said is that Cameroon is still in the early stages of nation building and it would be too early for anyone to sing the swan song.

Driving home this point from another angle, Professor Carlson Anyangwe argues forcefully, firmly, historically, legally and logically that:

> The Southern Cameroons did not vote, and could not have voted for annihilation of its own personality and identity and for treatment of its citizens as stateless, as persons of lesser order. That would not have been self-determination but self-destruction.[110]

In his open letter to the people of Southern Cameroons, Foncha expressly and resolutely put it in historical terms:

> We did not come cap in hand to be integrated to French Cameroon. French Cameroon people accepted the federal system. Ahidjo categorically declared before the UN that any policy on integration on the part of French Cameroon would sound the death knell on the hopes of the people of British Cameroons. *He further declared that they of French Cameroon were not annexationists.*[111]

So far it is clear that Southern Cameroonians were denied the option of independence "the Third Choice" during the plebiscite

---

[110] Ibid., See Anyangwe, p. 87.
[111] Idem., also, Foncha, Open Letter

through British intrigues. Furthermore, President Ahidjo reneged on every single promise he had made on the terms of reunification and finally proved himself with the "unilateral" abrogation of the FRC on 20 May 1972. This was his own contribution to inescapable traps for Southern Cameroons.

## Evolution of Southern Cameroons: Basic Mile Posts

The political evolution of Southern Cameroons is intertwined with its chequered colonial past. The territory to become Cameroons was annexed when the German flag was hoisted at Douala on 14 July 1884 as part of the general race that was raging among the European powers for the partition of Africa. Under its administration the expansion of German Kamerun reached its apogee during the period 1911-1915. This happened following the Agadir incident between Germany and France, the settlement of which was enacted at the Treaty of Fez, (Morocco) where France ceded 300.000sq.km of land which was added to German Kamerun. The emergent territory called "Neu Kamerun" vastly increased the size of German Kamerun almost comparable to that of Nigeria. However, with the defeat of Germany after World War I by the Allied powers, France seized the opportunity to retrieve the territory it had ceded to German Kamerun which was redistributed among the French territories of: Central Africa: Chad, Ubangi Chari, (present day Central African Republic) Gabon and Congo Brazzaville. Note should be taken of these dynamics when referring to "German Kamerun", which became so crucial in the struggle for reunification and found partial fulfilment in the plebiscite of 11 February 1961. It would be worthwhile finding out what Um Nyobe meant when he declared a return to Cameroon as it was under Germany. Did he anticipate bringing together these former German territories to form one united Cameroon? Conscious that these constitute the bulk of the states that presently constitute the States of Central Africa less Equatorial Guinea, the creation of a greater federated Cameroon (Neu-Kamerun) could be a practical approach in the process towards the realization of the United States of Africa.

## Partition of German Kamerun:

### Condominium 1915-1916: League of Nations Mandates 1922- 1946

In the course of World War I, Douala fell to the Allies on 26 September 1914, mainly to the British (and Belgian) forces but both powers (Britain and France) had not anticipated how it would be administered after German defeat. Consequently, the condominium principle was provisionally adopted on 24 September 1914 maintaining that a joint *ad hoc* administration by Britain and France would be implemented until Germany was completely defeated. Then on 4 March 1916, the remaining portion of German Kamerun was partitioned between Britain and France roughly in the ratio of 1:5 with France acquiring 4/5 or 80%, while Britain took 20% thus ending the so called Condominium. Territories ceded by France to Germany in 1911 reverted immediately to French Equatorial Africa. This was ratified by a French decree of 7 April 1916 which appointed General Aymerich as Commissioner to install a military government in French Cameroon, while General Dobell took charge of the disjointed British Cameroons by a British Order in Council.

French civil administration was introduced on 5 September 1917 and its share of the territory was maintained as a consolidated whole while Britain further partitioned its narrow western portion into: British Southern Cameroons, administered as an integral part of the Eastern Region of its Nigeria Colony, while the other, British Northern Cameroons was administered as an integral part of that region. On 7 May 1919 the Supreme Allied Council in Europe officially allocated the German colonies in Africa to their respective conquerors. The French insisted on annexation pure and simple for their quota of German Cameroon and Togoland, refusing to subject them as Mandates of the League of Nations.[112] However, they finally submitted in to the League of Nations on 20 July 1922, which formalized the partition. Both

---

[112] It is important to note that following Article 119 of the Versailles Treaty signed on 28 June 1919; all German colonies were confiscated and placed under the League of Nations. This disturbed the British and the French who hurriedly met in London on 10 July 1919 and produced the Milner-Simon Agreement which they used to obtain the status of Mandatory powers over Cameroon from the League of Nations.

French and British Cameroons became Category "B" Mandated Territories of the League of Nations which lasted till 1946.

To France, Cameroon was a single political and economic unit attached to the metropole by Article 109 of the 1848 French Constitution which prescribed assimilation as the policy by which Cameroonians would become black French men. By the *politique de protectorat* French Cameroonians were divided into: *Francais, Assimile, Evolue and Quartre Communes*. These latter were further divided into *citoyens* and *sujets*. The *Sujets* were subject to: *Prestation* by which they supplied compulsory labour on specified fields and farms, to commercial companies and on railways and roads. *Corvée* was forced labour, only abolished by the Brazzaville Conference of 1944, while direct taxation, led to forced labour for the production of cash crops. The imposition of '*laissez passer*' or travel permits on the other hand greatly restricted mobility or freedom of movement by the '*sujets*'. Professor Ajaga Nji summarizes this in comparative terms:

> Participatory democracy through indirect rule prevailed in West Cameroon as opposed to the 'highly centralized state modelled on the French system of government 'and a policy of 'assimilation' that prevailed in East Cameroon.[113]

This phenomenon which in terms of forced labour was not very different from the German policy, largely explains the exodus of French Cameroonians to British Southern Cameroons especially along the fertile volcanic agro-pastoral and industrialized coastal areas of: Victoria, Tiko, Muyuka and Kumba but generally throughout the Anglophone sector. And, finally, it was within these plantation towns that the French Cameroon Welfare Union evolved.[114] On the burning desire of French Cameroonians for reunification and the extent to which Hitler's Germany generated anti- French propaganda to that effect, Professor Ajaga Nji quotes a pamphlet published on 21

---

[113] Ibid., Eden Xtra, p.24.
[114] This issue is analytically presented by Professor Daniel Abwa as: "Contributions of Francophone Cameroonians to the Reunification of the Cameroons," in Eden Xtra No. 001 October 2011.

February 1918, which referred to the fact that the Francophones were infuriated by:

> The "bad French policy", had taken refuge on the other side of the Mungo with their brothers. Furtherthey wrote that the bad treatment of the indigenous people by the French Administration had forced many men to desert their families and emigrate to the English speaking part where there was humane treatment, peace and tranquillity... the English Administration in Cameroon was treating the Blackman with a strict respect of justice.[?] [115]

**Foncha and UN VisitingMission in Nkambe**

**The Focus here was on Dairy Produce**

---

[115]Ibid., *Eden Xtra* No. 001 October 2011 p. 20. "Contributions of Francophone Cameroonians to the Reunification of the Cameroons"

United Nations Visiting Mission Received by Youth in Mamfe. They asked for scholarships and Education for Girls

However, the point he emphatically makes is that, notwithstanding whether the Cameroonians found themselves under French or British rule, they generally saw themselves above everything else, first as "Cameroonians" before considering who administered them. This is optimistically captured when Ajaga Nji further maintains that:

> The migrations of Francophones to the other side of the Mungo during colonization constitutes a crucial factor in favour of the subsequent reunification as it provided Cameroonians the forum to learn to live together, in spite of the desire of the colonial administration to separate them.[116]

In summary, these off-rooted French Cameroonian immigrants formalised and generated the thought of reunification although it was a felt need on both sides of the Mungo. The other point is that the

---

[116]Ibid., Eden Xtra,

"Patrimony" of the territory belonged to both British and French Cameroonians in equal measure.

## UN Trusteeship Period: 1946-60/61

With the defeat of Germany again in World War II and the transformation of the League of Nations into the United Nations there followed the creation of the "Trusteeship Council". British Southern and Northern Cameroons together with French Cameroun became UN Trust Territories. These statuses lasted from 1946 till January 1960 for French Cameroon and till 1 October 1961 for British Southern and Northern Cameroons on the attainment of independence by Nigeria. By the experience from the First World War (WWI) Africans unmistakably demonstrated their mettle in liberating France from German occupation. This was re-enforced after their massive contributions during WWII, 1939 -1945. Thus the road map by the Trusteeship Council for the preparation of the Trust Territories under the British and French administrations for ultimate socio-economic, cultural and political development leading to self-government and independence was established. The UN was to ensure that the administering authorities did their homework effectively; they had to report periodically to the Trusteeship Council of the UN answering a battery of questions. As a follow up, the territories were visited periodically by the UN Visiting Missions who keenly reported on the progress and development made in the areas indicated above.

It should be stressed that the creation of the United Nations Trusteeship Council and especially the UN Visiting Missions greatly facilitated and stimulated economic activity and political consciousness in both British and French Cameroons. The various socio-cultural, political and economic development associations in the territory had the freedom to petition against whatever they considered the administering authority was failing to do; which accusations the colonial masters had to defend before the UN Trusteeship Council and the UN General Assembly.

## The Rise of Nationalism

In other words, on either side of the Mungo, almost spontaneously there was evolving a fervent desire for Cameroon unification as demonstrated by the French Cameroons Welfare Union (FCWU) west of the Mungo and the UPC in French Cameroon, which favoured a more urgent and radical approach demanding for immediate independence and reunification. The Kamerun United National Congress, (KUNC) the epitome of all the Anglophone Southern Cameroons political associations bore the ideology of the FCWU and subsequently transposed into the KNC, the first truly political party in Southern Cameroons led by Dr. Endeley. Actually, by the late 1940s there were joint meetings of the nationalists on both sides of the Mungo variously at Tiko, Buea, Bamenda and Kumba, which was the hub of political activity.

It was in the course of organizing themselves to attain these objectives that political consciousness was stimulated since the various socio-cultural, economic, tribal and development associations transformed themselves into 'pressure groups' and then into 'proto nationalist' groups. However, to fully become (political) nationalist associations, there first had to arise among them the genuine concept of a "nation" (a motherland or fatherland) with which they could identify and whose autonomy they sought. This called for patriotism as much as for nationalism, causes for which individuals were ready for any form of sacrifice even of their lives as was the case of the UPC in French Cameroon.

Thus French Cameroonians first identified themselves in terms of Moslem north and Christian south based on religious and ethnic divides. In British Southern and Northern Cameroons administered as integral parts and provinces of Nigeria, it was not so straight forward although political consciousness developed there faster and earlier than in French Cameroon. This was because the pace of political evolution was fostered largely through constitutional developments instituted by Britain in their African colonies from experience in America, Canada, New Zealand and India adapted to local Nigerian demands. These led to the organization of political groups and associations reaching out as the mouthpiece of the masses or common people.

As can be construed, political consciousness depended largely also on the level of education, which in Southern Cameroons during the colonial period was almost exclusively in the hands of various major Christian missionary denominations acting as "Voluntary Agencies". This in no small way explains the degree of discipline and infusion of moral values in the lives of Southern Cameroonian politicians without exception. In other words, the socio-economic and cultural development raised the level of political consciousness and either in anticipation or in response to these, the British Colonial administration drew up constitutions beginning in Nigeria with the Clifford Constitution in 1922, the Richard's Constitution in 1946, the Macpherson Constitution in 1951 and finally the Lytlleton Constitution of 1954, which for the most part applied to Southern Cameroons. Each of them raised the territories closer to autonomy. Thus, there was no cause for violence.

As a consequence of its attachment to the Eastern Region of Nigeria, political awareness in Southern Cameroons first took root in Nigeria, precisely in Lagos the political and economic capital. It was spearheaded by Paul M Kale, then supervisor, teaching in the Salvation Army School at Lagos together with EML Endeley, John Ngu Foncha, Nerius N Mbile, NN Namme and others. They formed the Cameroon Youth League (CYL) structured after the example of the Nigerian Youth League, (NYL) a similar organization in Nigeria. The CYL was attached to the National Council of Nigeria and the Cameroons (NCNC) 1944, the first Nigerian political party which fought for the political rights of Nigerians and Cameroonians led by Dr. Benjamin Nnamdi Azikiwe.

Note of course should be taken of Mr. GJ Mbene, President of the Cameroon Welfare Union (CWU) formed at Victoria in 1939. It had branches throughout Southern Cameroons and Lagos and was active for some years fighting for representation of Southern Cameroons in the Legislative Council failing which it petered out. The transition from the Cameroons Youth League (CYL), through the Cameroon National Federation (CNF) and the Kamerun United National Congress (KUNC) to the Kamerun National Congress (KNC) was mostly led by Dr. EML Endeley. The Kamerun National Congress, the first truly Southern Cameroons national party which sought independence for

Southern Cameroons and reunification with French Cameroon to form a Cameroon nation took place at the All Party Convention in Mamfe in 1953. The Kamerun People's Party of Kale and Mbile formed at the same time and venue, stood for integration with Nigeria. Thus talk about reunification is limited only to the KNC.

**Role of Native Authorities (NAs)**

**Some native authorities (NA) in Bamenda Province**

**The Fons of Bali, Nso, Bafut and Ndu**

As earlier indicated national consciousness throughout Africa was aroused after WWII experiences and generally fostered by the UN. In the case of African Trusteeship Territories, in addition to Kamerun there were: Togo, Tanganyika, Ruanda and Burundi, and German South West Africa (Namibia). They were given greater impetus by the Trusteeship Council. However, in the Cameroons, the colonial methods and policies of the administering powers, France and Great Britain differed appreciably. The British from long experience of imperial administration of their colonies including America (1600-1776), Canada, India and Nigeria were conscious of the fact that their African colonies like the others before them would at some 'faraway' date in the future attain autonomy. Consequently, they applied it in their policy of 'Indirect Rule' hoping eventually to hand power over to traditional or "natural rulers (chiefs)" at independence through whom they administered their colonies as "Native Authorities". In other words, by this system, administration of British Northern and Southern Cameroons remained largely in the hands of the Chiefs, Emirs, Sultans and Councils of Elders, much as before, minimizing interference even by the colonial administrators. Initially, the British deliberately ignored and minimised the educated elite, who were regarded as impostors or mere "verandah boys". The system therefore positively fostered traditional cultural values.

However, it was these educated elite, almost exclusively, Mission educated, who finally, took over power from the colonial masters and not the traditional rulers as expected at independence. As concerned the law in; East and West Cameroon Ajaga Nji maintains in comparison that:

> West Cameroon operated on the basis of the British common law while "east Cameroon legal system was modelled on the French code". Courts in former west Cameroon considered not only the law but also British judicial precedent and concepts of protection against self-incrimination.[117]

In practice, this made a whole world of difference between being considered "innocent" until proven guilty by the courts on the Anglophone side and where proof of innocence was incumbent on the accused by the French based legal system. This certainly influenced the hostility and brutality by the forces of law and order there and became a serious issue after reunification as exemplified by the wild behaviour of the gendarmes.

**French Policy of Assimilation**

The French keen on the promotion of their cultural values on the other hand, envisaged a situation in which all their colonies would become parts of "Greater France", the 'French Union' or France Overseas. Consequently, they adopted the policy of 'Assimilation' by

---

[117] *Eden Xtra*, p.27.

which French Cameroonians would qualify to become French citizens. For this purpose, they used direct administration with little elbow room for traditional rulers with Cameroonian traditions and cultures which were considered rustic. Since they were out to form French citizens, the mass of Cameroonians were excluded by reason of policies such as the *indigenat*, *corvée*, use of *laissez passé* which constituted obstacles whereas the British Cameroonians enjoyed literally unfettered freedom within the law and the payment of taxes.

Victor T Levine, best summarizes this when he says that French colonial policy reflected:

> The distorted image of the mythical 'African' in whose name and on whose behalf France claimed to have undertaken her 'civilizing mission' in Africa. The image persisted in the Cameroun until the eve of World War II; it was the image held by those who saw the African in the paternalistic light of the earlier epoch and one that blinded French officialdom to the extent that any rapid advance in the political education of the Cameroonians' was virtually precluded.[118]

Another close study of the French colonial policy was made by David Gardinier, in his book entitled, *Cameroon: United Nations Challenge to French Policy*. Of how French Cameroonians fared under this system with regard to freedom, he notes:

> Their lives were governed by the system known as *indigenat*, which literally deprived them of the liberties of criticism, association, and movement, and gave to the French administrator power to inflict disciplinary penalties without trial for a wide range of minor offences.[119]

Furthermore, the Cameroonians were subject to the *Prestation*. This was a sort of labour tax under which adult males were obliged to furnish

---

[118] Victor T LeVine, The Cameroons from Mandate to Independence, University of California, Los Angeles. 1964, p. 91.
[119] David Gardinier, Cameroon: United Nations Challenge to French Policy, (London: Institute of Race Relations, 1963), p.16.

the administration with up to ten days of unpaid labour every year. They were also liable to conscription for public services at wages set by the administration.[120]

Compared to life under the British policy of Indirect Rule with emphasis on freedom of speech, association, religion, and much more, this was tantamount to "Slavery" of sorts. This should be borne in mind when contemplating the large number of French Cameroonians who migrated and settled in Southern Cameroons. They were mostly attracted to the plantation towns at the coast. In these also lie the seeds of reunification. However, in terms of economic investment and development, since the large number of French citizens saw Cameroon as an extension of France, they settled there in large numbers and invested freely unlike in British Southern Cameroons, where there were restrictions. This of course, only heightened the thrifty British policy in the territory reason why there was such a wide disparity between the levels of development between the two Trust Territories. One side (British) had 'freedom' with little development while the other (French) had suppression and a heavy measure of economic development, which however, was largely in the interest of the settlers.

**Policies: Socio-Economic and Political**

Further, while the British policy did not favour British citizens acquiring property and settling in British Cameroons, in French Cameroon, where the French citizens settled, acquired and owned elaborate property they also participated extensively in local and national politics since they saw themselves as Cameroonians pure and simple. By the same logic, the French Government invested without reserve since Cameroon was part of France Overseas. *Loi Cadre* of 23 June 1956 provided for vast development projects in French Equatorial Africa including French Cameroun economically, socially and politically towards internal self-government. For a population of nearly five million Africans there were 25.000 resident Europeans almost exclusively French as compared to less than 100 Englishmen in British Southern Cameroons. This in no small way explains the

---

[120]Ibid.

disparity in the economic development of French and British Cameroons. It should also be noted that French Cameroonians on the balance, were elected to and sat in the French parliament as French citizens. This was unthinkable in British Cameroons.

French Colonial Policy in French Cameroon and elsewhere did not envisage separate national independence until 1958. French Guinea under Mohammed Sekou Touré, inspired by the example of Ghanaian independence under Kwame Nkrumah a year earlier in 1957, bolted out of the French Union and with the assistance of his political ally and mentor, Kwame Nkrumah. Guinee boldly rejected De Gualles' referendum of 1958 and declared independence outside the French Union. This example stampeded France unpreparedly into granting independence to French Cameroun and other French territories.

So far the basic objective has been to demonstrate factors in the widening differences between British and French Cameroons arising from extensively different socio-economic, cultural and political colonial policies. These were the compelling considerations at reunification for a federal constitution that could better accommodate these differences.

**Seeding Reunification**

The broad vision of the path to independence was already the distinct goal of Nigerian and British Cameroonian nationalists. In fact, all the British West African colonies including: the Gambia, Sierra Leone, the Gold Coast and Nigeria right from the mid-1940s were already bracing themselves for eventual independence. It should be recalled that the National Congress of British West Africa (NCBWA) representing these colonies with headquarters in the Gold Coast, (Ghana) already existed as early as 1928. The formation of the National Council of Nigeria and Cameroons (NCNC) in 1944 a truly nationalist party with the goal of attaining independence was patterned after it. Hence by 1954, Southern Cameroons as a "Quasi Federal State" was already enjoying a large measure, of self-government with its own House of Assembly and later a House of Chiefs.

However, French policy which envisaged French Union for all its overseas territories made it possible for Cameroonians to militate in

French political parties and trade unions affording them the privilege of sitting in the French parliament and participating in French political party activities in the metropolis. This explains the origins of the radical communist attachments of the UPC since they had to fight against French policy in favour of "immediate independence and reunification". While British Cameroonians were not unanimous over the issue of reunification, the French Cameroonian stand towards that goal was apparently unequivocal or at least faced no visible opposition. This was expressed before the UN Visiting Mission in 1958 and the major reason why they unlike Southern Cameroons were not required to undergo the process of a plebiscite.

Consequently, French Cameroonian political parties and trade unions became extensions of those in metropolitan France at the same time as the nationalists were interacting with their British Southern Cameroonian 'brothers' across the Mungo discussing 'reunification' based on their common German colonial experience and history. The idea of reunification based on German colonial heritage was fostered by the UPC, which demanded immediate reunification and independence of both French and British Cameroons. In Southern Cameroons, the large number of French Cameroonian immigrants who fled forced labour and other constraints, settled in the fertile coastal towns of Victoria, Tiko, Muyuka and Kumba. From among them evolved the French Cameroon Welfare Union, which was eventually led by Mr. Robert JK Dibongue with the major objective of reunification like the UPC but with modified conditions. Under Dibongue, these ideas evolved through the CNF, KUNC, KNC, and were finally, ironically realized by the KNDP, while all the earlier parties and leaders that had embraced reunification opted out.

## Southern Cameroonian Roots: Victoria Colony (1858-1886)

The background to the establishment of Victoria Colony in 1858 stretches as far back as to 1472, when Fernando Po (Malabo) was "discovered" by the Portuguese and named after the Portuguese sailor Fernado Pao. From there they ventured up the River Wouri estuary which they named *Rio dos Cameroes* (River of prawns). The Portuguese whose major interest was trade in slaves, ivory and gold never penetrated into the interior and actually did not establish any permanent stations at the coast. Between 1530 and 1827, slaves became the most important commodity along the Atlantic coast from Douala, Bimbia and Rio del Rey to Calabar in the hands of: the Portuguese, Dutch, French, English, Swedish, Danes and Brandenburger slave dealers. The first purchase of land in Bimbia had to do with the abolition of slave trade. On signing the treaty abolishing the slave trade with the British Government on 31 March 1843, on the southern edge of Ambas Bay in return for 1.200 pounds, King William declared:

> I, King William and all the chiefs of Bimbia, do solemnly promise to do away with the inhuman and unchristian- like custom of sacrificing human lives on account of death of any of the chiefs, or on account of any of their superstitious practices".[121]

It is probably on this land that Man O'War Bay was founded. With the abolition of the slave trade, the British obtained permission from the Spanish to occupy Fernando Po, 25 miles off the mainland for the purpose of controlling slave ships. They next acquired Man O'war Bay, between Bimbia and Victoria for use by the British navy to suppress the nefarious trade. The first settlements on Cameroon soil were made by the London Baptist Mission, led by Rev.Joseph Merrick a black Jamaican missionary who secured land at Bimbia. He soon established a small Christian community and by 1849 had acquired land for the Baptist Mission, which he called "Jubilee" in honour of the Jamaican Mission, which had sent them out to Africa. He built a kiln for burnt bricks and erected the first printing press, where biblical translations were made into Isubu. With his death in 1849 on his way home to Jamaica and the return of other followers to the West Indies, the printing press was transferred to Douala and the Bimbia Mission closed.

This bit of Cameroon history is repeatedly told and is found in most history books but the profound link between 'Victoria Colony' and Southern Cameroons, which certainly makes it unique, is not

---

[121] Ibid., Victor Le Vine, p.94.

sufficiently emphasized. German annexation as already observed is centred on the fact that on 14 July 1884, the German flag was hoisted in Douala following a treaty signed two days earlier on 12 July. German traders had signed treaties with Kings Bell and Akwa along the Wouri River on behalf of Dr. Gustav Nachtigal by which it was to become the beachhead of German Kamerun stretching from the Wouri right up to Lake Chad.

The truth also is that Victoria Colony founded by Rev. Alfred Saker in 1858 existed as a "theocracy" enjoying all the rights, privileges and prerogatives of a 'micro-state' exercised by the Baptist Missionary in-charge for full 36 years before this German annexation. The celebration of the Victoria Centenary in 1958 in confirmation of this fact was a gigantic international affair that brought to that Port Town in particular and Southern Cameroons in general the Governor General of Nigeria, the Prime Minister and representatives from Great Britain with a mounted monument that bears testimony to that event till today. As well, a chain of Baptist churches, educational and high profiled health establishments and popular secondary schools like Saker Baptist College, Victoria (Limbe) and Joseph Merrick Baptist College, Ndu in Donga-Mantung Division cannot be mistaken.

Strangely, the occasion of its 150th Jubilee in 2008 slipped away inauspiciously despite the powerful historical reminder for its public anniversary celebration made by the late Emeritus Archbishop Paul Verdzekov.[122] This only helped to bring back questionable memories of the undisclosed reasons for the quiet erasure of the famous, historical appellation of "Victoria" replaced with "Limbe" in 1982. Interestingly, this took place on the eve of President Ahidjo's maiden visit to Great Britain and at the same time as the vibrant economic life of this Port Town was shamelessly being dismantled with the closure of banks, commercial houses and companies such as RW and King, Printania, Emens Textiles, and corporations like the Marketing Board among others. Victoria became a shadow of its old self. One gigantic journalist, who mourned the demise of "good, old Victoria", was Tataw Obenson, whose lone voice refused to be silenced even by the

---

[122] Ibid., L'Effort Camerounais.

harassment and short terms of imprisonment that characterized press censorship under the Ahidjo regime.

However, turning to the historical antecedents to that event; the London Baptist Missionaries led by Rev. Alfred Saker and their Jamaican 'brethren' were expelled from Fernando Po (Malabo), a Spanish island they had occupied since 1841 by its Catholic Governor, Don Carlos Chacon under the principle of "cujus regio ejus religio" (Religion follows the crown).[123] Saker acquired the territory (Ambas Bay) on the mainland of Cameroons from Chief Bile (King William) of Bimbia in 1858, where like the Pilgrim Fathers of old, they could worship in freedom or in Saker's own words: "Where freedom of conscience and civil liberty could be enjoyed".[124] The actual establishment took place on 9 and 10 August 1858 and he named it "Victoria" after the reigning Queen of England. As the settlement grew with converts gathered in from Bimbia, Bota, the neighbouring Bakweri villages and islands, Saker drew up a constitution, established a Town Council, a Court for the administration of justice and of course churches and schools. Victoria received administrative and legal guidance from the British Consul at Fernando Po, as well as from visiting Men – of – War ships. In 1866, Mr. Horton Johnson was appointed the first President of Victoria Colony; otherwise, its leading missionary performed the functions of Governor. Owing to its ideal location, Victoria Colony became prominent and soon attracted several traders, philanthropists, scientists, sailors and adventurers.

---

[123] Llyod E Kwast, The Disciplining of West Cameroon: a Study in Baptist Growth, (Michigan: William Eerdmans Publishing Coy), 1976.
[124] *Victoria Centenary Committee, the Victoria Centenary, Southern Cameroons, 1858-1958, (Victoria*: Basel Mission Book Depot, 1958). p. 19.

**Rev. Alfred Saker: London Baptist Missionary Society. Founder of Victoria Colony August 1858**

On 24 March 1883, a meeting of the Council holding in the Court House unanimously resolved to petition Consul Hewett asking him to use his influence to officially obtain British rule over Victoria Colony. The petition was signed by Councillors: SR Brew, Joseph Michael, Stephen Burnley, James Michael, William Johnson, Thomas H Johnson, George P Beckley, Jacob C Haddison, Edward Williams, Marcelina Sylvester and Samuel Johnson. These ancestral names still resonate among the citizens of this iconic Port City today. The territory for which they requested protection stretched from Bimbia to Rio del Rey. The Cameroon district it was claimed, was the healthiest spot along the whole West African coast with the great Cameroon Mountain rising to 13.350 feet, affording every advantage as on its slopes, where vegetables and fruits could be grown and sanatoriums for health resorts constructed.

Owing to indisposition but above all, because of reluctance by the British Government and British trading interests to lend financial support for such a project, Consul Hewett was only able to reach Victoria on 19 July 1884, far too late as Dr. Gustav Nachtigal, the Imperial German Consul General had already hoisted the German flag at Douala precisely on 14 July 1884. This was after completing treaties with Kings Bell and Akwa on the Cameroons River territory, which British traders had controlled almost singlehandedly for over a century. The German Government had notified the British Government that they were dispatching Dr. Nachtigal to conduct negotiations concerning certain matters. However, this caused no alarm as Chancellor Otto von Bismarck had previously disclaimed all desire to acquire colonial possessions. Consul Hewett, who had prepared the deed for the annexation of Victoria, was so distraught that he merely handed it over to the leading missionary, Thomas Lewis to post in a public place. It read:

> I, Edward Hyde Hewett, Her Britannic Majesty's consul for the Bights of Benin and Biafra, do hereby notify to all whom it may concern that, in compliance with the wishes of the inhabitants, the territory, which has long been in the possession and occupation of certain British subjects, viz. The Baptist missionary society at Amboizes Bay, has now been taken over by her majesty the Queen of Great Britain and Ireland and forms an integral part of her dominion. Given under my hand on board Her Britannic Majesty's Ship Opal, anchored at this 19th day of July 1884.[125]

However, the "midget" Victoria Colony was formally claimed for Her Britannic Majesty's Consul Edward Hyde Hewett as part of its dominion on 19 July 1884. Saker right from the onset had a clear vision of what he expected Victoria would become; a centre for civilization, freedom, and light. It would essentially be a religious, enlightened colony. And "here also, under British protection, the Lord's people may worship without molestation".[126]

---

[125] *Victoria Centenary* p.26.
[126] Underhill 1958:101, see also, *Victoria centenary celebrations, 1858-1958*, Victoria, London and Colchester, 1958.

## Alfred Saker's Hinterland Vision

Alfred Saker's hinterland vision stretched far beyond the slopes of Buea Mountain. In fact as early as then the missionaries, especially Rev. T Comber had explored 65 miles from Victoria to as far to 'Kumba'.[127] Furthermore, in Saker's vision, Victoria was to become a trade centre from where a highway would run deep into the interior and from where Cameroonian goods could be shipped to Europe. British navy and ships would occupy the still waters of Ambas Bay with provisions and ship building yards. Right from the beginning as he drew up the constitution for the fledgling colony, Saker hoped the new settlement would become: "A centre of civilization, freedom and light. It will be essentially a religious, enlightened colony. And, here also under British protection, the Lord's people may worship God without molestation".[128]

About the success and progress of education, Quentin Thomson who concentrated on the schools in Victoria noted:

> I prayed for these things: first that l may see at least one Bakweri brought to Christ, secondly the converted Bakweri should be able to read the bible( also in his own tongue) and thirdly that he should understand without assistance from another what he read.[129]

Saker and his immediate successors did not realize these dreams, which only began coming thirty years later and are still unfolding. Prophesies and predictions are not within the realms of history. However, when approached systematically, critically and analytically historical foresights can be fairly reliable. This is the case with the Saker predictions which though stultified in the late 1960s, close to two centuries later are slowly but surely unfolding with an eye on all that is taking place in good old "Victoria" and the road and communication infrastructure gradually underway into the hinterland. This gives

---

[127] Is it possible there is a link in the names?
[128] Edward Bean Underhill, Alfred Saker, Missionary to Africa, (London, the Carey Kinsgate Press Ltd, 1958), p. 101.
[129] Victoria Centenary, p. 22.

credence to the view that certain historical processes once started may be slowed down but cannot be halted as they gather a momentum of their own. In the area of the economy at the time, there was flourishing legitimate trade in palm produce and general goods with no desire for slaves anymore.

## Victoria Centenary Monument Unveiled by theGovernor General of Nigeria 1958

**Down Beach Victoria (Limbe)**

As indicated during Saker's time, the colony attracted numerous philanthropists, scientists, and adventurers as well. These included: the German botanist, Mann, who in 1861 climbed and explored Buea Mountain. George Thomson on the other hand, who had come to study flora and fauna, built Brook Mount Mission House, which still stands solidly. The Pole, Rogozinski, who occupied Mondoleh Island, was a typical adventurer. In this range were: Roger Casement, Purser of the Elder Dempster and Harry Johnston, the British Vice Consul, who took over Mondoleh Island after the relocation of Rogozinski to Fernando Po. But just as their hopes and dreams had been dashed at Fernando Po in 1858, there was a repeat performance on being let down this time not by the Spanish Administration but by their own

British Government which surrendered the promising colony without justification to the Germans.

In the meantime, suffocated by the Germans and unable to expand inland, the London Baptist Missionary Society sold their Victoria property to the German Basel Mission and moved out to new missionary territory in the Congo. This deed was done on 23 December 1886 and the British surrendered their century old hold over the territory to the Germans.[130] This ended the British Chapter in Victoria which was to be revived only after World War I in 1916 but the ancestral links with Southern Cameroons remained indelible.

**A Broad Conclusion**

It should not be forgotten that the two former "Provinces", now Regions were never remotely consulted before their separation nor reasons advanced before, or after that decision was taken and implemented. As has been demonstrated, the only significant change that took place transforming the Federal Republic of Cameroon into a Unitary State was the splitting up of the State of West Cameroon in two, while the rest of Cameroon remained intact until 1984. Ultimately, placed in the Cameroon context, these two Regions remain the most compatible pair as proven by history, which can collaborate in any meaningful way.

Elaborate studies have been made about the six broad categories of ethnic groups that make up Cameroon: the Bamileke, Bamoun, Douala, the Central Peoples, the Foulbe and Kirdi by various scholars and carefully summarised by Willard Johnson. The Bulu, Ewondo, Eton; the So-Called Beti or Pahouin branch of the Fang, maintain what he describes as, "a pattern of ethnic conflict and tribal hostilities among themselves" and collectively intensified especially with the Douala and the Bamileke, as loudly expressed under Andre Marie Mbida in his time. The Foulbes are portrayed as, "incorrigible tribalists, incapable of overcoming ethnic divisions in order to unite around a political programme", while the relations between the Bamileke and other groups are classified among the most hostile in the country. Put

---

[130]Feeble attempts by Rogozinski to sign treaties with local chiefs. Actually he signed 35 with chiefs around Buea Mountain by 1885.

together, the Bamileke and the Bamoun, "almost have no sense of community"; while the Douala with a population of 25.000 (1965) distantly related to the Bakweri, Bamboko, Bota and Subu groups are regarded as unimportant owing to their numerical inferiority and disparity.[131]

In relative terms therefore, these other ethnic groups which became even more polarised following the fratricidal civil war that engulfed French/Republic of Cameroon from 1955-1971 can in no way be compared with Southern Cameroons, which was ruled as a unit for some fifty years, from 1916-1972 without any untowardincidents. The final recourse from reconstructing the arguments raised above has been in favour of resorting to the intersection of history, law and reason: righting the incalculable wrongs done to an unsuspecting peace - loving people of southern Cameroons. This would be in recognition of the irreconcilable differences that mark out the two cultural systems, French and British fashioned out by colonial masters, who for all their existence never lost any love between them. Here, Southern Cameroons would merely be using the templates of Quebec and Ottawa in Canada, which have savoured the experience for the past 250 years, and, acknowledging the reality that devolution and identity are universally in vogue. If it has not worked between Britain and France and fallen through in Canada, the wheel cannot be reinvented in Cameroon. Besides, history abounds with examples of unitary states that have decentralised in favour of federations and not federations being forced into centralised systems. Above all, in the instance of Cameroon, "Southern Cameroons" already enjoyed self-government to the point of securing full autonomy for close to two decades and all that is required is the political will by the predators as finally advised by Malcolm Milne to redress the wrongs done to these nice little people, restoring unity not in uniformity but in diversity for greater flexibility and prosperity of the entire nation.

---

[131] For details see Johnson, Part II; Edwin Ardener, "The Kamerun Idea" West Africa, June 7and 14, 1958; Ardener, EO8C9oastal Bantu of the Cameroons, Part XI, Daryll Forde, ed.( London, International African institute), 1956.

# Chapter 4

## Southern Cameroons: Political Maturity

### An Evolved Political Culture

This chapter, elaborately, and in comparative terms demonstrates using various parameters, the extent to which Southern Cameroons up to the mid-1960s, had extensively developed an evolved, mature, political culture. It was remarkably led by a range of: simple, visionary, austere, honest, peace-loving and realistic leaders almost without exception – vintage products of their epoch. Distinguished by good governance; throughout it organized regular free, fair and transparent elections, peaceful handover of power and enjoyed free primary and adult education. It was further crowned with an ideal, efficient civil service, comparatively corruption free. In fact, the period, 1955-68 in the history of Southern Cameroons qualifies as a "Golden Age"[132] for that nostalgic State, whose citizens were repeatedly referred to as "nice, peace loving, loyal, good and hospitable people" by administrators, missionaries, visitors and those who got to know them closely.

However, the most extraordinary observation was that finally made by Malcolm Milne himself. He noted with satisfaction that during the last couple of years in the Southern Cameroons Administration, he dealt with: "People of high intelligence who knew exactly what they wanted."[133] Unfortunately, in the interview repeated and derogatory references are made of the people in general and to the fact that: "Foncha and Muna were not well educated;" the 'KNDP lacked sufficient qualified personnel, therefore their negotiations were weak. In yet another interview granted to the; *Time Scape* Magazine, Ngoh is blunt and categorical, maintaining that:

---

[132]Ibid., Ndi,*Golden Age of Southern (West) Cameroon – Impact of Christianity*,( Full Gospel Press, Bamenda, Cameroon), 2005.
[133]Ibid., No Telephone, p.254.

British Southern Cameroons came out with a very poor deal because the KNDP politicians were ignorant and self-centred. For example on the 20thof June 1961, Ahidjo and Foncha had a secret agreement that the latter would be made Vice President in the draft constitution of the Federal Republic of Cameroon, this secret arrangement was leaked and it scared Southern Cameroon politicians who quickly fought for their own interests.[134]

All of this squares up with the Colonial Office correspondence by Malcolm Milne which refers to:

The present government in Southern Cameroons made up almost totally ofinexperienced and naïve ex-primary school teachers with good intentions is incapable of grappling with the tremendous problems which face it, leadership in Southern Cameroons is inexperienced, untrained and naïve"(sic).[135]

The fact is that Malcolm Milne after his miraculous revelation finally corrected his earlier vengeful remarks confessing that the Foncha Regime was the best he had worked with throughout his long experience in the colonial service. The irony is that others continue to quote him long after he had recanted this bias statement made out of spite for the Foncha cabinet by his colleague at the Colonial Office, Foley Newn.

However, returning to the charge of low qualifications, the fact is that other than Endeley as an individual; on a one on one basis as will be seen shortly, the KNDP leadership was if not of the same calibre as their CPNC colleagues much better. In fact, described as "ex-primary school teachers", practically all of whom had served in the prestigious positions of "Headmasters". They were the best any locality could boast of across Nigeria and Southern Cameroons at the time. On the other hand, none of the CPNC leadership but for Dr. EML Endeley, held qualifications higher than the West African School Certificate, while others were Pastors and holders of the Standard Six certificate.

---

[134]Ibid., *Time Scape Magazine Vol: 02 no. 006*, March-April 2011, p.18. For more on the so-called Secret Deals, see Chapters Four and Five.

[135]Ibid., Epilogue, *Summit Magazine*.

Some of these were amateur journalists and newspaper vendors, who had access to, and maximally used the local press to lambast, criticize and ridicule their KNDP opponents as testified by the terse provocative newspaper captions crafted by Motomby Woleta and Nerius Mbile.[136] This is abundantly demonstrated in the Endeley cabinet of 1958 - 1959. On the whole, this could be taken simply as political verbiage deserving no serious comment[137] as the KNDP certainly comprised better qualified ministers in comparison.

Without in anyway belabouring the fact, going through the declassified British secret documents on Southern Cameroons, very little of positive value is said about Foncha's Administration and his party, the KNDP; since the British colonial officials unabashedly took sides with their CPNC opposition. To make sense, the above criticisms should be examined within their global, historical perspective beginning with political leadership generally; in Britain itself, as well as in the US, Nigeria, Cameroon Republic and then, Southern Cameroons. Regardless of the issue of educational qualifications, it was an acknowledged fact that Southern Cameroonian politicians were visionary leaders: intelligent, competent, simple, austere and realistic. Additionally, of the people generally and in areas as distant from Buea as Wum in the 1960s, Mr. John Percival, an Englishman and one of the twenty-five Plebiscite Officers recruited for the UN had lots of admirable things to say about the political maturity, honesty and level of reasoning of the masses. In earnest, they wanted neither integration nor unification and, he thought the British were simply escaping their responsibility by refusing to extend the Trusteeship period. It was clear

---

[136]Ibid., *Sunday Times* 21 June 1959, Foncha is referred to as: "Mr. 14:12- mockery of democracy" by Motomby Woleta, also, Mbile: "'If the KNDP does not stop its mad and heedless drive …its policy may result in disintegration", also, DT/W/18/59.

[137]Both Mbile and Motomby Woleta were School Leavers; Ajebe Sone was a Grade II Teacher while Jeremiah Kangsen and AndoSeh were pastors. Abel T Ngala, a Cattle Control Assistant was a First School Leaving Certificate holder as well as Vincent T Lainjo with experience as a treasurer. These were cabinet members of Endeley's KNC/KPP Government but strangely defended in the interview as being better qualified than those in the KNDP. It may be added that Grade Two Teachers taught in secondary schools, which produced GCE O/L or secondary school leavers of the calibres of Mbile and Woleta. In comparison, there was no KNDP Minister with a qualification below the Teacher's Grade 11 Certificate. See *Golden Age p.*59.

to him that; "the British had negligently administered this little patch of Africa", essentially because, "It was a United Nations Trust Territory and there was no profit in it".¹³⁸ The people in general were highly evolved ethically and politically. He was critical, keen and noted how:

> In those days in Southern Cameroons theft was almost unknown. I left the house unlocked, even though it was stuffed with things that might have seemed highly desirable to most of the population. There were violent incidents… but anyone who overstepped the mark was likely to be hauled in front of the local court by his neighbours. Nobody starved. Nobody was alone or uncared for.¹³⁹

Yet, Percival's was not an isolated observation. At the end of the day, Malcolm Milne himself reported even more affectionately of the people, whom he described as peace loving and trusting, and intelligent leaders, who knew exactly what to do and whose watch words were centred on service and dedication.¹⁴⁰

**Qualifications and Political Leadership**

The question also arises as to whether there is any direct correlation between academic qualifications, political performance and output. Cameroon and African examples indicate a very low, if not a negative correlation in this regard. The governments of most countries in Africa are currently run by highly qualified technocrats and academicians, but the complaints about massive corruption, fraud and rigging at elections are a daily occurrence.¹⁴¹ What has to be said is that

---

¹³⁸Ibid., John Percival, *The 1961 Cameroon Plebiscite, Choice or Betrayal*, (Langaa Research and Publishing CIG, Mankon, Bamenda), p. xiv. 2008.
¹³⁹Ibid.
¹⁴⁰Ibid., Milne, *No Telephone*, p. 447. Malcolm Milne wrote his autobiography systematically reaching a peak and making his final conclusions on p. 447. This in fact was an anticlimax to all that he had said and done.
¹⁴¹Despite appreciable efforts currently being made by President Paul Biya to bring about "transparency and good governance", Cameroon whichat one point (1998, 1999) topped the list as the most corrupt country in the world and is accused of rigging at elections is run largely by 'academics', professors and highly qualified

some education especially up to High School level, which affords aspiring politicians the competence of grasping complex socio-political, economic and cultural concepts could be an advantage but this may not be absolute. Intelligence, common sense and commitment are primordial. The biblical adage which holds that, "by their fruits we shall know them", applies in full measure to the KNDP leadership in disproving such unsound absolute assumptions. How could a government described so disparagingly with an assumed powerful opposition perform as brilliantly as the KNDP did consistently from 1959-1966 despite the fact that the CPNC opposition had the massive stealthy and overt support of the mighty British colonial administration.

**Endeley's Executive Government, 1958**
**Dr. EML Endeley Premier and Minister of Local Government**

---

technocrats. This is confirmed by the roll call of embezzlers and fraudsters behind bars in the Yaoundé and Douala Main Prisons. As an example, President Laurent Gbagbo, of Ivory Coast, who stuck to power after losing at elections thereby throwing his country into a bloody war until he was ignominiously overthrown, is not merely an intellectual but also a Professor of History as well. Newspaper captions without exception and the internet carry this information. The talk of the day is that of Marafa Hamidu Yaya, e.g. CONAC (the National Anti-Corruption body) wants two ministers arrested for embezzlement. These are named as Bernard Messengue Avom, Minister of Public Works and Jean Kuete, Vice Prime Minister in Charge of Agriculture. See, *The Post* no.01297 of Monday nov.14 2011. Fun is made of a parallel cabinet set up in the Kondengue Maximum Prison complete with a Prime Minister, Secretary General at the Presidency, Ministers of State and others!

**Peter Ndembo Motomby Woleta**
**Staunch KPP, later KNC/ KPP alliance,(CPNC) Stalwart**

In comparative terms the question may be just how much better qualified the British political leaders themselves were than their Southern Cameroonian counterparts. In comparative terms, the officials of the Colonial Office had no logical reason to make such derogatory remarks, when they had prominent Prime Ministers like John Major (1990 -1997) who had onlythree GCE O/L papers and had to patch up elsewhere. From all appearances it was a matter of the pot calling the kettle black.

However, there is a pertinent analytical study practically dealing with the role intellectual qualifications played in the process of decolonisation in Cameroon by David Mokam.[142] He quotes Professor Ali Mazrui, who maintains that: an intellectual is a person who has the capacity to be fascinated by ideas and has acquired the skills to handle some of these ideas effectively. He further classifies these into four categories, namely: general intellectuals, who can appreciate newspaper series, philosophies and ideas; public intellectuals, who have their own

---

[142]It is entitled; "Locally and Western Trained Intellectuals Facing Decolonisation in Cameroon, 1946-1961" in, *Annals of The Faculty of Arts, Lettersand Social Sciences,* The (University of Ngaoundere, Editions CLE, Yaoundé), 2011, pp. 61-81.

disciplines and communicate with others - interdisciplinary sort of; intellectuals specialised in ideas of governance and policy options and, finally, academic intellectuals fascinated by ideas and engaged in higher research and education. The other definition comes from Mandla Nkomfe, an African National Congress (ANC) Chief Whip in Gauteng Legislature, South Africa, who maintains that an intellectual is someone who invents ideas and helps others to analyse events. Such a one uses these skills to speak and write against injustice, shaping public opinion without affiliation to any political party. This is rather romantic and theoretical.

Putting these together Mokam draws the conclusion that the concept of an intellectual should include the acquisition of good skills and expertise acquired only through long and tedious studies. This classification he does based on "long pens" (*crayons*) ranging from ten to 100s used in education. He converts these into: basic intellectuals (basic pens); intermediate intellectuals (long pens) and advanced intellectuals (longest pens). Taking some leaders from French and British Cameroons, a few things are clear. Chances for education beyond primary school were more limited in French Cameroon, where any education higher than *CEPE* (the First School Leaving Certificate) and the Minor Seminary had to be done either in Congo Brazzaville or Senegal.

However, in British Southern Cameroons, which was integrated with Nigeria, the First School Leaving Certificate or better still, the highly prized "Standard Six Certificate", was a given, while most post primary and professional education besides the Government "Secondary/Normal Department" from the mid-1920s, which evolved into the Teacher's Training College (TTC) Kake, took place in Nigeria.[143]

The Voluntary Agencies especially the Roman Catholic Mission (RCM) spearheaded post primary education in the Trust Territory, beginning with the opening of St. Joseph's College, Sasse in 1939, St. Francis' Teachers' Training College, Fiango, Kumba (female) in 1947, TTC, Baseng (later Njinikom and St. Peter's Teachers Training College, Bambui, 1948) for professional teachers; followed by

---

[143]Ibid., Mokam.

Cameroon Protestant College, (CPC) Bali in 1949. In other words, before the 1950s, any serious post primary education was mostly available in Nigerian institutions such as: Government College, Umuahia, Government College, Ibadan and Government College, Zaria.

Prominent Southern Cameroonian political actors engaged in the decolonization process included: Paul M Kale, Emmanuel Liffaffe Endeley, Nerius Namaso Mbile, and Motomby Ndembo Woleta, who campaigned for integration with Nigeria; and, John Ngu Foncha, Augustine Ngom Jua and Solomon Tandeng Muna, who stood for reunification with Republic of Cameroon. Of these, except Muna and Jua, who had the same post –primary qualifications at home, all the others pursued further education, "abroad" in Nigeria and, by Mokam's classification, well qualified. By all comparisons this left no room for any criticism as this was finally confirmed by no other person than Malcolm Milne himself, who considered them the best small cabinet he ever had the privilege to work with.[144] They were competent, intelligent, dedicated and knew exactly what to do.

---

[144]Ibid., Milne, p. 434.

Endeley and Wife "Congratulate" JN Foncha.

This followed defeat of KNC /KPP alliance byKNDP and Replacement of Endeley by Foncha as Premier

In perspective, Endeley attended Government College, Umuahia, where he trained to become a Medical Doctor but got dismissed for impropriety in 1946. However, providentially, this accorded him the opportunity to take up active political leadership in Southern Cameroons; Kale, who initially was headed for further studies at Fourah Bay College in Sierra Leone ended up as a teacher in Salvation Army school, Lagos; Foncha attended St. Charles' TTC Onitsha, and continued to Moor Plantation, Ibadan for the professional specialisation in agriculture. Muna attended the Normal School, Buea and finished up at Kake, TTC as did Jua. Muna further attended the Institute of Education, University of London. Motomby Ndembo Woleta went to Baptist Boys' High School, Abeokuta, while Nerius Namaso Mbile attended Hope Waddell Institute Calabar, Nigeria. So, by Mokam's classification these leading Southern Cameroons political leaders of the decolonisation era qualified as "Intermediate Intellectuals," while Endeley was obviously an Advanced Intellectual.[145]

On the other hand in French Cameroon: Andre- Marie Mbida after Primary School, studied in the Minor Seminary at Akono and later on at the Major Seminary, Mvolye, after which he was appointed headmaster. Reuben um Nyobe attended Presbyterian schools in; Makak and Illange, in the Maritime Sanaga Region, and got the CEPE in 1929. He did Teacher Training at Foualassi, where after some difficulties and expulsion, he graduated as an external candidate. He taught as a Probationary Teacher in the Presbyterian School, passed the entrance examination for Junior Clerks and was engaged in pursuing Law through correspondence. Felix Roland Moumie, attended Protestant Primary School, Njisse near Foumban, moved to Government Primary School Bafoussam in 1935 and continued to Dschang Regional Primary School, where he passed out in 1940. He then went to Ecole Superieure, Edouard Renard, Brazzaville in 1941 before proceeding to William Ponty Higher School, Senegal from 1945-1947 for professional training and qualified as an African Physician. Ahmadou Ahidjo on the other hand, attended; Ecole Regionale Primaire, Garoua, where he failed and then moved to the Yaoundé Higher Primary School, where he got his CEPEand was recruited as an agent with Post and Telecommunications. Thus by Mokam's classification Ahmadou Ahidjo was the only person who failed to qualify as an intermediate intellectual. Paradoxically, heended up becoming the most enduring if not the most "successful" of all the politicians put together, having ruled for close to thirty years.However, Moka finally appropriately summarises:

> The advanced intellectuals played a very small role. The greatest role was played by locally trained intellectuals who were capable of couching ideas and was realistic enough to understand some needs. Cameroon obtained independence and reunification thanks to the work of locally trained intellectuals who constituted a chain made

---

[145]Ibid., Mokam.

of "basic" and "intermediate" intellectuals to spread nationalist ideas.[146]

**His Royal HighnessFon Achiribi II of Bafut**

**He was Chairman of the Fons' Conference in Bamenda**

Interestinglytherefore, Ahidjo who did not qualify either by Ngoh's expectations or by Mokam's analysis ended up becoming the most "successful" politician in Cameroon thus making nonsense of the correlation between educational qualification and political performance.

**Distinct Southern Cameroons Political Culture**

Given the fact that all within ten years (1951-1961), together with the plebiscite of 11 February 1961; Southern Cameroonians had been to the polls five times, this certainly had a significant impact on the political consciousness and maturity of the people. Outstanding among these was the 1959 election which led to a peaceful transfer of power

---

[146]Ibid., Mokam, p.79. For more on educational qualifications and political leadership, see appendix ii.

from the ruling KNC/KPP alliance to the opposition KNDP, despite the fact that the former enjoyed all the rights and privileges of incumbency. The prevailing atmosphere at the handing over of power characterized by cordiality was exceptional as the leaders and their spouses shook hands and embraced each other in public. This culture continued to evolve and mature as during the plebiscite, Southern Cameroonians overwhelmingly demonstrated their political readiness by deliberately choosing what was considered by all definitions as the 'most unpopular option' imposed on them at the UN – Reunification with Republic of Cameroon (and yet won massively). After the plebiscite Dr. Djalal Abdoh, the Iranian, UN Plebiscite Commissioner wrote back commending the people of Southern Cameroons for the "remarkable calm which had prevailed" during the process. These elections as well as the plebiscite were generally considered free, fair and transparent held in a calm and peaceful atmosphere as depicted in the photograph.

**Peaceful, Harmonious Transfer of Power in 1959**

Considering the frequency of these elections and the fact that they were always preceded by campaigns and sensitization of the people before the electors made their choices at the polls; the average Southern Cameroonians through frequently, in fact, biennially exercising their franchise definitely were better informed about their civic rights and responsibilities than their Nigerian or French Cameroonian neighbours, or for that matter, electors anywhere at all. One of those high points in the mature political culture of Southern Cameroons that deserves special mention was the peaceful handover of power after free, fair, transparent and peaceful elections in 1959. On that occasion as indicated above, the ruling KNC/KPP alliance leader was defeated by the KNDP opposition. Without ruffles of any kind, Dr. EML Endeley, the serving Prime Minister accompanied by his spouse, calmly and even with a measure of joviality embraced and shook hands with his victorious opponent, Mr. John Ngu Foncha, Leader of the Opposition in the glare of photographers and the press.

One wonders where else such a spectacular transfer of power could have taken place. Hence, the Southern Cameroonian politicians and electorate deserve far more than the derogatory descriptions cast at them. There are no known institutions where the electorate goes to for preparation to become better "voters". Southern Cameroons, already enjoying universal free primary education through "Education Rating" under the Foncha administration with 100% trained teachers by UNESCO standards in 1970, could not be considered anything less than among the best. Adult education classes were organized throughout the Territory to great effect, not only through the agency of the government but with the collaboration of the Christian denominations or Voluntary Agencies. These apart, while education such as desired in the interview could be an asset in imbibing political issues and complex concepts, it is definitely not an absolute necessity. Intelligence is not a monopoly of the literate and must be distinguished from literacy and the ability to read and write or what is derisively described as, empty "book knowledge".

**The Sagacity of Traditional Rulers**

Many of the so-called "illiterates" have a wonderful grasp of issues that affect their lives and society as a whole, which even the "well educated" persons may not adequately understand. Otherwise, the question may well arise as to where sagacious rulers of the stature of Fons: Achirimbi II of Bafut, Asonganyi of Fontem, Galega I of Bali or Mbinglo of Nso and countless others like them received the education to enable them administer their large Fondoms so tactfully, diligently and successfully with highly acclaimed systems of dispensing justice in the Native Courts for ages before the arrival of the colonial masters.

Rather, it is for this reason that the British colonial administration easily adapted the much glorified and idealized policy of "Indirect Rule" (or Native Administration (NA)) using the Traditional or "Natural" Rulers as a medium of retaining the highly treasured African traditional values and customs,while adapting them to modernism or what was referred to as the "Dual Mandate". In fact, it was initially the objective of British Colonial Policy by the Richard's Constitution of 1946, which, while dividing Nigeria into three regions was still NA centred. Rather, it was envisaged that at independence power would subtly glide over from the hands of the colonial masters into those of the Traditional Rulers, who constituted the Native Authorities. The Richard's Constitution deliberately side-lined and ignored the rapidly rising vocal educated elite and provoked widespread opposition to it in Nigeria and Southern Cameroons. Thus, it instigated and fuelled the rise of nationalism since the educated elite were contemptuously disregarded as mere "Verandah Boys"[147], of little consequence. Before being fully implemented it was superseded by the Macpherson Constitution of 1951, which made provision for democratic elections into the various assemblies. While it rejected a Regional status for Southern Cameroons, it however, enabled the territory to come to the forefront and for the first time precipitated democratic elections in Eastern Nigeria and Southern Cameroons with which it was jointly administered.

As a result, the Southern Cameroons intelligentsia as members of the CYL provided a ready recruiting pool for membership into the nascent NCNC of Nnamdi Azikiwe.[148] It will be recalled that led by Mr. PM Kale the early Southern Cameroons nationalists almost without exception, who began by enrolling in the CYL, were also members of the NCNC, which became a sort of nursery school for budding nationalists and political leadership in Southern Cameroons.[149]

## High Calibre Political Leaders: Products of their Time

In the interview it is maintained that Southern Cameroons 'Had a Raw Deal' because of the "greed" of Southern Cameroonian politicians in general and those of the KNDP in particular.[150] It is important to note that talking about the early Southern Cameroonian political leaders is not making reference to a set of superhuman beings: saints, sinners or villains, living in a unique and perfect world. They, like political leaders the world over were products of their time, place and circumstances with their shortcomings, strengths and weaknesses.

---

[147]JF Ade Ajayi & Michael Crowder eds. *History of West Africa Vol II*, Longman, 1974; See especially "Politics of Decolonisation in Bristish West Africa"p. 622-655.

[148]Ibid., Frederick Lugard, *The Dual Mandate in British Tropical Africa*, 1926, p.193. Even up to independence, Mbile, Motomby Woleta and others continued to identify with the NCNC and Nigeria.

[149]Ibid., Malcolm Milne, No Teleph1o0n6ee pp.424-427.

[150]Ibid., Epilogue; Malcolm Milne, pp.424-427.

However, they were the very best that their society could produce at the time and any comparisons made outside these parameters are bound to be lame and in historical terms "anachronistic."

The 1959 General Elections in Southern Cameroons were extremely polarised, as they introduced the worst divisions among the people and thus created a very dense and contagious political atmosphere. The platforms between the KNDP and the KNC/KPP alliance were as incompatible as between "fire" and "water" Nigeria and Republic of Cameroonand just how these parties were expected to collaborate as propounded in the interview is inconceivable. In fact, Mukong, expressly stated the view that at heart, it was not in Endeley's best interest for Foncha to succeed either at the Bamenda or Foumban Conferences, although there was no clear evidence to back this view after 1961. However, in 1960, Endeley, Mbile and Motomby Woleta fiercely kept taunting Foncha and the KNDP with Endeley openly admitting that he had held three nocturnal meetings with Ahidjo behind Foncha's back that year. In fact, Endeley was desperate for inclusion and was convinced long before 1966, that:

> We can operate a one party system, which would certainly guarantee that everybody has the right to express opinions within the party. This would make the best use of the talents we have in the country, and we could evolve a system of agreement without engendering animosity.[151]

This of course was stabbing Foncha in the back. Even so, it did not bar Foncha involving the CPNC, the Fons and Chiefs, as well as the OK at the Bamenda All Party and Foumban Conferences, where they made constructive contributions as borne by the memorable speeches they made at these meetings. The reaction here is best summarized by Dr. George Atem, who argues that accusations in the interview that the KNDP did not want to share power are untrue; he makes the point that:

---

[151]*Cameroon Times*, Monday 28 April, 1962; also, Johnson, p.62 ;Southern Cameroons,(Langaa Research and Publishing, CIG, Mankon, Bamenda, 2005), p .233.

The party had a mandate in the 1959 elections and was responsible to the people and not to any other political party whose politicians had been rejected at the polls. Foncha and the KNDP were even magnanimous, they took the opposition leaders to the UNO, invited all shades of opinions to The Mamfe Conference, Bamenda and Foumban Constitutional Conferences. Was it that Foncha should have formed a coalition government? Foncha did not attend the Tripartite Conference in Yaoundé alone.[152]

Perhaps, the only little addition would be that with hindsight, we now know that before the holding of the Tripartite Conference in Yaoundé, Britain had defied all the agreements and norms and openly colluded with and handed over power to Ahidjo instead of to a "body representing the federal government" subscribed to by the governments of Southern Cameroons and Republic of Cameroon. It would have made no difference if Foncha carried with him the CPNC leadership and all the suggested lawyers. Ahidjo simply invited his "ubiquitous French advisers to privately draw up a document which he got the legislature of the Republic of Cameroon to enact on 1 September 1961, and became the Federal Constitution including Southern Cameroons."[153] British open subversion of the final decolonization process in Southern Cameroons had begun at the aborted Buea Tripartite Conference in mid May 1961. In fact, defying UN Resolution 1608 of 21 April 1961, Her Majesty, the Queen wrote directly to Ahidjo and not to Foncha, declaring:

> On the occasion of the ending of the UK Trusteeship in Southern Cameroons, I send Your Excellency my sincere good wishes for the future of the united territories over which you now

---

[152]George Atem. "The celebration of the 50th Anniversary of the Cameroon Unification" *Cameroons Panorama*. No. 657 of Dec. 2012. p6.

[153]See, Carlson Anyangwe, *Betrayal of Too Trusting A People: The UN, The UK Cameroon*, Langaa Research and Publishing, CIG, Mankon, Bamenda. The draft of the Unity constitution of 1972 was overseen by Maurice Duverger a Frenchman hired to review the constitutions of 1960 and 1961 both of which had been drafted by Mr. Jacques Rousseau, Ahidjo's Technical Adviser on administrative and institutional matters p. 120.

preside. I am glad that friendly cooperation between our two countries should have made it possible for Southern Cameroons to attain independence in accordance with the result of the February plebiscite. I look forward to the continuation of our cordial relations in the future.[154]

To say the least, most of these political actors were exemplary, dedicated and selfless patriots with great visions for their "beloved motherland". Nor should it be forgotten that they were pioneers, the first fruits of the land. This applies to: Paul M Kale, Emmanuel ML Endeley, John Ngu Foncha, Nerius N Mbile, Augustine N Jua, Solomon T Muna, PM Kemcha and all the others. As pioneers, they were adventurers, sacrificial lambs and explorers who plodded virgin, unknown territory in the course of which they burnt out their lives in the dedicated service of their people and their Fatherland in accordance with the visions they conceived when forming proto nationalist organizations such as the CYL and the KUNC. Naturally, with all the zeal, in the course of pursuing these objectives they made their mistakes and learnt by them. It was a matter of trial and error as there were no precedents or blue prints to follow. This partially explains the apologies made by JN Foncha and ST Muna during AACI at Buea in 1993.

It cannot be over emphasized that all comparisons are lame and that is why in history they are usually made within context; juxtaposing such individuals or events with similar or dissimilar examples and never in isolation. This helps to put things in perspective and because history does not deal with absolutes, which in any case do not exist in this world of mortals. That is why a brief glance is taken of the situation with our compatriots across the border during the same period.

---

[154]They were forced to resort to violence by French colonial anti-nationalist measures. This was especially the caseduring the tenure of High Commissioner Roland Pré beginning in 1954. For more on this; see Daniel Abwa, *"Commissaires et Haut Commissaires au Cameroun"*.

## "Maquizzards", Rebels, Nationalists, or Freedom Fighters

It was one of the numerous positive aspects of British colonial policy in Nigeria and the Southern Cameroons that the violent and bloody conflicts described below never took place in "peace loving Southern Cameroons".[155] The point is beautifully made by Chief Obafemi Awolowo, who joked that the British did not give their colonial subjects the opportunity to practice something of nationalist martyrdom in Nigeria as was the case elsewhere. Rather, from experience in empire building, they remote censored the desires of the nationalists which were defused constitutionally. The emphasis was on the force of argument and use of the ballot box and not the argument of force and use bullets through the barrel of the gun.

### Individual UPC Leaders

**Reuben Um Nyobe and Family:**

Assassinated(ambushed) 13 Sept 1958

---

[155] *Eden Xtra*,pp. 19-22,Daniel Abwa,"Contributions of Francophone Cameroonians to Reunification of the Cameroons, also", Emmanuel Njoya Ibid, in Frontier Post p. 4.

Ernest Ouandji in Handcuffs

Faced firing squad 15 Jan. 1971 under Ahidjo

Dr. Felix Roland Moumie: succeeded Um Nyobe as President

Assassinated with rat poison in Geneva, Switzerland 3 Nov. 1960

Abel Kingue VicePresident

Died 16 April 1964

UPC Leaders

(L. to R.) Front row: Castor Osende Afana, Abel Kingué, Ruben Um Nyobé, Felix Moumié, and Ernest Ouandié

However, in comparison, just across the border in French Cameroun with which Southern Cameroons shared a common colonial origin and heritage, the political evolution was characteristically different. Consequently, the contemporaries of the Kales, Endeleys,

Mbiles, Fonchas, Munas, Juas and countless other Southern Cameroonian politicians; their counterparts in French Cameroun sought to acquire political power and leadership largely through the barrel of the gun by fighting against the French colonialmasters in a prolonged barbarian colonial war.[156] This explains why Ndeh Ntumazah, leader of the One Kamerun (OK) party, the Southern Cameroons version of the UPC, had such a contemptuous attitude towards all Southern Cameroons political leadership because he maintained, they never faced the baptism of fire through colonial battles against the British. That was his own crude yard stick for measuring the degree of nationalism.

Most of them paid the supreme prize by selflessly sacrificing their lives in the process. Such was the case with nearly all of the early leadership of the UPC: Reuben Um Nyobe, Felix Roland Moumie, Ernest Ouandie, Abel Kingue and countless others. Some of these leaders at different times held crucial meetings with their "British" Southern Cameroonian counterparts at venues in Kumba, Buea, Tiko and Bamenda during the initial stages of the reunification process. There can be little doubt that these contacts helped in no small way to sharpen and mould the political thought of their Southern Cameroonian counterparts one way or the other. At the time, these leaders were variously described as "terrorists", "rebels" and "maquissards"[157] by the French Colonial Administration. Consequently, they were hunted down and killed in the fratricidal conflict, while they justified their ferocious counter attacks against the French colonial masters and their supporters as the struggle for freedom (immediate reunification and independence) and wanted the French colonial masters expelled from Cameroun.[158]

After independence these clashes continued with the same ferocity characterized by burning, killing, looting, maiming, kidnapping and scorched earth tactics under the Ahidjo Administration. This is what

---

[156] Richard Joseph, *Radical Nationalism in Cameroun*, (Oxford at the Clarendon Press), 1977, pp. 349-50.

[157] This fact deserves due emphasis.

[158] Richard Joseph, *Radical Nationalism in Cameroun*, (Oxford at the Clarendon press, 1977), pp. 349-50

was responsible for the unattractive, literally dreaded "Second Option" of "Joining Independent French Cameroun" in the 1961 plebiscite. This should be borne in mind when mention is made of the 'warring' Southern Cameroonians; as there were never any open hostilities among the political parties. There were categorically no lives lost during the political wrangles that took place among and between the political parties even during the worst of times. The "wars" frequently referred to were nothing more than "verbal" tirades based on argument and not muscle.[159] In fact, it deserves to be emphasized that for all its existence as a Trust Territory and throughout the dense climate running up to the plebiscite, there was not a single recorded fatality anywhere. That is why the people earned the distinctionof being regarded by one and all, priests, pastors, visitors, administrators and above all by Malcolm Milne as the " little peace loving people" of Southern Cameroons.

## "Jocular" Not Bloody Fights

In typical Southern Cameroons style, opposing politicians were known to travel in the same vehicles or convoys usually Land Rovers during their political campaigns. They would chat, eat and drink together and then use the roofs of the same Land Rovers or soap boxes to "attack" each other's political platforms. These were pretty often, jocular "attacks" with nothing faintly approximating what was taking place across the border. They played the game of politics which in ordinary parlance meant the "force of argument and not the argument of force". While much is made of "warring Southern Cameroonian politicians"; the most glaring example was set beginning at the Bamenda All Party and Continuing at the Foumban Constitutional Conference in 1961, where Foncha and Endeley leading the KNDP and CPNC parties travelled as a team and spoke with one voice. Consequently, Endeley seized the opportunity to ask Ahidjo, who attended the conference only with members of his UC, where his opponents were.[160]

---

[159]This fact deserves due emphasis.
[160]See, the Foumban Conference chapter seven for appropriate excerpts.

Of course, leaders of the opposition parties in the Republic of Cameroon were all behind bars and Ahidjo came to Foumban with only his UC party. Most of the speeches and quotations in this exposition by Endeley, Foncha, Mbile, Mukong and Egbe depict these traits.[161] Mbile makes the point lucidly when he reiterates: "It is to our credit that even in the years of bitter politics; there was not a single case of extreme action like murder, violent assault or people "jumping into the bush." [i.e. *maqizzards* (terrorism)] and of the plebiscite he maintains: "We fought the plebiscite and we bowed to the will of the majority of our people right or wrong".[162] Today, these former "rebels," "terrorists" and "*maquizzards*" of Colonial French Cameroun have been rehabilitated and are hailed as "nationalists", freedom fighters and liberators, who sacrificed their lives for the freedom that Cameroon presently enjoys.[163] There were no such political martyrs in Southern Cameroons; nevertheless, it was replete with patriots and nationalists. Unfortunately, the picture painted of Southern Cameroons politicians in the interview is the exact opposite of this reality. If as historians we do not extol these exemplary virtues of our leaders for posterity we would be doing a disservice to nation building and national integrity. The challenge is for young historians to break the silence by researching into the lives and contributions of these patriotic ancestors, many of them statesmen, to the evolution of the Cameroon Fatherland.

**Political Leaders: Past, Present and Global**

Current events in some African countries and in the Arab world (the so-called Arab Spring) affecting leaders such as: Professor Laurent Gbagbo in Ivory Coast, Ben Ali in Tunisia, Hosni Mubarak in Egypt, Muammar Qaddaffi in Libya as well as those in Yemen and Syria are instructive. These are leaders some of whom had acquired the status of

---

[161] Ibid., Mbile, Eyewitness, p.322., Ndi, The Golden Age, pp.64-68.

[162] Ibid., p.322. It should however be remembered that he fought against the results of the plebiscite right to the UN, leading the Balundu 'Mokanya' Cult; Bakossi Secret Society NAB Ref. O.36/31/35 of12150, August 1962.

[163] Ibid., *Eden Xtra*, pp. 19-23 Daniel Abwa, "Contributions of Francophone Cameroonians to the Reunification of the Cameroons" in the *Summit Magazine*, Political life does not reflect this reality.

demi-gods in their countries, crumbled and are crumbling like packs of cards in the face of "people's power". To these could be added the examples of other dictatorial and tyrannical African leaders such as: General Idi Amin Dada of Uganda, Sanni Abacha of Nigeria, Mobutu Sassa Seko Wazabanga of Zaire and Charles Taylor of Liberia, who trampled on the rights of their people and squandered the wealth of their countries thus invoking war and misery on their own people.[164] Without exaggeration, in Southern Cameroons, the British Administration was benign and by the very nature of Indirect Rule was rather paternalistic in what Lord Lugard from the Nigerian experience described as the "paramountcy of African interests" or the "sacred trust" the exact opposite of the French policy of "assimilation". In this regard Lugard prescribed that:

> The task of the administrative officer is to clothe his principles in the garb of evolution, to make it apparent alike to the educated native, the conservative Moslem, and the primitive pagan, in his own degree, that the policy of the Government is not antagonistic but progressive-sympathetic to his aspiration and the guardian of his natural rights.[165]

By this definition, the African's way of life and outlook as far as it did not contravene any accepted modern norms was not to be interfered with. In other words, it aimed at striking the delicate balance between change and conservatism. And, for one thing, the British administrators were few and far in between. Come to imagine that Bamenda Division (the entire Present day North West Region) was administered by just one Senior Divisional Officer (SDO) with three assistants until 1948, where we now have seven Divisions administered by SDOs with numerous assistants and headed by a Governor.Lugard's reference to "evolution" reflected the prime

---

[164]*Time Scape Magazine* Vol: 02 No. 009 November/December 2011, article by John Akuroh on pp. 52-53, for updates on Qaddafi and Gbagbo; Jean –Emmanuel Pondi, *Life and Death of Al-Qadhafi, What Lessons for Africa?* (Editions Afric'Eveil), 2013

[165]Lugard, *The Dual Mandate in British Tropical Africa*, 1926, p.193.

objective and approach of Indirect Rule or Native Administration as applied in Nigeria and Southern Cameroons.

**Libyan Leader Muammar Qaddaffi**
**He called his compatriots rats and cockroaches**

The immediate antagonists with the approach of independence in Southern Cameroons therefore were not the British but Nigerians or specifically the Ibos, who attracted opprobrium by their all-pervading existence, grasping and arrogant attitudes. The missionaries and even administrators were generally warmly welcomed by the people. Though few in numbers most of the British colonial administrators in the field were unlike those at the headquarters at Buea or at the colonial office in London, directly involved with development in their specific areas of command. They generally wrote stimulating reports that closely reflected the local realities but these were hardly translated into action because of bottlenecks at the headquarters, by their superiors whoinstead transmitted politically tainted versions to London. That is how Malcolm Milne, JO Field, and CE King wrought damage to the political process in Southern Cameroons through biased reporting against the KNDP leadership because they opposed integration with Nigeria.

## Visionary Leaders: Simple, Austere, Honest and Realistic

Description of the commitment of Southern Cameroonian leadership to work is best encapsulated by Malcolm Milne who ultimately maintained that: "service was their watch word".[166] These examples clearly distinguish the high calibre of leaders who launched the political process in Southern Cameroons and whose credit should be seen in the context of their time, circumstances and in comparison with others elsewhere. Nothing in the lives of these leaders, even in the worst of them could remotely compare to the examples cited above. Put together, the early political leaders were practising Christians, a significant number of whom for that matter were even Church ministers.[167]

## The Foncha (KNDP) Government, 1959

**Sitting left to right JO Field, Commissioner, Sir James Robertson (High Commissioner) Governor General of Nigeria, JN Foncha and Malcolm Milne (Deputy Commissioner)**

Every single one of them lived a simple austere life. True to the game of politics there was ample room for "opportunism" and the

---

[166] Ibid., *No Telephone*, p. 409.
[167] Ibid., Ndi.*Golden Age.*

struggle to gain political power and influence, which in insignificant cases reached inordinate proportions, but nothing near qualifying the majority of them as "greedy". This is the proper context which should help in evaluating the former political leaders in Southern – West Cameroon practically none of whom accumulated inordinate, wealth, exhibited traits of conspicuous consumption to the point of "greed", a description repeatedly echoed in the interview. This view is also inappropriately used by NN Mbile in qualifying the KNDP for "going it alone" when they wielded power (1959-62) although the KNC/KPP alliance never shared power with the KNDP when they held the reins of government from 1957-1959. Mbile's allusion of course could be excused as ordinary political verbiage and his access to the press but in retrospect, no justification can be found for using it.

## Malcolm Milne Pays Glowing Tribute to Foncha Cabinet

Over and above all of this is the generous tribute from none other than Malcolm Milne himself. He not only extolled the exceptional quality of the political leadership but of the ordinary run of low to middle grade civil servants in Southern Cameroons as well. Here it deserves to be remarked that in perspective he had experience of service in Eden, Ghana and Nigeria before coming to Southern Cameroons. Consequently, his grading is highly significant. Of the top grade politicians, who, at this time, interestingly exclusively consisted of members of Foncha's KNDP Government, Malcolm Milne was keen to note and to declare his unqualified admiration for Southern Cameroonian Ministers without exception. He took note maintaining that:

> The situation has changed again during the last four or five years of my service when l was operating at permanent secretary level or above. Then l was dealing with individual ministers, with cabinet committees or in the case of Southern Cameroons with a

small government. Almost without exception they were people of high intelligence who knew exactly what they wanted.[168]

What is most remarkable here is that the calibre of people referred to above are exactly members of the Foncha cabinet, who elsewhere are referred to by his colleague Foley Newn as "naïve schoolmasters". Having examined the credentials of a vast sampling of political leaders it is easy to agree with Malcolm Milne that Southern Cameroonian leadership was among the best anywhere. Milne's thoughts again went to the Bamenda corps of messengers with whom he had worked closely earlier, dating back to the era of the "Anlu" in Njinikom. With current reports from Mr. ED Quan, Assistant Secretary for Establishment; from this corps only one person had retired, Mr. A Dinga. Of this valiant unit in 1961, Malcolm was passionate and emotional, noting, forty years later: "I felt vaguely then, and know for certain now, that working with these men had greatly enriched my time in the colonial service. There was something very special about that corps; their service was their watch word".[169] This is superlative tribute that cannot be surpassed given that it is made by Malcolm who is held as "exemplar" and an administrator par excellence by Professor Ngoh.

## A Unique Southern Cameroons Civil Service

The KNDP are charged with "weak negotiation skills" because of low education, greed and all. Here, it should be added that the Foncha Administration was always aware especially after the vengeful mass resignations of Nigerian civil servants followed by those of British expatriates from the Southern Cameroons civil service intended to bring down the KNDP Government. This was precisely what took place on the eve of 30 September, 1961 as Omer BB Sendze, a key actor and living witness recounts:

---

[168] Part of Mbile's verbosity may be understood in the sense that he was a journalist by profession and so was Motomby Woleta. Both men were ferocious in their taunts of the KNDP.

[169] Ibid., *No Telephone* p.254, My emphasis.

> The British after the plebiscite were very bitter and disappointed and were only interested in cutting their losses and taking off. ... On the night of the handover, the British in Buea ... really all British civil servants were evacuated to a warship which was anchored in Victoria Bay. Those who were working in the CDC were herded in areas closed by high fences. Thus in the Public Works Department the expatriate staff of 15 was reduced to two, all superintendents or technicians.[170]

It should immediately be added that he, Sendze was one of the two senior members ( the other being Ndumu) of this crucial department at the birth of the nation. The same situation obtained in all the other services. Quickly through his Cameroonisation policy, Foncha set up a Public Service Commission that worked tirelessly to recruit, promote, train and make urgent replacements. The operation was so swift and "efficient" that in terms of the smooth functioning of the various services, the only significance was that Cameroonians found that overnight they had been catapulted to higher ranks in their various services and departments to replace their former Nigerian and British bosses. In fact, this is the historical context in which Foncha made his apology at the AAC1 at Buea in 1993 as suddenly he had to replace these civil servants, who had deserted their posts.

This in itself was great motivation and before long, those promoted felt challenged and quickly squared up into their new positions of responsibility since it was an "on the job affair" and there was nothing so new to learn after all. This was strengthened by repatriates from Nigeria, recruits from the West Indies and young graduates coming back from studies abroad following the mass award of scholarships. In fact, this should constitute a good part of a chapter in any work dedicated to Foncha as the Southern Cameroons, later West Cameroon civil service. This is the context in which the Colonial Office criticisms of the Foncha government as an administration of former primary school teachers should be understood.[171] In context it was hollow and a sham because what was required was performance and delivery. The sordid details of what happened in some services

---

[170] Ibid., *No Telephone*, p.409.
[171] Ibid., Sendze, My reflections, He was one of the two superintendents

(e.g., the plots of British expatriates at Ombe) are again fertile ground for budding history researchers especially at the Masters and doctoral levels.

**Omar BB Sendze President Emeritus: National Order of Civil Engineers, Cameroon.**

**A main Actor: he lived throughthe early political experiences as a student in London, the FRC and Unitary State of Cameroon. He was one of two Cameroon Civil Engineers left after massive resignation of British expatriates**

**Cameroonisation**

The Government established the Southern Cameroons Recruitment Committee on 1 May 1959 with precise instructions to eliminate foreign domination in the civil service. The Cameroonisation policy was extended to the private sector, which led to a new breed of Cameroonian functionaries and bureaucrats. The Foncha Government applied this policy systematically and methodically; recuperating Cameroonians who were working elsewhere and integrating them into the new public service, while yet recruiting others afresh. Cameroonians with expertise of any form were sure to be engaged and even the untrained and unskilled got jobs as cleaners and watchmen. The idea was first to be a Cameroonian and then to train and excel on the job. Next, there was a massive education crusade. This involved training programmes to meet skilled manpower needs in the long and short run. Grants–in– aid to the various Voluntary Agencies were raised and scholarships granted to Cameroonians studying in Nigeria and abroad under the ASPAU, African American Institute (AAI) and various other scholarship programmes.

The comparatively large number of Southern Cameroonians awarded scholarships by the Foncha Government in particular, then together with the CDC, the various religious denominations and other bodies testifies for itself and can be seen on record.[172] In this connection, note should be taken of the secretly plotted and executed, massive resignations of Nigerian civil servants serving in the Southern Cameroons civil service followed by those of British expatriates all deliberately intended as vengeance against the plebiscite results that went in favour of reunification and also to embarrass and cause the collapse of the Foncha Administration. Foncha and his administration had to act without delay to fill in the gaps. All he could do in the circumstances was to deploy the best human resources at his disposal, who of course, were the school masters, whose mettle was proven in the manner in which they ran the primary schools and assisted in village administration. These were people with records to show off their competence as administrators.[173]

The competence of the Southern – West Cameroon civil service remains inestimably proverbial and nostalgic to those who savoured the experience. Operating at the time without computers but equipped with highly motivated, assiduous, honest and diligent personnel, a civil servant employed on the 29th of the month was sure to be paid his due salary at month end just as those who retired had their pensions and retirement benefits paid on the spot, or in monthly instalments as

---

[172]Ibid.., Ndi, *Golden Age*, pp 6-12, also, Sendze Memories.

[173]Cameroon Tribune Hors Serie Octobre 2011, "Reunification One Cameroon, A Dynamic Story" pp. 126-7. Professor Ngoh himself acknowledges the fact that most of the Cameroon students and intellectuals supported Foncha and the KNDP. In fact, he was variously invited to address their conferences at Kumba and Yaoundé. See interview by Professor Monekosso.

they quit the service without having to compile dossiers towards that objective. Retirement was a prospect to anticipate with satisfaction after a job well done marked by celebrations festooned with the award of medals, gifts and eulogies.

Mr. Emmanuel Tabi Egbe, repeatedly referred to in the interview easily was the first ever qualified Southern Cameroonian lawyer. He was not left out as insinuated but engaged immediately after graduation and became the "darling" of the Foncha administration.[174] Personally, he had great respect and admiration for the "man," Foncha, whom he considered as selfless, dedicated and honest: "One whose vocation was to serve and not to be served".[175] It is an acknowledged fact that most Cameroon students and intellectuals supported Foncha and the KNDP and Egbe was one of them. In this connection it should be mentioned that the West Cameroon Bar Association was only approved in 1963 and so could not have been consulted at the Bamenda, Foumban and the Tripartite Conferences at Buea and Yaoundé which held earlier, which in any case was attended by the Attorney General, Mr. BG Smith.

In fact, Foncha was variously invited to address Cameroon students at their conferences at Buea, Kumba and Yaoundé. Perhaps the other point worthy of note is the fact that the "Cameroonisation Policy" implemented by the Foncha administration though apparently starting with "substandard" personnel hurriedly recruited and promoted to fill in the vacuums created by the depleted civil service, in time and with meticulous in-service training produced the closest to the ideal civil service anywhere along the West African coast. Equally conscious of the very limited human, material and financial resources, emphasis was placed on self-reliance and self-actualization through the introduction of intensive adult education and community development projects. This together with education rating greatly raised the level of literacy, efficiency and productivity in the territory. It is a generally acknowledged fact except by the British whose duty was to establish it but who rather expected the Foncha Administration to collapse.[176]

---

[174] Bernard Fonlon, *A Simple Story Simply Told or The Rise of Dr. Pavel Verkovsky, First Archbishop of Bamenda*. (Yaoundé, CEPER, 1983).

[175] Ibid., Sendze, "My Reflections."

[176] Ibid., Tributes ET Egbe.

Southern Cameroonians serving in Nigeria or overseas were seconded on returning to the new Public Service as well as all recruits from overseas. Put together, this approach yielded enormous dividends to the extent that by 1962 – 65 there were more graduate civil servants engaged in the West Cameroon Civil Service than in East Cameroon. And for one thing, they were generally acknowledged to be efficient, diligent, assiduous, transparent and reliable. It would be a calamity that with such brilliant achievements, which have left an indelible trail on the sands of time, anything should be done to tarnish this record for posterity.

Without in any way imputing triumphalism it would be much worse playing the ostrich for any reason whatsoever. This is a highly cherished patrimony, indeed, an accomplishment for which all Southern Cameroonians deserve to be justifiably proud and which constitutes the essence of The Golden Age of Southern –West Cameroon.[177] Furthermore, it is a worthwhile challenge which budding historians and social scientists should take up for further and better investigation. This was a diligent, assiduous and dedicated civil service whose watch word as coined by Malcolm Milne was "service".[178] It is regrettable that this brilliant memorable indisputable legacy of Southern Cameroons deserving rooftop showcasing for posterity missed the vigilant radar of the *Summit Magazine* which sets out to extol the best of the Cameroon nation.

---

[177] Ibid., Sendze, "My Reflections"
[178] Ibid., Ndi, The Golden Age.

# Chapter 5

## President Ahidjo: Alpha And Omega

### A Larger than Life French Creation

In profile, President Ahmadou Ahidjo was immensely a larger than life French colonial creation intended to serve their primordial objectives in subjugating the Trust Territory of French Cameroon to the policy of assimilation. Initially, he was used as a surrogate to replace Andre Marie Mbida, the first French Cameroun Prime Minister, who had begun displaying inadmissible traits of arrogance and independence of character. However, soon afterwards Ahidjo became a useful front man in fighting the insurgents, the point at which he was granted full rein and control of the technical, military, financial, material and advisory assistance he needed to pursue the rebellion. From this position, Ahidjo discovered his inner resources and cultivated a unique personality, magnified and strengthened as the country approached independence and beyond. Continuously, propped up by the French but additionally with the conception of the ideology of the One Party system (*Partie Unifie*) intensified by an invidious secret security system; an aura of a lofty, mythical, invincible figure; literallyacult was created around him. With the title of *Grand Camarade*, he was dreaded and adored but hardly admired and loved by the masses he ruled with an iron hand.[179]

Bayart, holds that despite the views the praise singers had of him as: "Father of the nation", "Pioneer of negritude", "Prophet of Pan-Africanism," "Defender of African dignity" and much else:

> Ahidjo was never genuinely popular, or inspired popular love, or really connected' with his people. He was certainly feared and viewed with apprehension by friend and foe alike but was never regarded with affection".[180]

---

[179] Ibid., Richard Joseph, *Radical Nationalism*, also, *Gaullist Africa*.
[180] Ibid., Le Vine, p. 39

In his treatment of people, even those very close to him it was noted that, Ahidjo was a very unusual character:

> When he disgraces someone, he does so brutally, but such disgrace is generally of short term: Mr. Ahidjo uses men, casts them aside when they are no longer useful, and recalls them when they have been reformed to his satisfaction. He is neither a nepotist nor a tribalist, and does not encumber the apparatus of state with his friendships, difficult to influence, patient, cunning, secretive...[181]

**Alhaji Ahmadou Ahidjo President of Cameroon, 1958 - 1982**
**He ruled with an iron fist**

This was the all-powerful individual with whom the Southern Cameroonian leadership and people had to deal. Interestingly, his official biographers confess that no one could adequately write the truth about Ahidjo because of the numerous "No go" areas in his life. In other words, he remained a sort of mythically cocooned character – by choice and apparently enjoyed being regarded and treated as such.[182] Victor LeVine, who knew him pretty thoroughly 'from near and afar' for thirty years, remarks of him: "Ahidjo remained something of an enigma to both outsiders and Cameroonian insiders: no one ever quite

---

[181] Ibid., p. 37
[182] See, *'As Told by Ahidjo'*, Paul Bory.

knew what to make of him, or what he thought, or what he really wanted." These were attributes he deliberately created and cherished as they mystified him.[183]

The fact that Ahidjo's academic as well as Koranic education was low, coupled with the allegation that he was of doubtful paternity, gravely impaired his status both in the Fulani community and among his political peers. He therefore sought solace in constructing this mystic personality by avoiding any external display of piety. He maintained a dual personality; mystical, reserved and aloof in public, attitudes which heightened awe and trepidation for him from the masses.

Victor LeVine maintains that Ahidjo was: "publicly reserved, sparing in word and gesture, he admitted few people into his private world though he could be an agreeable companion. Despite the fact that he was a Moslem, he smoked, drank alcohol and chewed kola in the company of his closest confidants."[184] Deriving from the 1961 constitution, the President was an active, powerful, Chief Executive, who singlehandedly had the powers to constitute or dismiss state governments; appoint and dismiss all ministers, enact ordinances with the form of law; he was actually the source of all legislation.[185] Mongo Beti and Eyinga, his critics, additionally argue that the attributes of: his silences, his studied hesitations, his lowered voice, his almost formulaic responses were due not to wisdom of deliberation, but simply to his lack of education and to verbal poverty resulting from it.[186] The brief quotation that follows almost perfectly puts in a nutshell the individuality of President Ahmadou Ahidjo with regard to his amassing of power and authority. In fact, there are some political analysts, who would argue that this does not go far enough in that regard. JF Bayart who has studied in depth and written extensively on Cameroon

---

[183] Jean –Germain Gros, Ed., Cameroon: *Politics and Society in Critical Perspectives,* University Press of America Maryland, p. 33, 2003.

[184] Ibid.

[185] See, "Political Integration and the United Republic Of Cameroon", by Victor T Le Vine, in, *The Search For National Integration in Africa,* David R Smock and Kwamena Bentsi –Enchill, (the Free Press, Collier Macmillan Publishers, London, 1976), pp, 275-6.

[186] Ibid., p. 35.

captured this portrait of the President in his article on the Structure of Political Power. Of President Ahmadou Ahidjo he notes:

> It can be categorically asserted that there are no political or economic authorities in Cameroon which do not derive their authority, directly or indirectly, from the President of the Republic: Ahmadou Ahidjo is the source of all power in the state and governs in an active and personal manner.[187]

The President was a calm, self-effacing, shy but unruffled, perceptive and astute individual and was an enigma to the Cameroon public and even to himself.[188] He was generally unpredictable and seemed to enjoy the fact of being considered as mystical. On the whole, he was feared, revered and admired from a distance by many but not much loved. His astuteness and oratorical skills were awe- inspiring perhaps because his was the lone voice officially heard over the airwaves, face seen on TV and read in the papers; as all news programmes began and ended with reference to his great deeds. This went on *ad nauseam*, such that the foreign press began in jest referring not to his rule but to his *"reign"* and to his person as, "His Royal Majesty because his rule was a hybrid of a presidential and monarchical system.[189]

**Ahidjo: Solid Steps towards a Federal Constitution**

There were Draft Federal Constitutions which resulted from the work of powerful teams set up by the two governments of Southern Cameroons and Republic of Cameroun following Ahidjo's maiden visit to Southern Cameroons from 15-17 July 1960. The first signed on 17 July 1960 by President Ahidjo, John Ngu Foncha, Prime Minister of Southern Cameroons and Charles Assale, Prime Minister of Republic of Cameroun, came following President Ahidjo's maiden visit to

---

[187]Richard Joseph ed., *Gaullist Africa: Cameroon under Ahmadou Ahidjo*, Richard Joseph ed., (Fourth Dimension Publishers), 1976.
[188]He ruled by surprises and finally surprised even himself when he abruptly and causelessly resigned from office in November 1982
[189]See, *Post Newsmagazine*, October 2007,'How Southern Cameroons was usurped', p.10.

Southern Cameroons, in which he was accompanied by a powerful, impressive entourage comprising: the President of the National Assembly, the Prime Minister, cabinet ministers and Members of Parliament together with the British Ambassador to Cameroun. This was at the invitation of the PM of Southern Cameroons through the auspices of JO Field; the Commissioner with the purpose of holding preliminary discussions on the nature of unification should Southern Cameroons vote for reunification in the forthcoming plebiscite. Ahidjo was expected to demonstrate to the people of Southern Cameroons the stance of Cameroon Republic.

On landing at the Tiko International Airport, in response to the welcome address by the Commissioner, apparently overwhelmed by the impressive jubilant and exuberant crowd, Ahidjo volunteered the following momentous statement on behalf of himself and his delegation, one which was to be the recurrent theme in his subsequent speeches: "Our desire is unification not annexation. Since bigger nations are uniting, the time has come for Cameroons to unite and form a nation. Our aim is unification to form a united Cameroon nation within a united Africa."[190] At the formal reception in Buea, Foncha addressing the Southern Cameroons political elite and his august visitors pointed out that the purpose of the President's visit was to:

> Confer with me and my ministerial colleagues on what the people of British Cameroons should have should they vote for the second alternative to be put to them at the forthcoming plebiscite. ... However, we know our place in the Federation of Nigeria. The place which we hope to have in a unified Kamerun will not be the same. It will be like that of divided brothers, who having regained their liberty return home to their fatherland. Each of the brothers claims the citizenship as of right ... we will sacrifice any selfish ambition for the general good irrespective of race or creed.[191]

---

[190] Ibid., *Press Release No. 906* of 16 July 1960.

[191] Ibid., It was on the last day of the visit that the first draft federal constitution was signed.

To enable forthright implementation, a joint committee was immediately constituted to study the various constitutional problems that would result from reunification and how to deal with them. The peak of the visit was when Foncha took Ahidjo and his delegation to Victoria, where they were received by yet a larger crowd in excess of 5.000 on 17 July 1960. Here, protocol and security safeguards were thrown to the winds as the jubilant, excited crowds milled all over to shake hands and touch their youthful leaders. There, once again, Ahidjo fully overwhelmed, uttered the momentous declaration that:

> Unification was a natural cry and debt bequeathed to us by our parents. He repeated that his government's desire was reunification and not annexation and that reunification would be on a federal basis. In a final declaration before he took off he declared. I am not going into the French Union.[192]

This was a spontaneous declaration coming from the heart that was repeated countless times and most significantly at the crucial Foumban Constitutional Conference and was taken as such by the Anglophones. That Ahidjo turned round to say that reunification was a UN imposition is most bewildering.

**Work of the Joint Federal Consultation Committee**

To hasten progress on the draft Federal Constitution, the KNDP appointed members to work on the joint committee with the UC team which had come with Ahidjo. It Comprised:

ST Muna: Minister of Commerce and Industry

A.N. Jua: Minister of Social Affairs

PM Kemcha: Minister of Community Development

PT Fombo: PM's Private Secretary

---

[192] *Southern Cameroons Press Release No.* 911 of 19 July 1960.

SA Njosa: Southern Cameroons Information Service

EM Mbwaye: Photographer

TA Abanda: Press Representative and three Advisers

Together with their UC counterparts, at their second meeting the following month, August 1960, they agreed to yet a third meeting which held at Yaoundé from 10-14 October 1960. After this, another draft Federal Constitution for the reunification of the two states with provision for the inclusion of Northern Cameroons was signed by President Ahidjo, Prime Minister Foncha of Southern Cameroons and Prime Minister Charles Assale of Republic of Cameroun.[193]

As can vividly be identified in this draft constitutional outline the key words were "federal" and "federation". There was talk of 'confederation' but this was finally resolved to "federation" with a safety clause on equality entrenched with emphasis from Foncha and the KNDP. Actually, this was the substance of the first draft of the Joint Consultation Committee of 16 July, signed the following day 17 July 1960. On record and available in the National Archives at Buea are two solid federal drafts of the constitution formally signed by Ahidjo, Foncha and Assale following discussions by the joint consultation committee, which met routinely at least until October 1960.[194]

Just for the record, with reference to the Foumban Constitutional Conference, with two versions of the draft Federal Constitution solidly signed by Ahidjo himself, Charles Assale and Foncha, the most crucial and logical question to answer would be why Ahidjo should have

---

[193] See Appendix p. xx.
[194] It definitely becomes problematic when Foncha is openly accused of 'hiding' a draft constitution, which for all his life remained a matter of conjecture. The two draft constitutions are reproduced in the appendix as well as the federal constitution resulting from the Foumban Conference itself. It can be a near impossible challenge being asked to prove what did not exist. The most logical thing would have been to question why Ahidjo ignored the work that these powerful committees had been engaged in, the product of which he co-signed with Charles Assale and Foncha and instead embarrassed delegates by introducing the Republic of Cameroun constitution for discussion at Foumban. The real issue and nagging question therefore should have been just how credible and reliable he could be as a leader.

introduced a brand new version of a highly centralized Federal Constitution in Mbile's words. The expressions of surprise by Mbile and Endeley could have been genuine and could well be explained by the fact that as CPNC, belonging to neither the UC nor the KNDP "Working Group", they did not participate in the discussions leading to the draft constitutions and consequently were not privy to the information which was solely a KNDP/UC affair with Muna, Jua and Kemncha included. Another source of embarrassment is Charles Assale, Ahidjo's PM and closest associate, who signed both constitutions. He ultimately asserted that Ahidjo was not interested in reunification. The question then becomes where to find the truth.

However, with hindsight and existing evidence, knowing Ahidjo for who he was, he introduced a constitution that had not been discussed by the Joint Consultation Committee of which he was chairperson likely to embarrass Foncha and the Anglophone delegation at Foumban. Put together, this was a bizarre way of inaugurating a union of two vastly diverse peoples brought up under two diametrically opposing colonial systems. The Southern Cameroons delegates came to the talks open, willing, honest and trusting, ready to exchange ideas; in Foncha's words; to confer with their long lost brothers but were tricked, caged and everything done to 'blindfold' them. This was a lost opportunity for confidence building towards a "grand manifest destiny" for solid unity based on trust and honesty. No true national unity and confidence building could be built on deceit. This discovery unveiled and understood fifty years later on the occasion of celebrations marking the Golden Jubilee is unnerving and much like a couple discovering that the other partner in the union had all along been unfaithful and worse still, that the union had been built on sheer falsehood right at inception.

Indeed, with a little reflection it becomes obvious that Ahidjo like the proverbial tiger barely hid his claws, camouflaged his black spots and unleashed them at the appropriate moment. He faithfully maintained his traits of duplicity, falsehood and deceit. The traps laid against the Anglophone delegates at Foumban were simply the first in a series of intractable snares and hurdles that were systematically deployed by the Ahidjo Regime from 1961 till the dismantling of the federation in 1972. That Charles Assale, his PM, who survived him, finally declared that Ahidjo did not believe in unification is embarrassing but unfortunately true.

With hindsight, there is every reason to believe that at no point in time even before the Foumban Conference got underway, did President Ahmadou Ahidjo remotely believe in the federation or anything less than a highly centralized administration under his personal grip.[195] However, given the very neat stage management of events, few would have perceived the sinister intentions behind his pious declarations and actions. On the outside, at the onset he looked serene, calm, honest, unassuming and reassuring in his words and deeds.

Almost without exception, the Anglophones were largely taken in by his declarations and even Albert Mukong who expressed misgivings was not emphatic enough in doing so. Generally, therefore, West Cameroon politicians believed in and fully trusted "President Ahidjo" and in as many ways expressed their total confidence and loyalty to him believing that he was truly a "godsend" leader, indispensable and reliable. In this: Endeley, Foncha, Mbile, Muna, Egbe, Jua and all the others displayed this brand of blind confidence and adulation forhim to the point of hypocritical sycophancy. His entire rule was shrouded in the fabled "King's Beautiful Dress" by a mesmerized populace until too late,[196] when it became impossible to raise a finger against him and survive.

**Geopolitical Contradictions: Creation of Federal Inspectorates**

Barely three months after consolidating the resolutions of the Foumban Constitutional Conference at the Yaoundé Tripartite Conference, Ahidjo surprisingly issued a decree flagrantly contradicting the Federal Constitution. By his Decree No. 61-DF-15 of Dec. 20 1961, he went on to divide the two- State Federal Republic of Cameroon into six Administrative Inspectorates each placed under a "Federal Inspector" with indeterminate powers which could be interpreted variously, since they: represented the Federal Government

---

[195] Ibid., *The Frontier Post* p. 4.
[196] He was welcome and variously heralded as a 'God Send', Messenger of Peace, Father of Unity, Harbinger of Peace etc.

in all acts of civil life and in judicial matters. Besides, they were to supervise the observance of the Federal laws and regulations in force, having at their disposal the police, gendarmerie and federal services. Thus, in the case of West Cameroon, there were no clear distinctions in authority between the Prime Minister and the Federal Inspector to whom the gendarmes and sous-prefects reported directly and he alone reported confidentially and directly to the President of the Federal Republic without any reference to the Prime Minister. In other words, there were as it were, two parallel administrative set ups with the Federal Inspectorate additionally spying on the civilian administration headed by the PM, who presided over the West Cameroon House of Assembly, House of Chiefs and was Head of Government, while the Federal Inspector at best was basically an appointee of the President.

This totally flawed the provisions in the Federal Constitution; geopolitically, legally and logically. In fact, it subverted that constitution. This was especially the case as the Federal Inspector of West Cameroon was accorded extensive powers by the President that overlapped those of the constitutionally elected PM of that state. The position of the Federal Inspector was further buttressed by the fact that he was in charge of the security and the newly introduced gendarmerie, a "brutal" paramilitary corps. Apart from extreme savagery in dealing with civilians there were as well numerous clashes they had with their counterparts, the police whom they treated with scorn. The situation at the time is accurately captured by Justice Nyo' Wakai who lived the experience as a prime executor of the law. Referring to the new changes, he notes of the time:

> On the other hand, after October 1, 1961, Anglophone Cameroonians suffered from a cultural shock. Firstly, a new agent of law enforcement appeared on the scene. The gendarmes are a para-military force looked at from any stand point. They are armed and ruthless in their understanding of keeping the peace. Perhaps they are taught to be brutal in their manner of approaching

suspects. The use of force and a tendency to detain anyone who questioned their powers of arrest is part of their subculture. [197]

Further illustrating the brutality of this corps even to innocent civilians as recently as the late 1990s, he explains how "*operation cale cale*," carried out in big urban centres was organized. They broke into private homes around 5 am forced everyone into an open space or in the street, where they were systematically searched and beaten, the rationale being that there were bandits and dangerous elements hiding therein. In the treatment meted out in these circumstances he continues:

> In the street or open space, everyone and I mean everyone, man woman and child, is stripped to the pants and forced to sit on the ground. Sadistically, the wet places such as water pools are preferred. Any resistance by anyone is visited by flogging and kicks with military boots…. The gendarmes are among the law enforcement agents who are a hated and detested lot. No citizen is willing to cooperate or collaborate with them in the discharge of their supposed noble task.Obviously, the law we are dealing with neglects the very concept of human rights; the dignity of the human being is consistently abused. The citizen is denied the "unalienable rights … life, liberty and the pursuit of happiness.[198]

The argument raised in the defence of such action is that these laws derive directly from French law and convention and fall under "Administrative Law", in the realm of "Public Order" and consequently, could be and have been a source of serious Human Rights abuse. It will be recalled that at the Foumban Conference, the Human Rights guarantee introduced by the Anglophone delegates was inadvertently omitted, and when reminded, President Ahidjo promised to have them inserted in the preamble to the federal constitution but finally, conveniently forgot or ignored it.

---

[197]Justice Nyo' Wakai, *Under the Broken Scale of Justice: the Law and My Times,*(Mankon, Bamenda; Langaa Research & Publishing, CIG, Bamenda, 2009), pp. 22-24.
[198]Ibid., p. 27.

This confusion became a trade mark that characterized the Ahidjo Administration. Generally, those areas of the constitution which he wanted to subvert, he simply had the laws changed or twisted to suit the particular interest by decree without necessarily resorting to changing the constitution.[199] Reflecting on this rather messy, fluid and confusing state of affairs with the Fundamental Law of the Land in Cameroon up to 2010 Justice Nyo' Wakai again best summarizes the situation pointing out succinctly, how:

> Our constitutions have become the floor mats of the executive arm of government. Right now, we are under the non-implementation of very vital provisions of the constitution of 1996. Today we talk of two constitutions in use, the one of 1972 as amended and that of 1996. No individual, not even those who have sworn to uphold and abide by the constitution have dared to challenge it.[200]

In retrospect, it is discernible that the creation of the six Federal Inspectorates of Administration parallel to the constitutional two-State structure amounted to the fact that the Unitary State declared in 1972 basically confirmed the existing inspectorates created in December 1961; a shadow that all along overcast the FRC. Jean Claude Ngoh, the "almighty" Federal Inspector for West Cameroon at Buea, appears to have been appointed with a veiled mission to openly contest, challenge and undermine the power, authority and privileges of the constitutionally elected state PM. Most of all, he was a spy planted to report in detail on the activities of the West Cameroon Government using the services of the prefects, sub-prefects and gendarmes directly placed under him with Mr. RJK Dibongue as an underground self-appointed key informant on his political opponents.

In particular, Jean Claude Ngoh seemed to have specialized in coverage on Foncha and Jua using the national security. Complaints about his arrogant behaviour to the President by Hon. AN Jua the PM

---

[199] But even then the Cameroon constitution has been changed six times: 4th. March1960; 1st. October 1961; 2nd June 1972; revised in February 1984 and 18thJanuary 1996, with changes on April 6, 2008; six times three of which were under Ahidjo.

[200] Ibid., Justice Nyo' Wakai, p.114.

and Foncha the VP received a deaf ear. His powers were boundless. Wilfred Nkwenti recalls how, the Federal Inspector bolted into the Buea Radio Broadcasting Studios, which were close to his residence ready to throttle him. His excuse was that he heard the name "Dr. EML Endeley" mentioned in the broadcast, and Nkwenti was charged with supporting the opposition! Nkwenti who ran a programme on Farmers and the Rural World had to explain under threats, why he dared to have mentioned the name. His defence that it was in connection with Dr. Endeley's contributions to the BCUF (Bakweri Cooperative Union of Famers) were taken with a pinch of salt.[201] In other words, he personally could go physical and publicly boasted that he had more powers than the PM.

**Jean Claude Ngoh Federal Inspector of Administration 1961-1972**

**Presidential Appointee Competed with the elected PM of West Cameroon**

Incessant public complaints and petitions with abundant evidence, dispatched to the President about the Federal Inspector, who was overstepping his powers and undermining the constitutionally elected PM continuously and ignominiously were ignored until the abolition of

---

[201] Interview with Mr. Wilfred Nkwenti on 6/03/13

the FRC in 1972. Rather, what emerged was the declaration of the "Peaceful Revolution" of 20 May promulgated on 2 June 1972 creating the "United Republic of Cameroon", built around a strong Presidency.[202] This was practically an elaboration of the Inspectorates which were slightly increased from six to seven in the Unitary State. This feat was achieved simply by breaking up the former State of West Cameroon into two, namely; the "North West" and "South West" Provinces with the names changed from inspectorates to "Provinces." In other words, the "20th May 1972 Peaceful Revolution" geopolitically only affected "West Cameroon" which was split, while the rest of the territory of the former Republic of Cameroun stayed intact until the February 1984 Constitution in which the United Republic of Cameroon finally reverted to the 'Republic of Cameroon'. This was precisely what the Unitary State was about; divide West Cameroon to better rule. The road and air communications between the two provinces were left to fall into total disrepair and movement between them had to be circuitous through Western and Littoral Provinces. In all of these changes, the powers of the President were retained and further fortified.

This started with the creation of the CNU party in 1966, which firmly subordinated the State to the party, or as Bayart better put it,[203] "It is the party that emanates from the person of Mr. Ahidjo and not the other way round". His predilection for discarding solidly reached agreements without qualms, the absence of political will evident bad faith and megalomaniac tendencies were clearly demonstrated in his style of government. It was with the instrumentality of the CNU that the dismissals of Prime Minister Jua and Vice President, Foncha and their replacement by Muna all with an eye on what culminated on 20 May 1972 as the "Peaceful Revolution" brushing aside the impregnable Article 47(1) of the Federal Constitution was effected. Thus ST Muna became the sledge hammer President Ahmadou Ahidjo manipulated to scotch AN Jua, JN Foncha and finally dismantled the Federal Republic of Cameroon. Of Ahidjo's deceptive; benign, unassuming but astute

---

[202] Apum Aseh Samah Albert, *Introducing Nation Building and Human Rights*, (Mama Press Yaoundé, March 2010), pp. 84-87.
[203] Ibid., Piet Konings, p. 247.

countenance, Mark Delancey, who carried out close studies of his regime and his person iterates:

> Initially, he was considered by many to be a mere puppet of the French and an intermediary figure at most…. soon however Ahidjo displayed an unexpected political craftsmanship which enabled him to strengthen his originally weak position and eventually to construct a system of personal rule. Centralization, coalition building and repression were his major strategies to concentrate political power and economic power in his office and person.[204]

In fact, whenever the full account of Ahidjo's administration shall come to be written it shall be realized that it was by any measures a "reign that struck fear and terror". Thus the superficial reference to the all- pervasive negative role played by President Ahmadou Ahidjo in undermining the reunification process and concentration on the defects of the Foncha Regime rendered the epic *Summit Magazine* interview extremely bias and hollow.

**Emergency Laws: Opposition Leaders Jailed in East Cameroon**

In this connection, it should be added that prior to approaching the West Cameroon political party leaders in 1962 with his gorgeous olive branch canvassing for the formation of a *"Grand Partie Unifie"*, Ahidjo had already subverted the Federal Republic of Cameroon's judicial system by the introductionof a series of "Emergency Laws" which dramatically transferred the administration of justice from the jurisdiction of civil courts to newly constituted Military Tribunals between 4 October 1961 and 12 March 1962. In the military tribunals of Yaoundé and Douala alone by January 1964 not less than thirty UPC leaders including some who had earlier had their sentences commuted to life imprisonment or actually cleared in civil courts were sentenced to cruel public executions supposedly to act as a deterrent to other culprits.

---

[204]Delancey, quoted in Piet Konings p. 247.

Under this guise Ahidjo found excuses to deal squarely with those politicians who stood in his way. Accordingly, he put behind bars with stiff sentences of penal servitude and heavy fines: Messrs Andre-Marie Mbida, the first Prime Minister of French Cameroun and leader of the *Democates Camerounais* (DC) under whom Ahidjo himself served as Minister of Interior and his assistant; Charles Rene Guy Okala, his former Minister of Foreign Affairs, who was very close to Ahidjo and attended many important meetings and conferences with him, at the UN and with the Foncha cabinet e.g. the Buea Tripartite Conference. He also gallantly and ably defended the case for the loss of Northern Cameroons in the 1961 Plebiscite at the UN and at The Hague; Theodore Mayi Matip, Chairman of the Parliamentary Group of the UPC and Dr, Marcel Bebey Eyidi, leader of the Labour Party of Cameroon. Significantly, all of them were prominent opposition leaders of political parties, as well as Hon. Members of the Republic of Cameroon National Assembly.[205] Yet they were not immune to arrests and imprisonment under Ahidjo.

Their crime was simply that although in principle, they had accepted the proposed formation of "A Front for National Unity" by the UC and the KNDP; they dared to have questioned the strategies engaged by Ahidjo's UC for absorbing other political parties into its fold. This group had summarized their protest in a 12 page document dated 15 June 1962, which they duly signed. The Government's response was to arrest all the four who were tried before the new Corrective Tribunal by Ordinance No. 62/OF/18 of March 1962 under the new Subversive Activities Law. On 11 July 1962, they were each sentenced to thirty months imprisonment and a fine of 250.000 francs.[206] When they dared to appeal, the sentences were simply doubled. This was the gory state in which Ahidjo's hands were soiled as he came across to West Cameroon carrying an olive branch and preaching democracy, reconciliation and national unity. Five years later, in 1966, it was obvious that what had befallen the gander in Republic of Cameroun would befall the goose in West Cameroon. The traits of

---

[205] Presidential Decree No. 52 of 7 May, 1969; The Organic Law on the State of Emergency.

[206] Richard Joseph ed., *Gaullist Africa: Cameroon under Ahmadou Ahidjo*, (Fourth Dimension Publishers, 1976), pp.59-63.

double speak and in short veiled deceit inherent in the Cameroon National Union (CNU) into which the UC transformed itself were inherent in the parent seed. Shrewd as ever:

> Ahidjo did not plan to grant the opposition parties of East Cameroon the same privileges accorded John Foncha. On 17th May 1962 the enlarged executive committee of the UC bemoaned the fact that the other parties had rejected the formula of the partie unifié and urged them to join the UC, a party in which their various views would be respected.[207]

**Hon. Simon Ngeh Tamfu: StaunchKNC, CPNC, CNU and CPDM Member**

**He had a knack for Revealing Secrets and embarrassing opponents**

In fact, at the onset, the new *Partie Unifie* was most flexible. It was designed to admit all categories of people and meant different things to

---

[207] Ibid., p.62.

different people but finally was only understood by Ahidjo and Moussa Yaya, who launched it.

## The Ebolowa UC Congress, 1962

In retrospection, all that took place from 1966 to 1972 was part of a carefully set out time table only perhaps made more urgent with the confirmation of the existence of oil reserves in West Cameroon in 1969. The degree of seriousness with which Ahidjo had taken the Foumban accord came out very clearly when at the important policy making forum UC Congress at Ebolowa in 1962, he remarked, rather casually:

> It was unthinkable to tamper with the Republican form of the regime; it was the Republic which had to transform itself into a federation, taking into account the return to it of a part of its territory, a part possessing certain special characteristics. The question therefore was not one of the birth of a new Republic with federal form. Bowing to this logic, we decided, therefore, to amend the constitution of 21st February 1960, since language and cultural differences needed to be given legal consideration.[208]

This brief quotation bears the hallmarks of the sincerity and importance, Ahidjo attached to all that transpired at Foumban and the plans he had for implementing the decisions that had been taken there. In the same vein, a year later, on another important occasion, when opening the UC building at Yaoundé, in September 1963, Ahidjo passionately stated his unique version of democracy. He declared in an emotional outburst:

> For heaven's sake, let us adapt this democracy to our own realities, which are not the same as those of other countries. We have extolled the single and unified party in order to achieve indispensable national unity. In the old established countries it was necessary for them to achieve national unity. In order to achieve it

---

[208] Ebolowa Congress of UC, 4-8 July 1962, My emphasis.

... certain ones had to resort to dictatorship. The monarchy which existed there was, in my estimation, worse than the single party... the citizens because they were against the policy of the king or emperor, paid for their opposition with their lives, and were decapitated. Thank God, we haven't come to that.[209]

All of this should be understood in the context of the fact that regardless of how shrewd, astute and intelligent Ahidjo was, this did not replace basic post-primary or secondary education in his life which would have afforded him the necessary competence in understanding the highly charged political, historical and philosophical concepts in his bombastic address. As a holder of the *CEPE* (The First School Leaving Certificate), which he only passed on the second attempt[32] his notion of impregnated concepts such as; nationalism, democracy and benevolent despotism and their impact on medieval Europe at best could only have been hazy. It is difficult to gauge his understanding of the outlook of political life in Medieval Europe and even more complicatedly, how this could be translated to the Cameroonian and African situations. Yet, this was his bogus understanding and translation of the principles he engaged in the administration of Cameroon for a quarter century. Here it may be added that several philosophical, economic and political publications are ascribed to his authorship.

**Deceit, Falsehood and State Terror**

The interesting story is told of a stalwart CNU militant, who was the Headmaster of the Council School in Bamunka, Ndop (present day Ngoketunjia Division). He was a zealous promoter of party activity and never let go any opportunity, where he could showcase his support for the great CNU party and its God-given leader, *Grand Camarade* President Alhadj Ahmadou Ahidjo. Consequently, he made CNU uniforms *"ashwabi"* for his entire family including children of tender ages. This was a ubiquitous practice that gripped the party's rank and file throughout the nation as militants fought to outbid each other in

---

[209]Ibid., Johnson, p. 197. My emphasis

displaying their attachment to the party and its leadership. The Headmaster even got his twelve year old son to carry out multiple voting (rigging) at elections so as to boost the party image and strength in the area. As the account goes:

> As Headmaster of Council School, Bamunka, he was invited on 11th February 1972 ... to teach children who had failed their examinations and decided to abandon school. [He] thought there was no better anecdote than the one that even the then President of Cameroon, El Hadj Ahmadou Ahidjo had failed the First School Leaving Certificate examination, yet rose to become the Head of State.[210]

It was not merely pejorative but considered an abomination to have publicly stated that the Head of State, better known as *'Grand Camarade'*, in the first place was the holder of only the First School Leaving Certificate, and worse, that he had failed and had to repeat the *CEPE* examination in 1938. For this seditious crime plain clothes military officers swooped down and had the headmaster arrested and locked up in the dreaded *Brigade Mobile Mixte* (BMM) at Bamenda until he was able to show proof of the source of his information. The trauma from this experience never left the collective memory of the family and continued to haunt the mind-set of the twelve year old son`, who was a living witness of the drama and who released the story. On the whole, this is the reality that was lived in which deceit, falsehood and state terror reigned supreme.[211] As for the brutality of his rule, Victor le Vine points out that:

> Ahidjo could and often did act brutally, particularly against his political opponents and those who crossed him, and during his rule Cameroon's prisons housed a sizeable number of political detainees. Political murder has been put at his door, as has torture,

---

[210]Ibid., *Ahmadou Ahidjo '1958-1968 As Told By Ahmadou Ahidjo'*, edited by Paul Bory Monacao.

[211]*Cameroon Panorama*, this was pejorative and considered in bad taste in political circles.

and he has been accused of aiding and abetting a Cameroonian ethnocide.[212]

Asked to come clean on the nature and status of the reunification he was proposing between Republic of Cameroon and Southern Cameroons at the UN in 1960, Ahidjo declared without the slightest ambiguity:

> I would not like firmness and clarity of our stand to be interpreted as a desire for integration on my part which would sound the death knell to the hopes of our brothers under British administration. In other words, if our brothers of the British zone wish to unite with an independent Cameroon, we are ready to discuss the matter with them, but we will discuss it on a footing of equality.[213]

This was a straight forward, simple declaration freely made before the United Nations General Assembly and registered in the annals of that world body. However, in his true element, President Ahidjo was an accomplished double- speaker. Addressing the National Assembly of the Republic of Cameroon later, he declared outrageously and unashamedly that by: "Resolution 1608 (XV) of the UN had imposed on us the obligation to adjust the institutional structures of Cameroon Republic so as to receive back a dismembered part of our country."[214] This of course is explicit and requires no further comment as to what could be taken as serious in what he said regardless of where that was done even at the UN.

**The Unitary State Already Envisaged in 1964!**

Arriving from a meeting he attended at Buea on 24 July 1964, Hon Samuel Ngeh Tamfu disclosed at the CPNC Convention holding at

---

[212]See, George Ngwane, "There Was1West Cameroon", in *Cameroon Panorama* No. 655 of October 012, pp. 6-7.
[213]Ibid., p. 37.
[214]*Recueilles des Discours Presidentielles*, 1958-68, (Paris, *Les Nouvelles* Editions, 1979). Quoted in Foncha's Address, pp. 8-9. My emphasis

Wum in 1964, that plans were under way for converting the Federal Republic of Cameroon into a centralized unitary state. This was eight full years to the crucial event on 20 May1972, far too remote to raise any alarm.[215] At the time, barely three years after Ahidjo's passionate and solemn declarations at the Foumban Constitutional Conference of the necessity and inviolability for the choice of a "federation" in place of a "confederation" as the form of union considered suitable for the former British and French Cameroons with vastly different colonial experiences over the decades, were still fresh in peoples' minds.

Hence Hon. Tamfu's disclosure was disregarded as idle talk and given no further attention, save that providentially it went on record and can now be referred to as a fact of history, which came to pass christened paradoxically as the 'Peaceful Revolution' in 1972. As if a revolt of sorts was anticipated, the very name itself raises questions as well as the process within which it was implemented. Looking back, it has become obvious that in all that he did after 1961, Ahidjo had made up his mind about a tightly unitary state and was simply playing for the right moment, in fact, seeking excuses for landing his fatal blow on the FRC. This point is made clear by Jean –Germain Gros who discloses that:

> In all likelihood, one of the hidden causes of the creation of the united republic was the discovery of oil off the coast of west Cameroon. It is no accident that Cameroon went into the tapping of its crude oil soon after the 'peaceful revolution'. A unitary state allowed greater control of this essential product by the central government.[216]

Even thereafter, the ruling elite were mute to divulge how much was earned from crude oil and what share was used on the people. Until the installation of his successor, Paul Biya this was considered a Presidential privilege not open to public discussion.[217]

---

[215] Idem., *Recueilles des Discours Presidentielles*.
[216] NAB Vb (b1962)5.
[217] Ibid., Victor Le Vine on "AhmadoAhidjo Revisited," in Jean Germain-Gros, ed., *Cameroon politics and Society in Critical Perspectives* ( University of America, Oxford, 2003), p. 84., Note 3.

## Subverting the KNDP, "Unity Group" Partner

The UC-KNDP agreement of 27 April 1962 stopped short of merging the two ruling parties into a coalition. It created an alliance between them instead in the form of a "National Unity Group" in the Federal Assembly. A coordinating committee was established to work out the procedures for harmonizing their relations and actions. Furthermore, it was maintained that the KNDP as the major political party in West Cameroon was the only one with which Ahidjo's own party the *Union Camerounaise* (UC) the major political party and its counterpart in East Cameroon would do business. It was also agreed that neither party would interfere in the other's fief. But as it suited his temperament, it was disregarded both by Ahidjo and Moussa Yaya, Secretary General of the UC.[218] however while this obtained, Ahidjo was carrying out nocturnal overtures with Endeley for a Government of National Unity to the exclusion of the KNDP, especially as the KNDP got stronger and stronger after the elections of 1961. With recurrent defeats at the polls in 1959 and twice in 1961 in the plebiscite and in the elections into the enlarged parliament of 37 with four defections, there were only five members of parliament left in the opposition CPNC and Endeley felt threatened and excluded from the reins of power. In carrying out these nocturnal negotiations with Ahidjo, he was convinced that:

> We can operate a one party system, which would certainly guarantee that everybody has the right to express opinions within the party. This would make the best use of the talents we have in the country, and we could evolve a system of agreement without engendering animosity.[219]

However, in analysing President Ahidjo's political exploits with the politicians of Southern/West Cameroon and the manner in which this was done should not create an impression of predator and game

---

[218] Ibid., Anyangwe, p. 108; This was discovered by Elf SEREPCA in the late 1960s, around 1969.

[219] Confirmed in interview with Mr. Wilfred Nkwenti, who was Press Officer of the KNDP at the time, 6/03/13

relationship. While the indications point out unmistakably to a situation in which nothing could have prevented Ahidjo from achieving his passion for the unbridled acquisition of power and authority centralized on his person, it need not have been the simple pushover that it turned out to be. In fact, a good argument could be made for the fact that it was actually a question of mutual culpability because it was facilitated by the squabbling among the political parties and individuals within the parties themselves. The British Colonial Administration lent the CPNC surreptitious and open support.. Among other accusations, in the case of the KNDP, Willard Johnson observes that:

> There were perceptions of discrimination in the appointment and promotion of civil servants according to tribal or former party affiliation. It was widely believed among people in the forest areas that they were disadvantaged during the Foncha administration particularly if they had any history of association with opposition party members. Occasionally people were dismissed from their posts seemingly arbitrarily on the basis of rumours of support to the opposition party or its affiliates.[220]

The examples frequently cited were those of two Bakweri civil servants, Messrs Eric Quan and Peter M Efange, both of whom possessed London University degrees with several years of satisfactory service but who were summarily dismissed because of their support to the CPNC.[221]

On the other hand, by 1962 members of the CPNC, which had been in serious decline after losing the elections of 1959, the plebiscite and elections of 1961 began feeling totally left out and in the cold. Consequently, the leadership, through the CPNC mouthpiece, the *Cameroon Champion* of 11 August 1962, "with growing sympathy from Yaoundé [Ahidjo] published an ultimatum to the KNDP calling on it

---

[220]Ibid.,, Johnson, p. 262; *Cameroon Times*, Monday, 28 April, 1962. In fact, only Endeley and Mbile became the rump. To Johnson, Endeley admitted that he met Ahidjo thrice during his visit in April 1962.

[221]Ibid., Johnson, p. 270, see also Sylvester Ngemasong, "Crisis Within The KNDP".

to dissolve itself and join the UC by January 1 or the people would not take its policies seriously".[222]This was with reference to the KNDP-UC Unity Group accord of April that year. The paper followed this up with threats especially as President Ahidjo was expected to visit Buea shortly. Endeley opened up secret talks with Ahidjo to: reaffirm his commitment to the idea of a single party and his desire to play a constructive and loyal role in the political life of the country. It is clear that Ahidjo appreciated the CPNC's declared good faith and Ahidjo began to voice his assurance that "no one need be considered redundant" who sincerely wished to help build the nation.[223]

To the embarrassment of the KNDP, the CPNC tabled this issue on the floor of the WCHA in a motion introduced by Hon. SN Tamfu in February 1963 callingon: "President Ahidjo to intervene in order that all persons interested take immediately the proper measures to insure the realization of a single party through the absorption of all existing political parties in one single one"[224] In the meantime during that visit *Cameroon Champion* in its editorial of 11January1963, again, addressed to the President this time invitedhim to: "Come to our aid… tribalismis atits peak; nepotism in the civil service is a creed of a political party; political warfare and rivalry is the order of the day."[225] That President Ahidjo unlike in East Cameroon did not act immediately but bade his time was a mark of his astuteness and composure. Paradoxically, when Ahidjo finally asked all the parties to fuse with his UC in preparation for the *"Partie Unifie"* the CPNC was reluctant and became the last to give in.

**Attempted Reforms within the UC-KNDP Unity Group**

Stultified attempts were made towards bringing about internal reforms within the UC-KNDP Unity Group to resolve the unease that was brewing on the inside. The Foncha Regime continued to believe that there would be a general re-examination of the structures of the Federal constitution at the end of the transitional period. However,

---

[222]Ibid., p.270.
[223]Ibid., pp. 265-266.
[224]Ibid.
[225]Ibid., p. 266.

conscious of the practical problems of launching the new system, winning the peace and consolidating independence, they demonstrated restraint through good faith; but there was frequent reference to: "the tumultuous seas" and "unsuspected rocks" while, counselling patience and good will among their followers. However with the passage of time, it became essential to review the Foumban Constitution. This happened at the "closed door top leadership meeting" of the UC and KNDP in September 1964. At that forum Dr. Bernard Fonlon made explicit the fact that there were indeed: two communities, two political parties divided in the background, mentally, backed by the two historic-geographical entities, East and West Cameroon. To Fonlon's mind:

> They had expected to enjoytwo kinds of equality with Westerners in the Federation : the equality of freedom to rule themselves, and a sense of the moral equality of the two states as the dual embodiment of the Cameroon Nation, the latter was denied by President Ahidjo's approach to the procedures of constitution-making (the assertion of the "one Cameroon" slogan to maintain the continuity of East Cameroon's constitution) , and the former was eliminated by the product of constitution making (a highly centralized federal system). Since coming together, the KNDP had hardly done more than stand by and look on. He questioned what had been done jointly so far in the areas of education, internal affairs, and external affairs and concluded that there had been disillusionment, discontent and frustration and desperation that could become explosive.[226]

Fonlon proposed six fundamental areas for reform covering: a general frame work policy in all fields of government policy between UC and KNDP; effective KNDP participation in all aspects of government policy; permanent committees of both parties to elaborate Government policy; constitutional revision to ensure that Government policy decisions should be taken in a Council of Ministers before the set date of April 1965. The West Cameroon leaders sought for

---

[226] Idem.

positions of strict equality between KNDP and UC. Moussa Yaya rejected equality of UC and KNDP in the policy committees. It had to be proportional representation leaving the President the freedom to decide executive policy and procedures. The President and his Government were to be responsible directly to the people and not to parliament; it was not a parliamentary system. Moussa Yaya's views could not be contradicted, so they were final.

These rumblings coming from within the Unity Group with veiled Anglophone threats clearly indicated to Ahidjo and his cohorts that the KNDP had indeed become a nuisance and an obstacle to Ahidjo's quest for supreme power and authority and could no longer be tolerated. So, the "closed door top leadership meeting" of the UC and KNDP in September 1964, sounded one more death knell to the coffin of the FRC and brought closer the decision to destroy the KNDP and create the *Unique Party* that would become the oracle for the President. This was the task undertaken by Moussa Yaya for the UC through the creation of the CUC.

**The CUC**

Meanwhile as Foncha prepared moving over to Yaoundé to take up the position of the Vice President of the FRC, a serious power tussle for his replacement erupted within the top ranks of the KNDP and finally rested solely between ST Muna and AN Jua. Jua won at the Ninth and Tenth Conventions of the party holding at Bamenda and Kumba respectively and finally at the joint parliamentary meeting in Buea, but Muna insisted that only the President of the Federal Republic had the authority to appoint the PM of West Cameroon. However the real issue was that Foncha had been indecisive in his support for either candidate. It would appear he had initially indicated his leaning for ST Muna and finally turned his support with the party majority to AN Jua. After Muna's defeat in the parliamentary vote, Foncha asked him to step down. When he refused, Foncha had him expelled together with nine of his supporters, who had refused to abide by the party regulations from the KNDP. This was the sense in which Muna described Foncha as a devil second only to Nzoh-Ekhah

Nghaky. Muna's followers constituted some of the best brains in the KNDP.

It was this rusticated group with whom Muna founded the Cameroon United Congress (CUC) with substantial support from Ahidjo. It had a strong tendency towards his UC. As Johnson puts it Foncha was isolated:"lost control of his party ... and incurred the wrath not only of Jua and his supporters but the Muna camp as well."[227]

Thus far, not only was the KNDP torn apart, greatly mortified and weakened; the situation was made all the easier for Ahidjo to execute whatever plans he had for the demolition of the KNDP and subsequently the FRC. In the context of his nocturnal deals with Endeley behind Foncha's back and with total disregard for the Unity Group agreement with the KNDP, much could be discovered of the manner in which Ahidjo masterminded the shattering of the KNDP through the intrigues of Moussa Yaya. Put together, the West Cameroon political parties and their leadership had largely played into his hands and made matters a lot easier for President Ahmadou Ahidjo, who now posed as the incontestable mentor and dispenser of all patronage in the Federal Republic of Cameroon. He had everybody at his feet and proceeded to implement his policies with little obstruction and without compunction.[228]

In step, Ahidjo barely delayed appointing Muna as PM in 1965, because democratic fervour in West Cameroon was still far too strong to be compromised and so he reluctantly appointed Jua as PM that year, while playing for time. He then had Jua despite the fact that he had the support of the majority in the West Cameroon House of Assembly ignominiously replaced by Muna, who was not even a Member of the West Cameroon House of Assembly in 1968. Two years later, he used Muna again to replace Foncha himself not only as the Vice President of the FRC, but also as PM of West Cameroon; positions earlier proscribed by Article 9(3) in the case of Foncha. This read: "The offices of the President and Vice President of the Republic

---

[227]Idem. With Motomby Woleta and Nerius Mbile as Journalists, the CPNC fiercely attacked the KNDP

[228]There was also the Nzoh Ekhah-Nghaky/ET Egbe rift caused by the untimely demise of Zac Abendong, Secretary General of KNDP.

shall be incompatible with any other office." To attain this, President Ahidjo simply amended the Federal constitution.

From the onset, evidence was raised to prop the proposition that regardless of whatever happened; Ahidjo's quest to centralize all political power and authority in his hands and control in West Cameroon could only have been delayed but was, predictably, unstoppable. He had already brought all political leaders to heel in his own East Cameroon. How Ahidjo the master schemer organized the coup d'état to attain this feat in West Cameroon is best summarized by Bayart, who confirms the fact that:

> The President clearly favoured the humbling of Foncha and participated in the process by encouraging divisions among West Cameroonians. By advising moderation to the KNDP, he probably saved CPNC leaders from imprisonment thereby preventing the KNDP from gaining absolute control of the west. He then played skilfully on the confrontation between Muna and Jua, letting the former know he was the favoured one, yet accepting the latter as western prime minister, all the while permitting the temporarily eclipsed aspirant continued access to federal resources. Muna was thereby kept in reserve for the opportune moment when Ahidjo would pull the rug from under Jua.[229]

After this the West Cameroon Westminster parliamentary system was cast in shambles as what obtained thereafter was neither the conventional presidential nor parliamentary system but simply the politics of patronage and sycophancy unique to Ahidjo. This also marked the first step of Muna's meteoric ascendency to the pen-ultimate helm of power in Cameroon in which capacity he was to outlive even Ahidjo his mentor. All of West Cameroon was fully in his grip and Ahidjo's mirror image was the "*Prince*" in Machiavelli, which he might never have read but nevertheless epitomized.

---

[229] Johnson, p.274.

## Formation of the Cameroon National Union (CNU)

Like the so called "Peaceful Revolution" of 20 May 1972, the myth surrounding the creation of the Cameroon National Union (CNU) in September 1966 is one fertile area for serious research. President Ahidjo's dedication to the doctrine of "national unity" as the rationale for the creation of the Cameroon National Union (CNU), in 1966, actually an expansion of his *"Union Camerounais"* (UC) could be seen in his address in 1964 dealing with African Socialism, "The Task Before Us". Ahidjo, the philosopher-historian noted that national unity was the duty to be done before any consideration of ourselves as sons of the Cameroon fatherland. Towards this objective; he ranted:

> No obstacle, no material, sentimental or ideological consideration should be allowed to bar the road to national unity. Does history not teach us that national unity is never compatible with private interest?We have the duty to stifle certain sentiments in order to fight the necessary battle, in order to establish this union of hearts and minds from the base… The essential mission of the leaders of party cells, committees, subsections and sections is to keep alive a spirit of comradeship and brotherhood, to foster this spirit to the uttermost between the militant members. This preoccupation should come before everything else.[230]

What is most astonishing is that this address already alluding in such detail to the various organs and reality of the one party system was being made two long years before the actual creation of the CNU. It is evident that the anticipated unity party in the interest of national unity was to be created literally at gun point since nothing could be allowed that would bar the road for the good of the fatherland. "The divisions, the hatred aroused and kept alive for ambitious ends should be sought out exposed and their fomenters ostracized."[231] Apparently by implication, Jua and Foncha belonged to this category. Since the stultified UC- KNDP top secret meeting they had become the enemy within the Unity Group. Henceforth the KNDP was doomed.

---

[230] Ibid., *Golden Age*, p.84 for Moussa Yaya.
[231] Ibid., J F Bayart in *Gaullist Cameroon*, p.86.

It is claimed that all the parties freely and voluntarily surrendered their individuality and identity to form a *unique party* for the purpose of national unity and development but the historical facts do not match this assumption. The newly created Cameroons United Congress [CUC] of ST Muna became the bane of the KNDP, just as the CNU became the instrument Ahidjo used to demolish the Federal Republic of Cameroon. Foncha's popularity at the polls in West Cameroon and increasingly among the Bamilekes, who passionately wanted him to stand against Ahidjo as presidential candidate added to the fact that he and Jua were diehard federalists required that both men identified as obstacles be cleared from his path. But to do this Ahidjo needed to use Foncha's own immediate collaborators.

That he succeeded in doing this and systematically executed other such plots distinguishes Ahidjo as he has been described by most writers at best as: shrewd, astute, patient and far-seeing and in his true element, as a ruthless master schemer. However, the role of French advisers at all levels and in numerous departments especially in the key sectors of the economy, military, and social welfare was primordial. They were found in; agriculture, education and administration as technical advisers. In the case of the constitution, he had specialists like Mr. Jacques Rousseau, who drafted the French Cameroon and Federal Republic of Cameroon constitutions and Professor Maurice Duverger, who was hired to review them. These excluded those close to Ahidjo like François Sengat-Kuo, who wrote his speeches. Consequently, Ahidjo was not merely an individual, he was "Legion".

The role Ahidjo played in the creation of the CUC was further expressed by Peter Akum Fomum, an outspoken and vocal individual, who knew him closely, having become the Communications Officer of the CUC. During its short existence he used that privilege to launch himself into national politics and became an MP under the new dispensation.[232] What emerges in total is that on several occasions, Ahidjo had put forward his one party proposal in political discussions but this was strongly resisted by Foncha and Jua. Nor was this in the best interest of the KNDP which was at the apogee of its power and popularity, their plan was for greater democratization, far removed

---

[232] Ahmadou Ahidjo, *Contribution to National Construction*, (Presence Africaine, Paris, 196), pp. 26-29 My emphasis

from the "One Party" option. As Sendze a central actor at the time reminisces:

> It was when Jua and Fonlon saw Ahidjo's plan to use the CUC as a surrogate to stand elections with him [Muna] as an ally and renounce his understanding with the KNDP, [Unity Group] that they advised Foncha to succumb to the one party scheme. The divide and rule tactics of Ahidjo to break KNDP resistance had once more succeeded.[233]

Even more pertinently, as recently as November 1964, the KNDP at their Tenth National Convention meeting at Kumba had tackled the worrying issue of the *"Unique Party"* which Ahidjo had been floating since 1962. The convention took note of:

> The growing importance in the young independent and developing African states of the uniqueparty systemby which national unity ....can be consolidated and which erases the politics of hate, rancour, corruption and tribalism and ensures the utilization of the entire reserve of a nation's manpowerand fosters rapid economic development and social emancipation.[234]

---

[233] Ibid.

[234] Though Mr. Muna's spiritual Godson as well, Mr. Peter Akum Fomum spilled the beans when he fell out with his boss over traditional issues in the village. Discussions and phone conversation with Messrs Wilfred Nkwenti and Francis Nkwatoh, May 2013.

Malcolm Milne Receives President Ahidjo. Declaration of Southern Cameroons Independence at Tiko International Airport 30 September 1961

But then, on the manner in which such an objective could be attained, members unanimously agreed that "the KNDP in keeping with its democratic principles would like to see this achieved through a voluntary regrouping of interested political parties rather than by forced legislation".This was very much the same wording used by the four opposition leaders in East Cameroon which had led to their being double incarcerated and made to pay heavy fines. Referring to the strong standing of the KNDP in the territory and the fact that it had recently swept the board clean at the polls, the point was made emphatically that,where the government party won all the seats in a free and fair general election, thus obliging the opposition parties to wind up naturally: "The party is reassured thereby that a *Unique Party* could be born through the popular wish and verdict of a country's nationals expressed through democratic and constitutional channels and shall welcome such an eventuality".[235]

---

[235] Ibid., Sendze, My Reflections, als1o4, t7he10th KNDP National Congress. In all of this, Moussa Yaya played an invidious role, Also, KNDP, 10th Annual Convention, Kumba, November 1964 p. 71.

This talk of the "democratic approach"[236] was precisely what President Ahidjo was out to scorch. In effect, it was to put off majority votes and open debate, which he disliked that the idea of "The Grand Unified Party" was being propagated. In the election of December 1960 in the French Cameroun National Assembly, he had been elected by a slim majority of just a single vote, which was ominous. What the KNDP was craving for would defeat the most important rationale for creating the single or unique party of his dreams as declared by Moussa Yaya at the UC-KNDP conclave in 1964. Precisely, the one party system and the list system were the surest means of preventing dissenting voices and democratic processes for which the KNDP stood.

This must have reinforced Ahidjo's determination to break the back of the KNDP, and its leadership which was becoming too powerful for his comfort. The CNU became all-embracing and as Victor Le Vine saw it at the time: "With the exception of religious bodies, Cameroonian groups that were operating outside the country and such organizations as the Chamber of Commerce; all social, cultural, professional and commercial associations are now expected to fall, however loosely under some branch of the CNU." In other words, the party was all inclusive and achieved complete associational integration of Cameroon and, while outwardly professing plurality was the only one existing. Le Vine proceeds further, noting that the CNU:

> Despite its pretensions to being a truly national party failed to become a genuine mass party with power emanating from the people. Instead, the party appears to have become a secondary auxiliary of the state, its cadres behaving more like government agents and civil servants.[237]

---

[236] Report on the Tenth KNDP Convention holding at Kumba.
[237] *KNDP, 10th Annual Convention*, Kumba, November 1964 p. 71.

**British Ambassador to Cameroon, CE King at Buea Mountain Hotel 1 October 1961**

He Delivers the Queen's Speech handing overSouthern Cameroons to President Ahidjo

This was the first step in the destruction of West Cameroon's Anglo-Saxon, Westminster type parliamentary system. With Muna under his heel, Ahidjo created a huge crevice through which the sands of discord were sowed for West Cameroon to be shattered because what ensued soon afterwards was an administration which was neither of the Westminster parliamentary pedigree nor of the typical French and American presidential systems. Especially, after the formation of the CNU, what emerged was a freak; a governmental style peculiar to President Ahidjo alone, a sort of twentieth century "benevolent dictatorship". That is why it came to be styled a "Royal Presidency".

**Proof: CUC First to Fuse with UC**

Not unexpectedly the newly formed CUC, the flip side of the UC made the point when it became the first West Cameroon political party to dissolve, declare and fuse with Ahidjo's UC, thereby weakening the resolve of the KNDP and CPNC, which were patching up differences to face the UC as a united front. At the convention towards that objective holding at Tabenken, in 1965, Ahidjo warned the CPNC to disband stressing that the move by both parties to coalesce was against national interests. Already at this point in time, no one could raise a finger against Ahidjo and hope to survive. After that, both the KNDP and the CPNC followed the example of the CUC and only played second fiddle at the preparatory meetings which produced the famous Cameroon National Union (CNU) in September 1966, the CUC hardly one year old occupied all the leading posts in the structure. In essence, the CNU was at best a mere modification of the appellation of Ahidjo's UC intended to absorb the other parties.

All this calls into question the generally accepted notion that what took place in September 1966 was a "Voluntary Dissolution" of all the parties in favour of the Cameroon National Union (CNU). It became the impregnable machine and oracle through which Ahidjo manipulated his way "democratically" virtually unchallenged from 1966-1982. Without appearing to be dictatorial, he acted following the supreme directives of the CNU Party, which represented and was the acclaimed mouthpiece of the people. This was precisely what he had done with the judiciary to eliminate the opposition in East Cameroon.

With Muna staunchly by his side and the CNU in his grip, Ahidjo's tool kit for the dismantling of the Federal Republic of Cameroon edifice was complete. Thenceforth, using the CNU party, President Ahidjo had Muna, who had replaced Jua, the diehard federalist PM of West Cameroon in 1968, to again causelessly replace Foncha, architect of reunification in 1970. Ultimately, he used Muna, who since 1970 had been pivoted into the double pinnacle positions of Prime Minister of West Cameroon and Vice President of the Federal Republic of Cameroon, earlier forbidden under Foncha to become the sledge hammer which he (Ahidjo) used to drive the final nail into the coffin of the Federation.

Paradoxically at Foumban in 1961, Muna without equivocation had taken the extreme option in favouring a "confederation" and not merely a "federation" for the act of reunification. There, he had openly and passionately argued:

> Unification between Southern Cameroons and the Republic of Cameroon might take the form of a loose federation with the aim of preserving the individuality of the Southern Cameroons state

[and] the union should be a union from which both sides draw strength.[238]

However, on abolishing the Federal Republic of Cameroon structures in 1972, the most important excuse given by Muna personally was that the administration of the federation with two state assemblies, a House of Chiefs in West Cameroon and a Federal House of Assembly in Yaoundé had become top-heavy and too costly to run. This was conversely, not borne by the facts as the administrative costs only soared. In any case all along reunification had been a political decision endorsed by the impregnable will of the people and could not therefore, be dissolved on flimsy unproven economic grounds. In retrospect it sounded like readings taken out from George Orwell's (Eric Arthur Blair) satirical fiction, *Animal Farm*.

This demolition project initiated by Ahidjo was completed by President Paul Biya, who by a stroke of the pen in Presidential Decree No. 85/01 of 4 February 1984 dissolved the United Republic of Cameroon and resuscitated the Republic of Cameroun, which already had internationally recognized boundaries.[239] This replaced the United Republic of Cameroon (URC) with the Republic of Cameroon (RC) reverting to the name assumed by French Cameroun at independence on 1 January 1960. The destruction of the FRC (1961-72) and the URC, 1972-84 were aptly referred to in two words by Dr. JN Foncha as the "bad faith" of our Francophone brothers.[240] All these developments must be understood in the context of the iron clad dictatorial rule of President Ahmadou Ahidjo, where no form of opposition was brooked.

**Inexplicable Absence of the "Ahidjo Factor"**

Regrettably, this "Ahidjo Factor" was writ large by the near absence or rather skewed reference made to him in the epic *Summit Magazine* interview, while solace was found in planting blames,

---

[238]Idem.
[239]Ahidjo's warped definition of democracy at the Second UC Congress at Yaoundé Johnson, p. 197.
[240]Ibid., Victor LeVine, p.280.

accusations and indictments elsewhere. Together with the declassified British secret papers these two omissions historically represent inexcusable flaws in the discussion because, while the declassified secret British papers largely dismiss the charges levied against Foncha and his administration, Ahidjo's "bad faith" coupled with the lack of political will, which drove him to introduce a highly centralized authoritarian constitution pivoted on himself, explains the demolition of the Federal Republic of Cameroon barely within a decade of its creation without a fair trial period. As demonstrated, Ahidjo not only did not believe in democratic principles and federalism because it was not part of French administrative tradition but even more strongly by virtue of his own upbringing and innate dictatorial tendencies.[241]

This was almost immediately demonstrated in his carefully calculated introduction of "Federal Inspectorates," which diametrically defied and contradicted the fundamental concept, vision and spirit for which the federation was created. Then followed the introduction of "Emergency Laws", that mortally subverted the judiciary; the defiant denunciation made at the Ebolowa UC conference; next was the subtle but ruthless sabotaging of the KNDP to pave the way for the CNU, which became the oracle for his devious machinations. Addressing the over five thousand people who thronged the stadium to receive him at Victoria on 17 July 1960, Ahidjo had freely declared that reunification was a "debt bequeathed to us by our grandparents" and "federalism" was the indestructible machine to run it. However, addressing the National Assembly of Cameroon Republic, sometime later without in any way "biting his tongue", in his characteristic double speak, the President declared disparagingly that the United Nations, by Resolution 1608 (XV) "imposed on us the obligation to adjust the institutional structures of Cameroon Republic so as to receive back a dismembered part of our country".[242]

---

[241] Ibid., Aka p. 246.

[242] Reason why the SCNC have argued that by that act, one of two things had happened: a] the Republic of Cameroon had seceded, thereby liberating Southern Cameroons, or b] that Southern Cameroons had annexed, pure and simple. See, The Case for Southern Cameroons, ed. Albert W Mukong CAMFECO, USA p. 21

## Malcolm Milne and President Ahidjo- Soul Mates

That Malcolm Milne and Ahmadou Ahidjo bonded as perfect conspirators and accomplices over the demolition of Southern Cameroons is borne by all the proceeding disclosures and finally bythe fact that both men presided over the celebrations at Tiko International Airport and together proceeded to complete the process at Buea Mountain Hotel. There, the reins of power and authority were made over to Ahidjo by Malcolm Milne and CE King to the exclusion of Foncha, who did no more than watch a process that had nearly cost him his life and was to spell doom to his people.[243] The consummation of the union of these predator soul mates had commenced as Malcolm Milne drove President Ahidjo from Tiko to Buea in the Commissioners' land rover; he felt most delighted and declared it was his most pleasant and fulfilling moment because for once, Foncha was placed out of the lime light and President Ahidjo had taken central stage.[244] By all counts, Malcolm Milne and President Ahidjo were great friends. Milne maintains that: "He was a friendly and dignified personality with the impeccable manners of his Fulani ancestors. He was a pleasure to deal with and the last thing we wanted was for ill to come to him."[245]

Hence Southern Cameroons was safely packaged and handed over to him to seal Anglo-Cameroonian Friendship as professed in the Queen's Address. In their final bid further to laying traps to teach Foncha and Southern Cameroons a lasting lesson through the agency of JO Field and Malcolm Milne, HMG found a perfect accomplice in the person of President Ahmadou Ahidjo. He was adept at ensuring that there was no let off for Southern Cameroons, which he kept strictly under his heel by all manner of exploitation and suppression.

---

[243] Foncha's Speech 1994; also, Discussion with him in April 1999, just before his passing on. He emphasized the fact that 'our brothers' do not keep their word but still hoped for reconciliation given the right atmosphere.

[244] Not much is known about his father, but his mother took great maternal concern of her son's education, general welfare and Moslem feudal culture. Actually, Ahidjo postulated that Cameroon unity would be better instituted through Islam which would progress right to the shores of the Atlantic Ocean, Gaullist Africa pp.61-63.

[245] Ibid., *No Telephone*; p.147

In retrospect, Ahidjo gravely and systematically undermined all the pious declarations he personally had made at the UN and the Foumban Constitutional Conference barely a year earlier and began axing down the tree of the federal structures at its roots within the first year of its inauguration. This was manifested in the introduction of "Federal Inspectorates" which diametrically defied and contradicted the federation; followed by the introduction of Emergency Laws, which lethally subverted the judiciary; the defiant denunciation made at the Ebolowa UC Conference of October 1962, followed by the subtle sabotaging of the KNDP to create the CNU which became the oracle for his devious machinations. Addressing the over five thousand people who thronged the stadium to receive him at Victoria on 17 July 1960, Ahidjo had liberally declared that reunification was a "debt bequeathed to us by our grandparents." However, addressing the National Assembly Republic of Cameroon, sometime later without in any way "biting his tongue", in his characteristic double speak, the President declared that the United Nations, by Resolution 160 8 (XV); "imposed on us the obligation to adjust the institutional structures of Cameroon Republic so as to receive back a dismembered part of our country."[246]

The utter absence of political will, manifest bad faith, and the practice of double speak characterized most of his pronouncements and deeds.[247] In the final bid further to laying traps to teach Foncha and Southern Cameroons a lasting lesson through the agency of JO Field and Malcolm Milne, HMG found a perfect accomplice in the person of President Ahmadou Ahidjo. He was adept at ensuring that there was no let off for Southern Cameroons, which he kept strictly under his heel by all manner of exploitation and suppression.

## Conclusion

In Perspective, the yearning for Cameroon reunification on both sides of the Mungo goes back some 130 years to 12 July 1884, when by the act of annexation, Germany put together a collection of some 300 disparate ethnic groups. These were accorded a corporate identity

---

[246]Ibid., No Telephone; p.446.
[247]Ibid.,

which survived two World Wars and forty-five years of colonial fostering by Britain and France. When eventually nationalism took root, it thrived on the "Kamerun idea" shaped by its German roots. By the same token, colonial traditions left indelible cultural impressions in British and French Cameroon that were recognized and respected at Foumban. This was the kernel of the Foumban Constitutional Conference in 1961, where the founding fathers thoughtfully choose the Federal Republic of Cameroon as the formula for uniting the two Trust Territories with vastly distinct, dissimilar cultural backgrounds. Which were further safe guarded by Article 47(1) in the Federal Constitution? Since the abolition of the Federation in 1972, the Anglophones have clamoured for a return to the legality of 1961.

One of the most significant acts at Foumban was the insistence by the Anglophone delegates that the clause, "one and indivisible" proposed in the highly centralised draft federal constitution submitted by Ahidjo be deleted, which he (President Ahidjo) quickly and politely obliged asked to be cancelled immediately. Understandably, having fought valiantly and relentlessly since 1950 for session from Nigeria, acquired internal selfhood within Nigeria from 1954 - 1961 and evolvedas "West Cameroon" in the Federal Republic of Cameroon; it is only logical that Southern Cameroonians could not have voted as massively as they did on 11 February 1961 for "Self-annihilation".

Finally, when the declarations of Ahidjo's close collaborations such as Moussa Yaya, Charles Okala, Charles Assale and several others are juxtaposed, it becomes problematic to apportion and label responsibility for all that befell and is continuing to bedevil Southern Cameroonians; whether it was specifically an Ahidjo syndrome or a systemic policy. In fact, the utterances of powerful cohorts like Moussa Yaya carried the force of decrees or dogmas as they were hardly even controverted. This would rather lead to the conclusion that it was actually a result of collegial, regime policy. When to this is added the reserves of French advisers, then Ahidjo was not more than a flagstaff on whom all tributes, blames and praises were hung. Thus he could be correctly be described as "Legion". Interestingly, typical of his enigmatic character, Ahidjo systematically sacked every single one of this cabal and finally, not even Moussa Yaya was spared.

# Postscript

Let me start this postscript with a quote from: *God's Little Devotional Book for Graduates.*

> When Honorius was Emperor of Rome, the great Coliseum was often filled to overflowing with spectators who came from far and wide to watch the state-sponsored games. Part of the sport venue consisted of human beings doing battle with wild beasts or with one another, to the point where one was killed. The assembled multitude made holiday of such sport and found the greatest delight when a human being died. On just such a day, a Syrian monk named Telemachus was part of the vast crowd in the arena. Telemachus was cut to the core of his heart by the utter disregard he saw for the value of human life. He leaped from the spectator stands into the arena during a gladiatorial show and cried out, "This thing is not right! This thing must stop!" Because he had interfered, the authorities commanded that Telemachus should be run through with a sword, which was done. He died, but not in vain. His cry kindled a small flame in the nearly burnt out conscience of the people and within a matter of months the gladiatorial combats came to an end. The greater the wrong, the louder we must cry out against it. The finer the cause, the louder we must applaud.[248]

Following the reunification/unification of the two Cameroons on October 1, 1961, and the derailment of the intended purpose of the project, Fonlon, Foncha, Jua, Gorji Dinka, Mukong, and many others kept shouting from the public arena: "This thing is not right! This thing must stop!" Some of them explained with anger, passion and persuasion that what was being done to erase the history of Southern Cameroons from the bosom of the new country of October 1, 1961 would inevitably affect the endurance of the unification mission. They said that the reunification agenda would crumble from the weight of

---

[248] *God's Little Devotional Book for Graduates* n.d.

the apparent ignorance and conceit of nationalists of "Republic of Cameroon." In response, those who were in charge sent some of them to jail; others like Foncha were just pushed aside with arrogance and disdain.

Number 16 of Summit Magazine (April- June 2011) carried an interview with Professor Victor Julius Ngoh, the Deputy Vice Chancellor for Research and Cooperation, University of Buea on the subject, "Reunification Fifty Years After." The interview seemed to tell Southern Cameroonians in a veiled manner that it is their fault that they are suffering the fate they are suffering in the united Cameroon today, since they are the ones who put the rope around their own neck and handed the end to those they are complaining about today! This book by Anthony Ndi is a mark of the seriousness with which the academic community has taken his comments. The book titled "Southern Cameroons Revisited, 1950-1972: Unveiling Inescapable Traps," presents the facts of the matter from an "insider" perspective. Indeed, the book can be said to be another shout from the open arena: "This thing is not right! This thing must stop!"

In one of the themes in the book, Anthony Ndi discusses "Methodology: the nature of history." A science can only consider itself a science if its tenets are universally applicable. History is usually said to be the province of selfless servants of the truth. Truth is universal, and is unchanged by the fact of being known by one, many or none. Diversity cannot be applied to the truth, since there can be no multiple or diverse truths. There could be many possible interpretations of the truth, but some things are simply not true. A lie is a lie, no matter how loudly it is argued or how persuasively it is phrased. In historical and scientific discussions it is possible to overemphasize the achievement of some people, and downplay those of others; most historians write with some amount of bias – that is why history must always be rewritten. Although not all bias amounts to distortion, it is clear that the approach of the Summit Magazine interview results in a serious distortion of the truth about Foncha's achievements as a leader of the Southern Cameroons struggle. In history, it is important and necessary to support with facts and evidence, texts or formulae, what one says about a subject. The purpose such rigour, at least in academe, is to ensure that history does not become a vehicle for indoctrination and manipulation of public opinion.

Hindsight usually enjoys more knowledge than is available at decision point. Memory is usually known to play many tricks on some historians and actors. So from the vantage point of hindsight many journalists and historians usually construct their theories using paper-thin foundations of interviews and sources to allow them to revise their initial wisdom long discredited by unfolding events. For the same reasons, many details in personal memoirs are usually not even slips of memory but self-serving fiction. The scientific method requires that such "sources" be treated with caution.

It usually takes only one commanding personality per generation to change a city, a state, a nation. Such personalities rise above the flow of events only when thrust up by forces under the surface. A rare personality like Foncha that was thrust up by the urge for independence of Southern Cameroons and its reunification with the Republic of Cameroon definitely altered the direction of many forces in society at that time. He succeeded to steer events towards the course he wanted. He changed the course of events, meaning that his personality had a vitality that moved history. Like many such personalities in history, he was carried up or borne down by forces outside himself. It is known that every human being has both a weak and needy part of their soul, and a part of their soul that is strong and filled with resolve. To treat Foncha as if he lacked this duality, and was only weak and needy is unfair. This work by Anthony Ndi allows not only the academic world but also every interested party to crosscheck some "facts" about Foncha and reach more valid conclusions than has been possible before now.

History usually unfolds as humans live their lives in the melee called politics. Politics is a domain where the interaction of individual wills in various domains leads to the creation of a common will. Neither the interviewer nor the interviewee of the Summit Magazine interview is a political virgin. They are both living in the present in Cameroon. Unfortunately, they did not seem to have proceeded from the cognitive dissonance that this is supposed to induce. The Cameroon we are living in today is the product of the interaction of individual wills during a period that extends from the Foncha times to today. To treat the individual will of Foncha as if it was played out in a vacuum is obviously a most unscientific exercise. A historian should always maintain a lively intellectual curiosity and an interest in everything "historical," in what other people think and why they think the way they think, because everything really is related to everything else.

The political is the way in which a society and its members come to understand themselves as this society rather than some society of accidental coexistence willed on them by some outside forces. The political is a process by which a society expresses its autonomy, giving itself its own mode of existence. The political is the condition of the possibility of politics. The distinction between the political and politics creates the space within which democracy becomes possible. The creation and preservation of that space in society is a daunting political task which demands the avoidance of the always-present temptation which Ahidjo fell prey to, either to reduce the political to politics, or to overcome their distinction in a higher unity that eliminates divisions within the body politics of society.

A wrong impression is given in the Summit Magazine interview that the unification agenda failed because of the weaknesses of Foncha, or because it was a "gamble," or because "Foncha and Muna were not well educated" and "KNDP lacked sufficient qualified personnel, therefore their negotiations were weak." This book by Anthony Ndi argues forcefully and convincingly that "Ahidjo's 'bad faith' and determination to introduce centralized personal authoritarian rule largely explains the failure of the Federal Republic of Cameroon barely within a decade of its creation without a fair trial period." Indeed, the obstacles on the unification road were effectively the abolition by Ahidjo of the space in which democracy was possible. He did this by "unifying" society into a higher synthesis that human nature makes impossible: he signed his Ordinances of exception, and created a one-party state!

Justice Nyo'Wakai, a legal luminary in his book The Law and My Times questions why although Cameroon has known no crisis since independence that put parliament out of service, the Chief Executive – Ahidjo - "tended to request the legislative arm to surrender to him (to sign ordinances) and they too seem to do so with relish…"[249] Immediately following unification on 1October 1961, Ordinance No. 062/OF/18 of 19 March 1962 on subversion was signed instituting tight restraints on freedom of expression and association, and allowing the security forces to arrest, torture and send citizens who voiced dissent to prison with abysmal prison conditions - all of which served to intimidate them. The Ordinance established new offences termed "subversion" or "rebellion" which all prohibited free expression of opinion, making it a crime for anyone to oppose or criticize any government action. Thus, barely five months after unification on October 1, 1961, people like Albert Mukong, Gorji Dinka and others who dared to shout from the public arena that "This thing is not right! This thing must stop!" were bundled up and sent to jail, or intimidated to submission. Indeed, we are told by the author that because of the effect of the Ordinances and one party rule, the claim that "all the parties voluntarily surrendered their individuality to form a unique party for the purpose of national unity and development" is false because "the historical facts do not match this assumption." He further states that: "The entire life of the Federal Republic of Cameroon, (1961-1972) and beyond, on the other hand, was dominated by the unnerving intrigues of President Alhadji Ahmadou Ahidjo, who could not brood any form of opposition to his authority.

If "fate" can be accepted as part of a people's history, then these were the determinants that got factored into the developments that have shaped the destiny of Southern and subsequently former West Cameroonians so far…"[250] One-party rule was tantamount to totalitarianism and violated human rights, human dignity, and communal autonomy. Ahidjo's one party regime was a totalitarian attempt to overcome opposition between the democratic individual and the community of which he or she was a member. It removed the space in which individuals would have engaged in the travails of nation building through autonomous self-interpretation or critical reflection. As is always the case, it came about either because there was a hidden agenda (to wipe out the identity of Southern Cameroons), or because

---

[249] Justice Nyo' Wakai, *Under The Broken Scale of Justice: The Law And My Times* (Langaa Research and Publishing CIG, Mankon, Bamenda 2009), p. x.
[250] Albert Mukong, *What's To Be Done?* (Bamenda, July 1985), p. 4.

he felt that the tension between the likes of Foncha, Mukong, Dinka, Fonlon, and others, and himself following the achievements of the Foumban Conference would not be managed by him democratically. As a result, a synthesis was sought, the result of which was the loss of both freedom and communal autonomy, the eradication of the culture of democracy, and the expansion of one-man or group power. A political culture was created in which those who questioned the justice of the action of the regime looked like mentally deranged people.

Ahidjo's power was expanded not by force but by corrupting a self-interested, easily beguiled, and sometimes irresponsible citizenry in exchange for material reward or social honours. We are informed that "Jua preponderantly won repeatedly in the party's conventions at Kumba and Bamenda and even in parliament; Muna assured of Ahidjo's support, was adamant that only the President of the Federal Republic of Cameroon (FRC) had the right and authority to appoint the Prime Minister of West Cameroon and not the party's conventions and parliamentary majorities, norms totally anathema to the British parliamentary system which obtained in West Cameroon. ...Ahidjo then had Jua despite his parliamentary majority as expected replaced by Muna, who was not even a Member of the West Cameroon House of Assembly in 1968. After this the West Cameroon Westminster parliamentary system was thrown to the winds and chaos set in as what obtained thereafter was neither the presidential or parliamentary system but simply the politics of patronage and sycophancy...."[251]

Thus, Ahidjo's totalitarian adventure was a well thought-out strategy, not an accident, an historical aberration, an irrational folly or some childhood illness! It was not imposed on a unanimously resistant people, since it was supported from within by Muna and others. As put by Anthony Ndi, "The newly created Cameroons United Congress [CUC] of ST Muna became the bane for the destruction of the KNDP... the Cameroon United Congress (CUC), the West Cameroon version of Ahidjo's UC party ... undercut and weakened the KNDP and especially its leadership. This was the first step in the destruction of West Cameroon's Anglo-Saxon, Westminster parliamentary system. With Muna under his heel, Ahidjo created a huge crevice through

---

[251] 4Idem.

which the seeds of discord were sown for West Cameroon to be shattered because what ensued soon afterwards was an administration which was neither of the Westminster parliamentary pedigree nor of the typical French and American presidential systems..." To gain favours a new breed of people not known in Southern Cameroons until then, came on stage: selfish, cowardly people raising flattery and lies into authorized currency of the time. It can be said that German Kamerun created a sort of "common sense" in both French and English-ruled Cameroons. Reason why there was a plethora of political parties, all bearing the letter "K"[Kamerun]: KNDP, KNC, KPP, OK, KUP, etc. But the existence of a shared or common sense does not exclude the autonomy of the individual or groups, which is in fact the premise of the common sense. The essence of a common sense is to create a political bond based on mutual recognition by autonomous individuals and groups; to create a solidarity based on responsibility towards other autonomous individuals and groups, as a pre-condition for confronting the fundamental critical questions facing society.

Political action in society is usually divided into periods, described as "lived experience", "reflection" on lived experience, and "conception" of new action or new beginnings. The "new" action always constitutes the first stage of the next political "period." The human spirit is very powerful, indomitable, and is capable of achieving any aim it sets itself, including challenging any odd that props up on the road of its evolution. This is why in human history new beginnings are always possible. Unfortunately, Ahidjo seemed to believe that empirical political choices are caused by empirical considerations. This was in ignorance of this normative sense in which the political binds rights- bearing individuals into an autonomous "reflective" community that endures, evolves over time and generates responses to new challenges that arise in their society. History shows that individual conception of the nation may at any time become political when the conditions of the possibility of their self-affirmation challenge the previously assumed definition of politics that surrounded the concept. This could create tension between the political and politics –as is already the case in Cameroon in relation to unification/reunification - and open up the public space in which society (and its members) can reflect on what it is and what it wants to be.

The Ordinances and one-party state may have acted like a vast refrigerator that reduced the reunification zeal into a condition of torpor. There was no doubt that the refrigerator would breakdown with time. Apparently, to prepare for such an eventuality, the problematic gift Ahidjo deposited on the seat of power as his parting gift, "set out at dawn" as Wole Soyinka would put it. He went as far as possible to legalise Ahidjo's turpitudes with his problematic and provocative change of name of the country back to "Republic of Cameroon" using law N° 84-1 of February 4, 1984! Now the debate on the wisdom of the acts is right in the public domain, and it is robust and wide-open. It has to be dealt with very seriously, at the risk of compromising the whole unification agenda. It is always good to have more than one side of a story. Anthony Ndi's multifaceted association with Foncha give him insight into the man; Professor Ngoh's academic forays with the history of Cameroon give him an outsider's perspective of the man. Each of them has painted a picture of the man John Ngu Foncha. It is left to the academic world, and the public at large to draw their conclusions. As for me, I can state unequivocally that I am happy I read the work of Anthony Ndi, because of the way previous writings I had read had influenced my thinking about Foncha. I can now state with confidence that I am convinced the man did his best about the course he set himself. His best might not be the best, but that is completely another matter.

In order to open up space for this kind of debate and clarification, and for possible new beginnings, it is necessary to establish historical facts, and clarify how these facts, patterns and choices became possible. Nothing can be said to be pre-ordained. The Summit Magazine interview and this book which is a sort of "rejoinder" by Anthony Ndi constitute action in the public space that has been opened for the re-examination of the unification project, if it has to continue to endure and prosper. This self-critique and self-interrogation of the seemingly failed unification/ reunification agenda will not be helped by any efforts by any zealots – known and closet nationalists - to set the agenda.

# Historiography

## A Brief Note about History

History is written following set principles defined by "It is History and not the Historians that Society Requires" (Marwick) and not merely the presentation of a catalogue of facts. Isolated facts in history make no sense. They must be seen in the context of place, time and circumstance. That is why similar facts and events occurring or happening in the same place, affecting the same or different persons at different times are characteristically different. History, therefore, cannot and does not repeat itself as it is impossible to re-enact past experiences, no second, no minute, nothing exactly repeats itself. This makes all historical comparisons at best, lame, and 'casual comparisons' dangerous. It is an "art" and "science" best handled by those trained in the craft. History is far more than just recounting the past, and credible history results from constructed solid facts and principles coded in historiography, the science of the craft of history. This requires stringent effort and as Ensor posits:

> The Historian must be determined to play the game, to deal in facts, not fiction. And as part of that he must strive to do his best to be impartial. I doubt if impartiality comes naturally to anybody; but it is possible to acquire a large measure of it by trying.[252]

In other words, few are born with these professional ethics, which comprise: distinguishing between facts, fiction and opinion, embellishments, propaganda, defence, denigration and self-projection. These have to be consciously cultivated through rigorous exposure to peer review and subjection to critical examination.

---

[252]RCK Ensor, in: *Why We Study History* Manson Publishing Company, Oron 1990

## Levels of History

At the level of the primary school, history is defined simply as "the story of the past" children are taught basic facts based on people, place, time and circumstances which they retain by rote memory. This tends to make the study of history boring and discourages many. In the secondary school as they get older and their horizons widen children are taught to distinguish facts from opinion. They are introduced to causes or reasons course results and effects of historical events. They are equally taught to reason, analyse and categorize historical data. At the General Certificate of Education (GCE) A/L, they are more mature adults and history is no longer just a "story of the past"; its wider dimensions and ramifications are introduced. They are equally introduced to serious critical, logical thinking as they have to analyse, criticize, compare, and contrast and even to "compare and contrast" thereby being challenged to form objective opinions in concluding their essays or answering exam questions.

At the undergraduate or tertiary level in the university, they are introduced to still greater, critical, logical reasoning, as well as to historiography; the craft of history. History is far more than just recounting or narrating facts, dates and names at the tertiary level. Here critical analysis and interpretation is called for, reading, digging beyond the facts that catch the eye but sorting, classifying and presenting logical incontestable information that can stand the test of time. They are introduced to research methodology through writing reports, term essays and finally long essays. It takes a more solid formation and background by drawing from kindred disciplines in the humanities and social sciences (Archaeology, Anthropology, Sociology, Geography, Economics, Philosophy, Law and Logic). That is why history, described as the repository or "collective memory" of a community is classified as second only to the Bible (Koran) in providing wisdom from its rich store of common knowledge. In this connection, Richard TA Murphy articulates it: "History is a jewel with a thousand faces and Bible History is in a class by itself: clever, sophisticated, creative, often poetic, almost always entertaining and instructive." He further quotes Toynbee, who holds that, "History is a vision ... of God revealing Himself in action to souls that were sincerely seeking him".[253] However, unlike the Bible, History though abiding by eternal, universal values, is unyieldingly neutral and does not forgive those who do not learn from its lessons.

## History should be Logical, Chronological and Credible

It is for this reason that anything classified as history or as historical should of necessity be credible, a reference point for posterity, clarifying doubts and placing people and events in their correct and proper perspectives. To be factual, these must be based on scientific, statistical, concrete and verifiable sources. While historians may differ in their opinions and interpretation of facts of history, the facts themselves should never be in dispute because of their analytical, scientific, concrete, chronological and logical origins. No level of education or qualification can replace source material for the points of view presented by any historian of worth. The word "History" is derived from Greek and Latin, "Historia", and means, "I report on /after inquiry, investigation or research." Thus nobody speaks as a historian on his own authority. Nor are historical facts the preserve of any category of people - they should be available to the public or they are not historical. Arthur Marwick cautions on the historian and his work: "It is history rather than the historian which society requires: the historian who is too conscious of social needs may well produce bad history".[254]

## Functional History

Another important point to note in this connection is that history and historical facts are not about perfect human beings; 'saints, sinners or devils' living in some ethereal world. No, it is about ordinary human beings with their short comings, strengths and weaknesses. These Southern Cameroons leaders like political leaders the world over, were naturally products of their time, place and circumstances. In other words, they were the best that their society could offer and any

---

[253] Richard TA Murphy, *Background to the Bible, An Introduction To Scripture Study*, Servant Books, AN Arbor, Michigan, p.196. (By courtesy of Mr. Francis Nkwatoh).
[254] Arthur Marwick, *The Nature of History,* Macmillan Publishers Ltd.1985, p. 16,

comparisons made outside this context are lame and in historical terms "anachronistic". The bulk of them were patriots, dedicated and selfless with great visions for their "beloved motherland".[255] They burnt out their lives and made enormous sacrifices in the service of their people and their community and in so doing, made their mistakes and learnt by them. It cannot be over emphasized that all comparisons in history are made within context; juxtaposed with similar examples and never in isolation.

**Pseudo-History**

This is slanted and inadmissible history. Writing history based on prejudice "Conspiracy Theories", gossips, skewed or biased information such as in Nazi Germany under Hitler, Fascist Italy under Mussolini, Communist Russia under Stalin, Communist North Korea. This type of history has led whole countries like China and Japan into serious conflicts or even threats of war and some of them have had to be officially re-written. Talk about Nazi Germany's genocide of the Jews, Armenian genocide or Rwandan genocide have entered the realm of legality punishable by law, when denounced by any individual. Other qualities of pseudo-history include work that uncritically accepts myths and anecdotal evidence without scepticism or work with political, racial, religious or other ideological agenda. Pseudo History includes: selecting or ignoring evidence contrary to healthy views or work that is speculative, controversial, facts without foundation, unjustified interpretations; facts taken out of context; giving undue weight, distorted either innocently, accidentally or fraudulently playing on ignorance of the masses. History has a way of auto –correcting itself and pseudo- history sooner or later gets caught up with the truth either after further research or simply with time, after the dust settles and the facts are laid bare. Currently, we are witnesses to the fact that George Bush and Tony Blair have been tried for their policies in the Iraqi and Afghanistani wars in the "court of popular opinion".

This background commentary arises from the need to place the issues surrounding the Reunification regarded as a Gamble raised in

---

[255] Ibid., P M Kale.

the Summit Magazine interview in their accurate historical perspective. Basic knowledge of History as can be observed is imperative for all citizens, who desire and deserve to understand the background to the daily events touching not only Cameroon but Africa and the world. For this reason history is not the preserve of any special category of people. It should be read for pleasure, as well as for information or above all, as a profession for those opting to teach or to engage in diplomacy or other liberal professions. In some cases it is basic for survival; Fanso aptly captures this sense when he says:

> History is an interesting but delicate subject because the past we are writing about is never dead to the present and also because it is written and rewritten. Whoever thinks that the dead do not bite and that the past is gone for good does not think history.[256]

It is also known that history has a way of auto-correction arising from the fact that every generation is challenged to rewrite its history in the light of new discoveries such as those in the declassified British secret papers, memoirs, debates, archae1o7l9ogical findings or simply through peer review processes. Consequently, like in all intellectual pursuits, no one has ever put a final full stop to any topic in history since it is dynamic and forever under regeneration and research. Though it deals with the past, history is continuous, alive, and dynamic; everything that "exists" is a subject of history and actually nothing exists outside history, whether active, passive or indifferent. As historians writing the history of our fatherland or any other history we owe it in trust to our venerable ancestors and, as an obligation to posterity to render nothing but what is credible, factual and balanced. Perfect history as such may remain elusive but this objective remains inalienable to the discipline. Knowledge of basic history is every citizen's right. All said and done, history should be inspiring; it should be read for pleasure, entertainment and relaxation.

---

[256]See open letter: Professor Fanso's remarks to Professor VJ Ngoh's Reaction to his Valediction Address of Friday 23 September 2011, p.3.

# Epilogue

Below is the *Summit Magazine* No. 16 April –June 2011 interview with Professor, Victor Julius Ngoh anchored by Kange Williams Wasaloko (Publisher, Acting Editor-in-Chief) Reproduced in full.

"Fifty Years after Reunification: Southern Cameroons Had a Raw Deal Because of the Greed of KNDP Politicians.

Foreword - The Reunification Gamble: Setting the Records Straight (sic)

Professor Victor Ngoh epitomizes history, history of Cameroon, and especially the history of sentiments that are goading Cameroon's English population. In featuring an exclusive interview with this un-assuming but well-versed intellectual, we would be attempting to find answers to the numerous "why" that has cast doubts on the honesty of those we have referred to as the fathers of Reunification.

In accepting the deals that were struck between Foncha and Ahidjo how much ofthe people's interest was considered? Fifty years after Reunification, can anyone say that there was a balance in the negotiation leading to this union?

There doesn't seem to be any turning back now; but were you to bring back to life the Fonchas, Munas, Endeleys, Egbe Tabis, Fonlons, Mbiles and others, what account will they give to their people? Will they regret their selfish attitudes to the detriment of the people who heartedly hailed them? Or are they rolling in their tombs in total disarray for leaving their people in a disparaging mood? Why were the negotiations for the independence of Southern Cameroons as a separate and sovereign state torpedoed? Why were the constitutional talks in Foumban so one-sided as though the Southern Cameroons had no legal or constitutional experts?

Why were our leaders so blind-folded as to say "yes" to everything that was proposed to them?

Why did they seem to have been so ignorant and exposed their fool- hardiness because of a larger morsel of bread?

Why did they not listen to the counsel of some British experts who warned that they will be "swallowed" by the "locust-like" invasion from the East?.

Why were negotiations not based on equal partnership?

Why was the house of the negotiation so divided thus opening large loopholes for the other negotiator to manipulate their intelligence?

Why did the name of the country have to change at every bat of the eye? Fifty years down the line these questions have continued to haunt us.

The eventuality as is the case now is to "let the sleeping dogs lie"

Those who could have given us a clarification have bowed out of the scene. All we can do today is to speculate. However, we feel blessed to be endowed with historians despite some controversies in relating the sequence of events leading to Reunification; give us some food for thought.

Professor Victor Ngoh is one of them and we should benefit from his intellectual largesse. **Peter Esoka (Editorial Adviser)**

## 50yrs after Reunification - Southern Cameroons Had a Raw Deal Because of the Greed of KNDP Politicians

Prof Victor Julius Ngoh is one of the few authoritative researchers in Cameroon history. At the time when Cameroon history is polluted by some writers who have used their cultural background to distort facts about our history, Professor Victor Julius Ngoh has always stood firm on the truth about the process towards reunification, laying emphasis on the role of southern Cameroons politicians at the time. His stand that the KNDP politicians placed their personal interest ahead of their followers did not auger well to some people who tainted his public image tagging him a persona non-grata in his own country.

However today his position is being amplified by even those who blackmailed him. Professor Victor Ngoh still maintains today that the greed of the southern Cameroons politicians was responsible for the raw deal in the process towards reunification coupled with the fact that John Ngu Foncha the southern Cameroons leader in the reunification struggle had struck a deal with Ahidjo that should the reunification process go through, he will be made vice president. Professor Victor Ngoh who is currently deputy vice-chancellor/research, corporation and relations with the business world, has written over twenty research publications on Cameroon Africa and the World. He is currently writing an essay titled" The hidden facts about the reunification of Cameroon. When we sat down to chat with him in his office at UB, the learned professor took time to release certain revelations amongst them was the fact that Foncha received material and financial support from Douala based billionaire, late Soppo Priso. He also revealed that ghost voters were imported from the Republic of Cameroon to vote in favour of reunification. This is just the tip of the interview we conducted for your documentation. Excepts.(sic)

**Summit Magazine:** *The Venue for the celebration of the 50th anniversary Cameroon's reunification is up in the air pending the announcement of the Head of State, Paul Biya. Some people talk of Buea, others say Kumba, Bamenda and Foumban. As a historian where should the celebrations take place?*

**Professor Victor Julius Ngoh**: Well I think it should be made absolutely clear, the reunification event was between British Southern Cameroons and the Republic of Cameroon. The centre of the power in British Southern Cameroon was in Buea. All negotiations between Ahidjo and Foncha in British Southern Cameroons were held in Buea. So there is absolutely no reason to say Kumba, Bamenda or Foumban should host the event. It should be made clear that even in in the days of the German colonial administration in 1904, the capital of German Cameroon was transferred from Douala to Buea. So nobody should think of another place except Buea. As a historian, I will say Buea is the natural host for the celebrations. It is now left for the politicians, elites, traditional leaders and opinion leaders to lobby the Head of State to announce the choice of Buea as the venue early enough.

*As someone who has written extensively on Cameroon, what briefly are the reasons that were advanced by politicians at the time in favour of reunification?*

For the purpose of clarification, I wish to mention that reunification was the least popular option. The most popular option was secession and independence of Southern Cameroons as a separate entity, followed by independence in association with Nigeria. The problem with reunification was that, the KNDP led by Dr. John Ngu Foncha was very smart and it tailored its messages according to the audience it was addressing at the time. This was enhanced by the confusion that emerged after the London Conference of November 1960, when Foncha and a good number of Southern Cameroonians went to London to impress on the Her Majesty's Government to reverse the United Nations' decision of 1959 and grant Southern Cameroons independence as a separate state. That request was rejected but the population though that the request was granted and this was also compounded by the fact that the KNDP made the population believe that there was a transitional period of five years, during which should reunification fail, Southern Cameroons will walk out from the union. The politicians, however, failed to understand that section 47 of the Federal Constitution ruled out the possibility of secession. So, on the day of election, most Southern Cameroons' voters thought they were voting for Southern Cameroons as a separate state or that they had five-year- trial period. You have to also bear in mind that the very popular area in favour of reunification was the Northwest or Grassfield population. The plebiscite options were twisted to be a struggle between the Grassfield led by Foncha and the Forest Zone led by Dr. E.M. L. Endeley. It is important to note that at that time, a good proportion of the workers in the plantation in the Forest zone came from the Grassfield and this tilted the population.

Unfortunately, the Cameroon peoples National Congress Party, the CPNC, led by Dr. EML Endeley did a very poor job as far as the campaigning was concerned. They relied a lot on the insecurity in the Republic of Cameroon and they felt that the intense insecurity in the Republic of Cameroon will naturally influence the voters to vote against reunification whereas Foncha and the KNDP whipped up the anti-Ibo scare and most of the electorate voted for reunification partly because of the fear of the Ibos at the time.

*One other argument the politicians put forward factor for reunification was that the salary scale in Southern Cameroons was lower than what obtained in La République du Cameroun. How much did this influence the move towards reunification?*

That was absolutely no factor because there wasn't any contact between the civil servants in British Southern Cameroons and the civil servants of La Republique du Cameroun to the extent that they were able to discuss their salary scales. So, the issues of salary scale between the two entities had no part to play in the reunification exercise.

*Contemporary politicians increasingly blame the architects of reunification. It is that they lacked negotiation skills or that personal interest was put before that of the region?*

All the issues were put on the table. Unfortunately, the KNDP decided to do the negotiation alone. The KNDP even refused to take along the British experts whom the Colonial Office had put at their disposal. You also have to understand that the KNDP government

lacked sufficient qualified personnel and therefore their negotiation skills were weak, and for one reason or the other which is difficult to understand, is that the KNDP did not follow the advice of the colonial master to take along the Southern Cameroons Bar Association. This was very detrimental to the KNDP at the Yaoundé Tripartite Conference Talks of 2-7 August 1961 because this conference, which came after the Foumban Conference of 17-21 July 1961, was meant to put the proposals from the Foumban Conference into legal form. The delegation that the KNDP took to the Tripartite Conference did not include the Southern Cameroons Bar Association in spite of the fact that the KNDP was advised to take along legal/constitutional experts from the Bar Association. This was enough proof that a deal had been concluded between Ahidjo and Foncha to the effect that should the Federal system succeed, Foncha would be Vice President and Muna the Federal Minister, and if Foncha stepped down as Prime Minister of West Cameroon, A.N.Jua would become Prime Minister.

*Apart from Foncha and Munawho were not well educated there were other figures like E. T Egbe, Engo and Gorgi Dinka who were lawyers. Were their views not consulted?*

In fact, Southern Cameroons had quite a handful of lawyers at the time. Why was the Southern Cameroons Bar Association not invited? Surprisingly, Emmanuel Tabi Egbe was an influential member of the pro-KNDP think tank. He was not invited, and if you do recall, during the All Anglophone Conference in Buea in 1993, Foncha and Muna told participants that they had a poor deal because they lacked the lawyers. That is not true. The lawyers were there but they were not consulted. They did not even invite the Attorney General, E. K Mensah.

*According to you, as a historian, where did the error really come from?*

The error was that at the end of the day, the Southern Cameroons politicians were more interested in promoting their personal interest. There is something which is very tricky in the whole exercise. The draft Federal Constitution was discussed in the National Assembly of the Republic of Cameroon in August 1961 and President Ahmadou Ahidjo signed it into law on September 1st, 1961. So the Federal Constitution was signed into law on September 1, 1961. There was nothing as the Federal Republic of Cameroon then. So Ahidjo signed the Federal Constitution as the President of the Republic of Cameroon and when the Southern Cameroons House of Assembly discussed it, it was not to adopt or ratify it. Rather, S.T Muna tabled a motion on September 18, 1961 calling on the House to approve the method and the brotherly co-operation which the governments of Southern Cameroons and the Republic of Cameroon displayed to have the Federal Constitution. That was a major problem.

*Fifty years after reunification. Do you think that the Anglophones have had a fair share of this political marriage?*

You see, we have to be very careful. If we take off by saying that former Southern Cameroons and the Republic of Cameroon reunited as equal partners, then we are deceiving ourselves. The harsh realities that most of us do not want to accept for one reason or the other is that the reunification did not take place between two equal partners. The Republic of Cameroon was independent, had a national anthem, a flag and a motto. It had all the attributes of sovereignty and was a member of the United Nations. It sent its ambassadors to other sovereign countries and also received theirs. Southern Cameroons had no flag, no national anthem nor motto; in fact, no attributes of sovereignty. It was still a UN Trust Territory. So for public consumption, Ahmadou Ahidjo said the two would come together as equal partners. But the hard and unpleasant reality was that one was independent and the other was not. Let me tell you a sad story, in 1959, the British Secretary of State for Colonies asked one of his officials to undertake a study trip to the Southern Cameroons. After his five – day stay in Southern Cameroons, he wrote a report in which he said the Republic of Cameroon might swallow Southern Cameroons and that the people of the Republic of Cameroon were more sophisticated that those in Southern Cameroons. He used the word "swallow' and referred to Southern Cameroonians as these nice little people. And 50 years later, you can draw your own conclusion on the above prophetic words. It should be pointed out that Foncha was not really in favour of Southern Cameroons attaining independence as a separate state. In March 1956, Foncha told Eastwood of the Colonial Office, in confidence, that he did not see Southern Cameroons as being an independent separate political entity as a permanent solution. This is what Cameroonians do not know.

*Where did Ahidjo draw his strength in terms of negotiation? Was it only with the support of French advisors. Some people go as far as saying that, French businessmen bribed Southern Cameroon's politicians?*

First of all, it should be understood that Ahidjo was not very interested in reunification. What he wanted was reunification with British Northern Cameroons only because of the Moslem population. If that option was not accepted, he would reluctantly accept reunification with both British Southern and Northern Cameroons. Reunification with Southern Cameroons only was a last resort to Ahidjo. This came out very clearly on January 1, 1960 during the independence anniversary when Foncha led a 12-man delegation to Yaoundé. During the celebration, Foncha talked about the virtues of reunification unlike Ahidjo whose address hadn't a single sentence on reunification. So to answer your question as to where Ahidjo got his strength, he was very much aware that Foncha was in a desperate position. As far back as October 1956, Foncha had written a confidential letter to Soppo Priso begging for financial and material assistance to be used against the KNC and the KPP which wanted independence with Nigeria unlike the KNDP which wanted independence with their brothers of Eastern Cameroon. Soppo Priso and the Pro-reunificationist groups in the Republic of Cameroon provided material and financial support to the KNDP.

*Why was the idea of Southern Cameroons gaining independence with Nigeria not very popular amongst people of the Grassfield region?*

The idea was not very popular due to the harsh treatment Southern Cameroonians received from Nigerians especially the Ibos at the time. Secondly, the battle was seen as being between the Grassfield led by Foncha and the Forest Zone led by Dr. E.M.L Endeley. Those who were from the Grassfield naturally supported their own person and since they had the numerical strength, they normally won the day. It is important to mention that in some areas like in Nso where you had Vincent Lainjo of the KNC, for several years, he had the support of the KNC in that area.

*Let's talk about the London Conference of November 1960 and the role in the reunification process?*

You see, in October 1959, the KNDP, KNC and KPP accepted that the plebiscite question should be reunification with French Cameroon or association with Nigeria. The KNDP militants felt that Foncha had betrayed them because Foncha had promised that the question would not be reunification versus association with Nigeria. Foncha had told them that he would get a trusteeship extended for two to three years. When he went to London and it was nailed down that the question would be reunification with the Republic of Cameroon or association with Nigeria, it got to a point where Augustine Ngom Jua sent him a telegram saying what he had done was very unpopular. In fact, things got to a stage where moves to force Foncha to resign as President of the KNDP but he was able to weather the storm. So that option of reunification with the Republic of Cameroon was very unpopular. It got to a point where the CPNC and KNDP convinced Foncha and the Southern Cameroons Commissioner J O Field that it would be better that they should go back to London and revisit the UN compromise. Precisely at this time, you had the Kamerun United Party, KUP, of PM Kale who came out strongly for independence as a separate state. So these politicians with J O Field went to London to request the British government to revisit the plebiscite option. At one time it was thought that the Southern Cameroons delegation would get their request accepted but things changed because the British government found out from its representatives at the UN that the plebiscite option would not be reviewed. In addition, the Afro-Asian bloc was very much against small African countries having independence since the Afro-Asian bloc was against the balkanization of Africa. So then they came back from the London Conference they did not really explain to the population that what they went for, had failed. Immediately after their return, Foncha went to Yaoundé and met Ahidjo; and they signed the two Alternatives reaffirming the October 1959 plebiscite compromise.

*Let's talk about the plebiscite. How did it go?*

The Plebiscite was well conducted. In September 1960, the Southern Cameroons Order-in-Council was signed; dividing British Southern Cameroons into 26 constituencies or electoral districts and the campaign went on smoothly. As I said earlier, the CPNC had a very poor campaign strategy. Their whole message was that blood was flowing in the Republic of Cameroon, "the UPC terrorists are killing people there – is that where you want to go?" etc… Such as Campaign was not very convincing at the time. The KNDP was more aggressive in the field especially as they had financial and material support from the Republic of Cameroon. What is not well known is that some people came from the Republic of Cameroon and voted for KNDP. These voters were, for instance, transported from Loum, Nkongsamba, and Mbanga.

*Let's look at the heart of the negotiation process. Is it true that Foncha refused to present the draft constitution to his Anglophone peers before the Foumban conference?*

In fact, I do recall when I first wrote that in 1990, it created a whole lot of problems to the extent that in certain areas, I was declared persona non grata. I have a copy of the threatening letter in my library. How the writer declared me a persona non grata in my own country beats my imagination. But today, everybody is saying that it is true. Yes, it is true. In Dr. E. M. L. Endeley's opening speech at the Foumban conference of July 17-21, 1961, he said "some of us are seeing this document" here for the first time. I had the privilege of interviewing S. T. Muna, N. N. Mbile and Moussa Yaya. They all confirmed that. There is a confidential note that the British Commissioner at the time, J O Field, sent to London also confirming that. It is important to note that J O Field's confidential note goes further to say that based on reliable information, Foncha and Ahidjo had struck a deal.

The first point is that no actual discussion of substance took place because the southern Cameroons delegates. They were shocked to discover that after preparing their position in the Bamenda "All-

Constitutional Conference" of June 1961 with the understanding that then they got to Foumban, they would place their document on the table together with that of the Republic of Cameroon and both sides would debate and reach a consensus. But they were shocked when Ahidjo told them that "this is what you have to work on. I gave this document to Foncha a long time ago." What makes it worse was that the document presented to them in Foumban was in French. So they had to take time to work on the translation. While that was being done, the delegates from La Republique were bored and were walking about. Confirmed reports say the delegates from Southern Cameroons were well treated. They were given all what they wanted and I use the words all what they wanted. So they felt at ease and believed that these were really our brothers who would take care of us.

*To whom was the sovereignty of the Southern Cameroons given?*

This is an issue which the SCNC has been playing about a lot. Some books say the sovereignty of the Southern Cameroons was handed over to Ahmadou Ahidjo or to the Republic of Cameroon. This is not true. I am working on an essay that will soon be published. It is titled: "The Untold Story of Cameroon's Reunification". Let me say that the issue of sovereignty was one of the burning issues that were discussed at the Yaoundé Tripartite Conference of the August 2 - 7 1961. at one time, Foncha proposed that the sovereignty should be transferred to Southern Cameroons while Ahidjo was held that the sovereignty should be given to him. It got to a point where Foncha asked the Attorney- General of Southern Cameroons to prepare a legal brief on that subject. The brief was prepared in which it was stated that sovereignty should be transferred to the body representing the two territories. That was rejected by Ahidjo. Ahidjo was able to do that because Southern Cameroons politicians were divided. Following the disagreement, it was agreed that an exchange of notes be done on September 27th 1961 to settle the issue. The exchange of notes in summary was thus: "The British Ambassador in London at the time, C.E. King wrote to Ahidjo saying that at mid-night on September 30, 1961, Southern Cameroons would become independent and Ahidjo replied, "Yes I acknowledge receipt of your Note. On the 1st of October 1961, Southern Cameroons will become independent."

*A lot has been written about reunification to the extent that some historians have been accused of distortion of facts. What are some of the issues that you as a senior historian will like to address so as to help clarify public opinion?*

The first is that sovereignty of the Southern Cameroons was not transferred to Ahidjo. Secondly, Foncha was given a draft constitution and it was meant for him to discuss it with his colleagues in Bamenda which he never did. Thirdly, there wasn't an over whelming support for reunification per se even within the KNDP. In fact, the KNDP was able to get votes because it played on the fears of Southern Cameroonians and also exploited the numerical superiority of the Grass Field population where most of the people voted KNDP. I will give you a simple example: in 1957, Fon Galega II wrote and told his people that Dr. E. M. L Endeley used him as a house boy in London by asking him to carry his bag. That story is false. It never took place but it spread like wild fire and if you do understand what it meant in those days, to humiliate a Fon then you can understand. This is an issue that was not true but worked against the KNC, KPP and in favour of KNDP. The KNDP fellows also said Dr. E.M. L Endeley never respected the Chiefs. This is not true. When the Prime Minister or President goes to an event, he is not the one to choose where to sit. To say that he sat on chairs reserved for chiefs, where and when? Finally, it should also be made clear that southern Cameroons had a raw deal because of the greedy approach of the KNDP politicians. The KNDP never wanted to share power in spite of the fact that they had agreed in New York in April 1961 to work together with the CPNC to ensure that reunification would take place smoothly. But immediately they came back, of course, everything fell apart.

*It was alleged that the Bamenda Conference was intended to prepare the constitutional talks in Foumban. What happened at the conference that the delegates still went ill-prepared to Foumban?*

It was not that it was not an allegation. The essence of the Bamenda Conference in June, 1961 was to prepare the Southern Cameroons delegation for the Foumban Constitutional Conference. It meant that the Southern Cameroons delegation would come with their own proposals. So the conference was meant for the Southern Cameroons delegation; CPNC, KNDP and the rest to come with their draft, with the understanding that in Foumban, they would present the draft and the Republic of Cameroon, led by Ahmadou Ahidjo would also present theirs and the two delegations would arrive at a consensus. The Bamenda Conference provided the unique opportunity for the Southern Cameroons delegation to say exactly what they wanted. They asked for a Senate and a House amongst others. They deliberately gave powers to the West Cameroon State and the East Cameroon State. The Federal government was not supposed to be strongly centralized. Unfortunately, while they were discussing all of these lofty ideas, Foncha did not tell them that what they were discussing was completely a sharp contrast to what Ahidjo had handed to him. The Federal draft constitution was a slightly modified constitution of the Republic of Cameroon. Foncha decided to hide this draft constitution from Southern Cameroonian politicians because he had already made a deal with Ahidjo to the effect that should the Federal constitution go through, he would be made Vice President. While they were discussing all of these, he sat quiet and allowed them to discuss and adopted the draft. So when they got to Foumban, they were surprised when they wanted to present their own draft for discussion. Ahmadou Ahidjo said no! I have already given a draft to Foncha and that is what, we are going to discuss now.

*After the entire hullabaloo about re-unification, the Anglophones met in Buea in 1993 for the All Anglophone Conference, AAC1 and moved over to Bamenda for AAC2. From the discussions, was the Anglophone problem addressed?*

The sad part of AAC, I belief very strongly, is that it was an opportunity that the Fonchas and the Munas wanted to polish up the mistakes they made in 1959, 1960, 1961.Surprisingly, in that same hall in Buea, there were politicians as well as civil servants and civil society members, who knew exactly what the situation was in 1959 and the 1960s. I am still surprised that when they were told that they had a poor deal with Ahidjo because they did not have lawyers, none of them raised a finger. [Whereas] there were seasoned lawyers like Egbe Tabi, Gorji Dinka and Engo whose services were not solicited. It was argued very strongly that the Southern Cameroons delegation should make use of the Southern Cameroons Bar Association. They never did. This became very important when they met in Yaoundé for the Yaoundé tripartite Conference, which comprised; the Southern Cameroons, the Republic of Cameroon and the UK. The principal goal of the Yaoundé Tripartite Conference, from 2-7 August 1961 was to put into legal form the Foumban constitutional proposals. So, how could they be putting proposals into a legal form, when the Southern Cameroons delegation did not have a lawyer?

*After that came the birth of the Southern Cameroon National Council, SCNC launched by Barrister Ekontang Elad. What are they preaching?*

I have great respect for almost all the members of the SCNC, as Cameroonian patriots. But my problem is that either deliberately or out of ignorance, some of them distort the history. And secondly, one is tempted to conclude that the SCNC is a collection of a mixed bag of politicians, and disgruntled civil servants, who somehow thought that they did not get that they wanted. It is interesting to ask why most of those who are strong in the SCNC are retired civil servants. I am not saying all, I say most. Why did they not complain when the going was good? I think this is a where I may be reluctant to go along with them. Some of their ideas are good. You may have a good idea, but the way you go about it, will spoil it. It is strange that for quite some time, they were able to convince some Anglophones that they went to the UN and the UN gave them a flag, promising that the UN would reopen discussions on the Southern Cameroons' problem. That was not true. You can go to the UN shop in New York and buy all what you find there. I have been there and bought all those things. The idea of saying that the UN will reopen Southern Cameroons' question is deceitful. Southern Cameroons achieved independence following the UN Resolution 1514 and UN resolution 1541 of December 1960 which clarified UN Article 76B of the UN Charter.

*The view of SCNC notwithstanding, Is there an Anglophone Problem in Cameroon?*

You have to understand who is an Anglophone before you move along. In Cameroon there are three definitions of who an Anglophone is. One group holds that an Anglophone is somebody whose parents, both mother and father, are either from the present – day South west or Northwest Regions. Another school of thought holds that an Anglophone is someone, although born somewhere in former East Cameroon, has developed the Anglo-Saxon culture. Another group holds that some of the parents should be of either from the Northwest or Southwest Region. There is even a third group of those whose grandparents migrated from East Cameroon, even before German Cameroon was split into two. I am referring to the Doualas, the Bamilekes, the Ewondos, the Bassas, the Bamouns. They came as far back as 1916 to work in the German plantations. They got married here, they had their kids here. That is another group. This group feels and believes that they are Anglophones. It depends on how you look at it.

*Let's narrow the definition to those from the Southwest and Northwest Regions of Cameroon, is there any bias on them?*

If we look at the fact that they form a totality of one group and Cameroon was split in 1916 into two parts; the French took one part and the English the other. It was believed that this provisional partition was not supposed to be permanent. The League of Nations, the UN, administered their respective parts of former German Cameroon as equal parts. It was not said that the French part was superior to the English part. The fact that the French took a larger portion and therefore a greater population doesn't mean that the English part of former German Cameroon was inferior. When they united in 1961, it was believed that they were coming as equal partners. And coming as equal partners, meant they had had to be treated equally. Unfortunately, the realities on the ground did not promote that so called equality. That is where we have this problem. It has been reinforced and compounded by the lack of the political will on the part of some Anglophone and Francophone politicians to the extent that you find and hear some prominent Anglophone politicians say that there is no Anglophone Problem. If you look at it from the standpoint that the Northwest and Southwest Regions are just like the other region in Cameroon, then you will be tempted to say there is no Anglophone problem. We should bear in mind that the Northwest and Southwest Regions are not just like any other region in Cameroon. The other regions; North, Far North, Adamawa, West, Centre and South were never administered as a separate entity by the League of Nations or the UN. So, you cannot equate the Northwest and Southwest as being equal to the West or East Regions. They came in as a separate group, joining another separate group.

*50 years after re-unification, what are we celebrating?*

Cameroonians, both French and English are celebrating the 50th anniversary of the coming together of the two territories, which were provisionally partitioned in February 1916 and re-united on October 1st, 1961. It is that which is to be celebrated, the 50thanniversary of reunification.

*As a Historian, how will you react if someone says reunification has been a marriage of convenience?*

It is not correct to say it was a marriage of convenience. If you say it was a marriage of convenience, it gives the false impression that either former British Southern Cameroon's or former French had no choice. So, to make things move smoothly they just accepted. It should be made clear that the British Southern Cameroons had a choice; either joining Nigeria or joining former French Cameroon. Before the UN decision in October 1959, Southern Cameroons had three options; independence as a separate state, independence by joining Nigeria or independence by joining French Cameroon. Finally, Southern Cameroon politicians decided on the two options: independence by joining Nigeria or independence by joining French Cameroon. So, one cannot say re- unification was a marriage of convenience. No it was not.

**Interviewed by Kange Williams Wasaloko**

# Appendix I

## Declassified British Secret Documents (Excerpts on Foncha and Southern Cameroons these made compelling reading)

Note: The numbering is basically intended for easy reference and convenience and has no bearing to the original arrangement.

1. "Our policy remains strongly against a separate Southern Cameroons state  ...if Cameroons political parties combine to take action to establish an independent state, this would place us in a very embarrassing position. With support of moderate Afro-Asians and others, we have always argued that separate independence would produce an entirely unviable state." (Sir Andrew Cohen in a secret Brief of 11 October, 1960 to the secretary of state at the Foreign office).

2. "What would worry me is if a sequel to the Southern Cameroons' try for independence was that the Northern Cameroons went the same way. That would really, I think, upset our relationship with Nigeria as a whole and for which we must, at all costs, avoid. The Southern Cameroons and its inhabitants are undoubtedly expendable in relation to this"(Lord Perth, British Minister of state at the colonial office in a minute of 12thOctober 1960 to Sir John Marten of the same office.)

3. One question was always asked. This was "why have we not had a third choice?…..Why can we not stand alone? Why should a poor man sell his independence to join with bigger and richer men?
….. There was widespread ignorance of what exactly the Republic of Cameroon was; particularly in the remote area". Mr. K. Lees, Plebiscite Supervisory Officer, Bamenda, in a Report on the first plebiscite Enlightenment Campaign dated 28th October, 1960, to the Deputy Plebiscite Administrator, Buea.)

4. "We are as anxious as the French that the Southern Cameroons should join the Cameroun Republic effectively on 1stOctober 1961 ... the French may be right that we should not give the Southern Cameroons authorities too much reign." (Mr. E.B. Booth by, in a confidential Memo of 4th July 1961, to the British Permanent Under-Secretary.)

5. In particular we must be very careful about independence and temporary sovereignty lest Northern Cameroons is likely influenced not to join Nigeria. This, I believe is the overriding consideration so we must be more or less tough with Foncha that joining Cameroun Republic does not allow sovereignty for a term (sic) of years and then a Federation,"

6 "Mr. Hammerskjold was afraid lest a difficult security situation should arise and was anxious to avoid any thing in the nature of a "contest between two independent states" (Nigeria and Cameroun Republic) he was wondering therefore whether it would not be a good thing for him to summon about March a "round table discussion" between Ahidjo, Foncha, Endeley and representatives of Nigeria. It might then be possible to work out a formula, which would avoid the necessity for any plebiscite. The formula could however be tested by a plebiscite if the United Nations so wanted. We criticized this idea rather sharply."

7. "First of all I take it that objections hitherto seen as establishment of a separate Southern Cameroons state remain as strong as ever." .... I am therefore assuming in what follows that our policy remains strongly against such a solution. If Southern Cameroons political parties did combine to take action envisaged in paragraph 2 of telegram under reference, this would place us in a very embarrassing position. With support of moderate Afro-Asians and others, we have always argued that separate independence would produce an entire unviable state. We have supported a unanimous resolution prescribing plebiscite which involves choice between Nigeria and Cameroon Republic."

8. "There is an increasing movement in the Southern Cameroons in favour of a third choice in the plebiscite. Total independence with United Kingdom aid or continued United Kingdom Trusteeship. We have not supported this proposition."

9. "I realize of course that the Cameroons question is of such a nature that whatever line we take, we must make enemies. This is recognized in paragraphs 10 and 11 of brief for Colonial Secretary enclosed in Greenhill's letter of 17th November. This being so instead of trying to please everyone and failing might it not be worth while trying to please one side viz Nigeria? If we try to be impartial, both Nigeria and Afro-Asian bloc will believe that our real aim is to keep Southern Cameroons as a colony and military base. By coming down firmly against the "third question" we will keep Nigeria as a friend and blunt any teeth of our enemies."

10. "When I wrote my letter 1519/166/60 of June 7 about the Southern Cameroons, I had not seen Halls letter1847/s.6/112 of May 25 to Kale about the third question. The terms of the last sentence of that letter cause me some concern. It seems to me that they amount to a statement that the United Nations, may well be prepared to reconsider its decision on the choices if a majority of the Southern Cameroons assembly wishes to do so. This seems to me likely to encourage Foncha, if he wants to ask for the questions to be changed, to come to the United Nations and do so. It is impossible to predict what reception he would in fact get there if he did any such thing. I think it quite likely that he would fail to secure the necessary two thirds majority but in the process, United Kingdom and the United Nations generally would be placed in an exceedingly difficult position, and need not elaborate on the possible complications for our relations with both Nigeria and the Cameroun. I must reiterate therefore what I said in my letter of June 7, that I think we ought now to use all our influence to prevent this third question idea being raised at the United Nations. This may mean saying publicly that we can see no likelihood of United Nations agreeing to changing its position on this matter."

11. I think it is important that we should not allow this matter to slide as may happen if we are not sufficiently firm with Foncha and perhaps also with Field about the "third question" matter movement. I believe a firm attitude on this now may save us a great deal of trouble later and think that H.M.G's position should be made abundantly clear to Foncha in an effort to scotch tendencies towards the third question."

12. "Can one argue the terms of the question; "Do you wish to attain independence by joining the Republic?" allow for an interim period during which the Southern Cameroons will virtually have its own separate and independent existence while, the terms of reunification with the Republic are being worked out? The words "by joining the Republic" taken literally appear to rule this out. But it may be that Foncha will seek to argue that if his solution having been argued to by Ahidjo is not opposed by the U.K, the U.N may be induced to wear it. Then would be the better grounds for this if Endeley were prepared also to agree to this interpretation of the question. We do not like this at all. But we kike the alternatives even less. To go for complete independence or to seek to insert a third choice in the plebiscite would create major difficulties."

13. But from the point of view of our relations with Nigerian delegation and of getting the most satisfactory result, it seems to us essential that, when we discuss tactics with them, they should be left in no doubt not only that we disagree with Foncha's interpretation of the second question but that whatever tactics we adopt, our objective in Assembly discussion will be to secure that question is not redefined as Foncha proposes, or changed, or supplemented by a third question. That does not mean of course that we would not accept Assembly decision to redefine the second question. It would mean that we should pursue tactics to prevent this."

14. "Our trusteeship over the Southern Cameroons is due to terminate on October 21(sic) upon the Southern Cameroons joining the Cameroon Republic." These last words are taken from the UN General Assembly resolution and are read by the Cameroon

Government as implying that sovereignty over the Southern Cameroon Republic on October I, and that a federal constitution should be worked out after wards. The Southern Cameroons view is that it has always been recognized that the association between the two territories would be a federal one and that it was on this basic that the people of the Southern Cameroons elected to join Cameroun. They think that, on October 1, they should transfer their sovereign powers to an organization representing the federation rather than to the Cameroun Government itself.

15. The problem is quite a complicated one, from a legal point of view and no doubt it is possible to hold different views about it. But from preliminary examination the Deputy legal Adviser thinks that the Southern Cameroons has quite a strong case. At the end of 1960 President Ahidjo of Cameroun and Prime Minister Foncha of the Southern Cameroons, subscribed to communiqués which emphasized that a federal state would be created and requested that "immediately after the plebiscite and in the event of the people voting for unification with the Cameroun Republic, a conference should be held attended by representatives of the Cameroun Republic and the Southern and Northern Cameroons ... which ...would have as its aim for the transfer of sovereignpowers to an organization representing the future federation." We are as anxious as the French, that the Southern Cameroons should join the Cameroun Republic effectively on that date. But it could be argued that we have a responsibility to the Southern Cameroons to that before we relinquish our trusteeship there is a provision for carrying out our engagement to which the two leaders subscribed before the plebiscite.

16. We very much hope that Foncha and Ahidjo will eventually reach an agreement on the question and save us the, embarrassment of taking a definite line on it ourselves. We have no intention of making things difficult for the Cameroons Government, so long as they can carry the Southern Cameroons authorities with them. But it would be difficult for us to approach the matter in the same black and white way as the French and the Cameroonians. Apart from legal difficulties, there is the question of what sort of tactics are likely to have the best

effects on Foncha. We are afraid if he is pressed too hard, opposition from certain circles in the Southern Cameroons might prevent the federation from taking place at all. This is a matter of guess work and the French may be right that we should not give the Southern Cameroons authority too much rein".

17. Independence for the Southern Cameroons would face us with considerable problems. They would expect financial support from us up to the tune of perhaps one million pounds a year and also that we should leave our troops in the country to defend them. If we met these requests it would be expensive for us financially and militarily and we would be accused of "neo- colonialism." If we refused the requests, Ghana, Guinea or the Russians would, no doubt, be only too pleased to help. In short this is not a course which we should at all encourage Foncha to adopt.

18. The department is strongly of the opinion that we should not encourage Foncha to go to the U.N. at all. In the telegram authorized by the African Committee, we have in fact said that "H.M.G. considers that this (ending of Trusteeship on 1stOctober.) must be regarded as final decision by the U.N. and will not be able to support any proposal for extension of U.K Trusteeship or any other arrangement other than that the Southern Cameroon joins the Cameroun Republic on October 1st. The French would be most strongly opposed to any approach to the U.N. M. Gorse repeated this to our Ambassador on Saturday and we should antagonize them if they thought that we were supporting it.

19.The Cameroon Government appear seriously worried about the possibility that Foncha or Jua may appeal to the United Nations for a ruling that reunification should come about on the terms set out in the joint communiqué and declarations issued on December 10th and used in the pre-plebiscite enlightenment campaign. At a farewell luncheon given for me by Mr. Okala, two members of the ministry of foreign Affairs, one of them in charge of U.N. Affairs pressed a member of my staff to indicate the line that would be taken by the United Kingdom delegation if the matter came up for debate in the United Nations. This impression has been confirmed by the American

Embassy who have told us that the Secretary General of the ministry of foreign Affairs agrees with the view expressed in paragraph 2 of your telegram to Paris No. 2472 saying that the Southern Cameroons would have quite a respectable legal case for opposing an unconditional transfer of sovereignty. In accordance with your telegram No. 197, we have been stressing that as far as we are concerned sovereignty will be transferred to the Republic on October 1 and that it is up to the Cameroonians to reach an agreement among themselves".

20. "Foncha is due to see Ahidjo again this week. The main purpose of the visit this time is to get Ahidjo's support for an economic mission to tour the capitals of Europe between now and October to get aid for various development projects after independence. I can't see Ahidjo being very enthusiastic about such a jaunt on the eve of unification but one never can tell and if he doesn't shoot it down, I suppose I shall be writing to you about it before long. I have naturally thrown what cold water I can on the idea at this stage."
" I agree generally with paragraphs 5 and 6 of your letter to the effect that if the southern Cameroons so chooses, sovereignty will have to be handed over to the United Kamerun when Trusteeship Agreement is terminated, and that this will involve the new federal Government having from the outset the necessary powers in foreign affairs. Otherwise Foncha might apply for U.N; membership? In other words Foncha will have to be told that the point in paragraph

6(4) of Milne's dispatch personal No.6 of October 18 is not possible. This is in accordance what I said in my telegram Brief 154 to John Martin. I of course, appreciate the need to drive Foncha back to no plebiscite and separate independence.

21."You asked me to discuss with Field the possibility of requiring the woman member to resign so that Foncha would no longer have a majority I find the situation here has changed. There now seems a distinct possibility that Government and Opposition may combine together to urge H.M.G to use their influence with the U.N to cut out plebiscite, and secure immediate independence for the Southern Cameroons on its own leaving the question of union with either of their neighbour over for settlement later. Field will be writing dispatch explaining background to this."

Reasons are:

• Realization by Endeley and co the vote is most likely for Nigeria.

• Doubts by all parties as to capacity of Republic to replace Nigeria Federal services and provide financial and economic support."

22. "I referred to the possibility of some positive and success full action to sway Cameroons to choose other than to re-join Nigeria."

23. "Most people in the Southern Cameroons do not want to be administered by the Republic; they do not want to have anything to do with French army or police (which they fear.) They do not want a French system of law, they do not the French language, they do not want to risk being pushed around by French officials and they do not want policy dictated to them by Republic politicians. Least of all they do not want the British connection to be completely severed or to be cut off from British help ... They fear being pushed into Nigeria as much as they fear being pushed into the Republic."

24. "Her majesty's Government position should be made abundantly clear to Foncha in an effort to scotch tendencies towards the third question. The policy of Her Majesty's Government is to discourage any tendency towards a "third question" very strongly".

25. "The Southern Cameroons is a frontier exposed….to communism– inspired influence whichcan become a danger of serious magnitude. This reason not to speak of its great potentialities makes the Southern Cameroons an area of serious concern for the United States. The present government in the Southern Cameroons made up of almost totally inexperienced and naïve ex-primary school teachers with good intentions is incapable of grappling with the tremendous problems which face it. Leadership in the Southern Cameroons is inexperienced, untrained and naïve …. The logical conclusion would

seem to be that the Southern Cameroons with its remoteness from Lagos, its complexities and its vulnerability, deserves increased attention on the part of the United States."

# Appendix II

## Attendants at the Buea Tripartite Conference: 15-17 May 1961

Republic of Cameroon (08)

    HE M, Ahmadou Ahidjo, President of the Republic
HE M. Charles Okala, Minister of Foreign Affairs
    M, Krob(?)Secretary General to the Presidency
    M, Betayene, Secretary General, Ministry of Foreign Affairs
    HE M, Oyono, Ambassador to Liberia
    M. Missomba, Sûreté Nationale
    M. Domissy, Conseiller Economique to the Presidency
    Colonel Blanc, Conseiller Technique

Government of Southern Cameroons: (05)
Hon. J N Foncha, Premier
Hon. A N Jua, Minister of Social Services
Hon. S T Muna, Minister of Commerce and Industry
 Hon. P M Kemcha, Minister of Natural Resources

United Kingdom: (08)
Sir Roger Stevens, Foreign Office
Mr. C G Eastwood, Colonial Office
Mr. A G H Gardner-Brown, Colonial Office
Mr. P M Johnston, Ambassador to Yaoundé
Mr. P M I-Ver H M Embassy, Yaoundé

Also present: British Ex Official (Malcolm Milne)
The Deputy Commissioner
The Attorney General The Financial Secretary Total: 20

# Appendix III

## The Constitution of the Federal Republic of Cameroon

Part I
The federal republic of Cameroon

1.
(1) With effect from the 1st October 1961, the federal republic of Cameroon shall be constituted from the territory of the Republic of Cameroon, hereafter to be styled East Cameroon, and the territory of the Southern Cameroon, formerly under British trusteeship, hereafter to be styled West Cameroon.

(2) The Federal Republic of Cameroon shall be democratic, secular and dedicated to social service.

It shall ensure the equality before law of all its citizens; and it proclaims its adherence to the fundamental freedoms written into the universal Declaration of Human Rights and the Charter of the United Nations.

(3) The official languages of the Federal Republic of Cameroon shall

be French and English.

(4) The motto shall be "Peace Work Fatherland"

(5) The flag shall be of three equal vertical stripes of green, red andyellow, charged with two gold stars on the green stripe. (6) The capital shall be Yaoundé

(7) The national anthem of the Federation shall be: O Cameroon, cradle of our forefathers."

(8) The seal of the Federal Republic of Cameroon shall be a circular on the reverse and in the centre the head of a girl in profile turned to the Dexter towards a coffee branch and flanked on the sinister by five cocoa pods, encircled beneath the upper edge by the words "Federal Republic of Cameroon" and above the lower edge by the national motto "Peace - Work - Fatherland".

(9) The subjects of the federal states shall be citizens of the Federal Republic with Cameroonian Nationality.

(1)National sovereignty shall be vested in the people of Cameroon who shall exercise it either through the members returned by it to the Federal Assembly or by way of referendum;

Nor may any section of the people or any individual arrogate to itself or to himself the exercise thereof.

(2)The Vote shall be equal and secret, and every citizen aged twenty- one years or over shall be entitled to it.

(3)The authorities responsible for the direction of the State shall hold their powers of the people by way of election by universal suffrage, direct or indirect.

(1)Political parties and groups may take part in elections;

And within the limits laid down by law and regulation their formation and their activities shall be free.

(2)Such parties shall be bound to respect the principles of democracy and of the national sovereignty.

4. Federal authority shall be exercised by

a) The President of the Federal Republic, and b) The Federal National Assembly.

Part II
Federal Jurisdiction

5. The following subjects shall be of Federal jurisdiction

(a)Nationality
(b)Status of Alien
(c)Rules governing the conflict of Laws
(d)National Defence
(e)Foreign Affairs
(f) Internal and External Security of the Federal
State, and Immigration and Emigration.

(7)Planning, Guidance of the Economy, Statistical Services, Supervision and Regulation of Credit, Foreign Economic Relations, in particular Trade Agreements.

(8) Currency, the Federal Budget, Taxation and other Revenue to meet federal expenditure

(9) Higher Education and Scientific Research.

(10) Press and Broadcasting

(11) Foreign Technical and Financial Assistance

(12) Aviation and Meteorology, Mines and Geological Research, Geographical Survey

(13) Conditions of Service of Federal Civil Servants, Members of the

Bench and Legal Officers

(14) Regulation as to procedure and otherwise of the Federal Court of

Justice

(15) Border between the Federal States.

(16) Regulation of services dealing with the above subjects

6.

(1) The following subjects shall also be of federal jurisdiction. a) Human Rights

b) Law of Persons and of Property

c) Law of Civil and Commercial Obligation and contracts.

d) Administration of Justice, including rules of Procedure in and Jurisdiction of all Courts (but not the Customary Courts of West Cameroon except for appeals from their decisions). e) Criminal Law

f) Means of Transport of Federal concern (roads, railways, inland, waterways, sea and air ports

g) Prison Administration h) Law of Public Property i) Labour Law

j) Public Health

k) Secondary and Technical Education

l) Regulation of Territorial Administration m) Weights and Measures

(2) The Federated States may continue to legislate on the subjects listed in this Article and to run the corresponding administrative services until the Federal National Assembly or the President of the Federal Republic in its or his field shall have determined to exercise the jurisdiction by this Article conferred.

(3) The executive or legislative authorities as the case may be of the Federated Starts shall cease to have jurisdiction over any such subject of which the Federal authorities shall have taken charge.

(1) Wherever under the last preceding Article the authorities of the Federated States shall have been temporarily enabled to deal with a federal subject, they may legislate on such subject only after consultation with the Federal Co-ordination Committee.

(2) The chairman of the said Committee shall be a Federal Minister, and the members shall be nominated by the President of the Federal Republic in view of their special knowledge.

Part III
The president of the Federal Republic

(1) The President of the Federal Republic of Cameroon, as head of the Federal State and head of the Federal Government, shall ensure respect for the Federal Constitution and integrity of the Federal, and shall be responsible for the conduct of the affairs of the Federal Republic.

(2) He shall be assisted in his task by the Vice President of the Federal Republic.

9.

(1) The President and the Vice President of the Federal Republic shall be elected together on the same list, both candidates on which may not come from the same Federated State, by universal suffrage and direct and secret ballot.

(2) Candidates for the offices of President and Vice President of the Federal Republic must be in possession of their civic and political rights, and have attained the age of thirty-five years by the date of the election, the nomination of candidate, the supervision of elections and the proclamation of the result being regulated by a federal law.

(3) The offices of President and Vice-President of the Republic may not be held together with any other office.

10.

(1) The President of the Federal Republic shall be elected for five yearsand may be re-elected.

(2) Election shall be by majority of votes cast, and shall be held not less than twenty or more than fifty days before the expiry of the term of the President in office.

(3) In the event of vacancy of the Presidency for whatever cause the powers of the President of the Federal Republic shall without more devolve upon the Vice President until election of a new President.

(4) Voting to elect a new President shall take place not less than twenty or more than fifty days after the vacancy.

(5) The President shall take oath in manner to be laid down by a Federal Law.

11.

(1) Ministers and Deputy Ministers shall be appointed by the President of the Federal Republic from each Federated state at his choice, to be responsible to him and liable to be dismissed by him.

(2) The office of Minister or Deputy Minister may not be held together with elective office in either Federated State, office as member of a body representing nationally and occupation or any public post or gainful activity.

12. The President of the Federal Republic shall

(1) Represent the Federal Republic in all public activity and be head of the armed forces.

(2) Accredit ambassadors and envoys extraordinary to foreign powers

(3) Receive letters of credence of ambassadors and envoys extraordinary from foreign power.

(4) Negotiate agreement and treaties

Provided that treaties dealing with sphere reserved by Article 24 to the Federal legislature shall be submitted before ratification for approval in the form of law by the Federal Assembly.

(5) Exercise the prerogative of clemency after consultation with the Federal Judicial Council.

(6) Confer the decorations of the Federal Republic

(7) Promulgate federal laws as provided by Article 31

(8) Be responsible for the enforcement of Federal Laws and also of such laws as may be passed by a federated State under the last paragraph of Article 6.

(9) Have the power to issue statutory rules and orders. (10) Appoint to federal civil and military posts

(11) Ensure the internal and external security of the federal republic. (12) Set up regulate and direct all administrative services necessary for the fulfilment of his task.

Provided that where he considers it advisable he may after consultation with the heads of the Government of the Federal States assume authority over such of their services as exercise federal jurisdiction as defined by Article 5 or 6 and may by Decree delegate any part of his functions to the Vice President of the Federal Republic

13. The Governments of the Federal States shall be bound before adopting any measure which may impinge upon the Federation as a whole, to consult the President of the Federal Republic who shall refer the matter to the Committee provided by Article 7 for its opinion.

14. The President of the Federal Republic shall refer to the Federal Court of Justice under Article 34 any federal law which he considers to be contrary to this Constitution, or any law passed by a Federated State which he considers to be in violation of the constitution or of a federal law.

15. The President of the Federal Republic may where circumstances require proclaim by Decree a State of Emergency, which will confer upon him such special powers as may be provided by federal law.

(2) In the event of gave peril threatening the nation's territorial integrity or its existence independence or institutions, the President of the Federal Republic may after consultation with the Prime Minister of the Federated States proclaim by Decree a State of Siege.

(3) He shall inform the nation by message of his decision

(4) The Federal National Assembly shall without more be in session throughout the state of siege.

Part IV
The Federal Legislature

16. The Federal National Assembly shall be renewed every five years, and shall be composed of members elected by universal suffrage and direct and secret ballot in each federated State in the proportion of one member to every eighty thousands of the population

17. Federal Laws shall be passed by simple majority of the members

18. Before promulgating any bill the President of the Federal Republic either State request a second reading, at which the law may not be passed unless the majority required by the last preceding Article shall include a majority of the votes of the members from each Federated State.

19. (1) The Federal National Assembly shall meet twice a year, the duration of each session being limited to thirty days and the opening date of each session being fixed by the Assembly's steering committee after consultation with the President of the Federal Republic

(2) In the course of one such session the Assembly shall approve the Federal Budget. Provided that in the event of the Budget not being approved before the end of the current financial year the President of the Federal Republic shall have power to act according to the old Budget at the rate of one twelfth for each month until the new budget is approved.

(3) On request of the President of the Federal Republic or of two thirds of its membership the Assembly shall be recalled to an extraordinary session, limited to fifteen days, to consider a specific programme of business.

20. The Federal National Assembly shall adopt its own standing orders, and at the opening of the first session of each year shall elect its Speaker and steering committee.

- The sittings of the Federal National Assembly shall be open to the public.
- Provided that in exceptional circumstances and on the request of the Federal Government or of a majority of its members strangers may be excluded.

21. Federal election shall be regulated by a federal law.

22. Parliamentary immunity, disqualification of candidates or of sitting members, and the allowances and privileges of members shall be governed by a federal law.

Part V
Relations between the federal executive and legislature

23. Bills may be introduced either by the President of the Federal Republic or by any member of the Federal Assembly

24. Or the subjects of federal jurisdiction under articles 5 and 6, the following shall be reserved to the legislature.

(1) The fundamental rights and duties of the citizen, including. a) Protection of the liberty of the subject.
b) Human rights
c) Labour and trade union law
d) Duties and obligations of the citizens in face of the necessities of national defence.

(2) The law of persons and property, including a) Nationality and personal status.
b) Law of moveable and immoveable property c) Law of civil and commercial obligations

(3) The political, administrative and judicial system in respect of. a) Election to the Federal Assembly
b) General regulation of national defence
c) The definition of criminal offences not triable summarily and the authorization of penalties of any kind, criminal procedure, civil procedure, execution procure, amnesty, the creation of new classes of courts.

(4) The following matters of finance and public property
a) Currency
b) Federal budget.
c) Imposition, assessment and rate of all federal dues and taxes d) Legislation on public property

(5) Long term commitments to economic and social policy, together with the general aims of such policy.

(6) The educational systemappropriate committee before debate on the floor of the House.

26. The text laid before the House shall be that proposed by the President of the Federal Republic when the proposal comes from him and otherwise the text as a mended in committee but in either case amendment may be move in the course of the debate.

27. The President of the Federal Republic may at his request address the Assembly in person, and may send messages to it, but no such address or message may be debated in his presence.

28. Federal Ministers and Deputy Ministers shall have access to the Assembly and may take part in debate.

29.(1) The programme of business in the Assembly shall be appointed by the chairman's conference, composed of party leaders, chairmen of committees and members of the steering committee of the Federal National Assembly, together with a Federal Minister or Deputy Minister.

(2) The programme of business may not include bills beyond the jurisdiction of the Assembly as defined by Articles 5, 6, and 24, nor may any bill introduced by a member or any amendment be included which if passed would result in a burden on public funds or an increase in public charges without a corresponding reduction in other expenditure or the grant of equivalent new supply.

(3) Any doubt or dispute on the admissibility of a bill or amendment shall be referred for decision by the Speaker or by the President of the Federal Republic to the Federal Court of Justice.

(4) The programme of business shall give priority, and in the order decided by the Government, to bills introduced or accepted by it.

(5) Any business shall on request by the Government be treated as urgent.

30. (1) The President of the Federal Republic shall promulgate laws passed by the Federal National Assembly within fifteen days of their being forwarded to him, unless he receive a request for a second reading, and at the expiry of such period the Speaker may record his failure to promulgate and do so himself.

(2) Laws shall be published in both official languages of the Federal Republic.

## Part VI
## The Judiciary

31. (1) Justice shall be administered in the Federation in the name of the people of Cameroon by the competent Courts of each State.

(2) The President of the Federal Republic shall ensure the independence of the judiciary and shall appoint to the bench and to the legal service of the Federated States.

(3) He shall be assisted in his task by the Federal Judicial council, which shall give him its opinion on all proposed appointments to the bench and shall have over member of the bench the powers of a Disciplinary Council; and which shall be regulated as to procedure and otherwise by a federal law.

32. (1) The Federal Court of Justice shall have jurisdiction

(a) to decide conflicts of jurisdiction between the highest Courts of the federated States;

(b) to give final judgment on such appeals as may be granted by federal law from the judgments of the superior Courts of the Federated Stated wherever the application, whether claiming federal law is in issue;

(c) to decide complaints against administrative acts of the federal authorities, whether claiming damages or on grounds of ultra vires;

(d) to decide disputes between the Federated States, or between either of them and the Federal Republic.

(2) The composition of, the taking of cognizance by and the procedure of the Federal Court of Justice shall be laid down by a federal law.

33. Where the Federal Court of Justice is called upon to give an opinion in the casescontemplated by Articles 14 or 29, its numbers shall be doubled by the addition of personalities nominated for one year by the President of the Federal Republic in view of their special knowledge or experience.

34. Warrants, orders and judgments of any Court of Justice in eitherFederated State shall be enforceable throughout the Federation.

PART VII IMPEACHMENT

35. (1) There shall be a Federal Court of Impeachment which shall be regulated as to composition and taking of cognizance and in other respects by a federal law.

(2) The Federal Court of Impeachment shall have jurisdiction, in respect of acts performed in the exercise of their offices, to try the President of the Federal Republic for high treason, and the vice President of the Republic and Federal Minister, Prime Ministers and Secretaries of State of the Federated States for conspiracy against the security of the State.

PART VIII
FEDERAL ECONOMIC AND SOCIAL COUNCIL

36. There shall be a Federal Economic and Social Council which shall be regulated as to powers and in other respects by a federal law.

PART IX
THE FEDERATED STATES

37. (1) Any subject not listed in Articles 5 and 6, and whose regulation is not specifically entrusted by this Constitution to a federal law shall be of exclusive jurisdiction of the Federated States, which within those limits, may adopt their own Constitution.

THE FEDERATED STATES

(3)The House of Chiefs of the Southern Cameroon shall be preserved

38. (1) The Prime Minister of each Federated State shall be nominated by the President of the Federal Republic and invested by a simple majority of the Legislative Assembly of that State.

(2) Secretaries of State shall be appointed to the Government by thedismissed.

39. (1) Legislative power shall be exercised in the Federated States by a Legislative Assembly, elected for five years by universal suffrage and direct and secret ballot in such manner as to ensure to each administrative unit representation in proportion to its population:

Provided that in West Cameroon the House of Chiefs may exercise specified legislative powers to by defined together with the manner of their exercise by a law of the Federated State in conformity with this Constitution

(3) There shall be one hundred representatives in the Legislative Assembly of East Cameroonand thirty seven representatives in the Legislative of West Cameroon

(4) The electoral system qualifications for candidates and disqualification of sitting members, parliamentary immunity and the allowances of representatives shall be regulated by a federal law

40. (1) Each Legislative Assembly shall adopt its own standing orders and shall annually elect its steering committee.

(2) It shall meet twice a year, the duration of each session being limited to thirty days, on dates to be fixed by the steering committee after consultation with the Prime Minister of the Federated State and so that the opening date of the budgetary session shall be later than the approval or the federal budget

(3) On request of the Prime Minister, of the President of the Federal Republic or of two thirds of its membership, it shall be recalled to an extraordinary session limited to fifteen days to consider a specific programme of business.

41. The sittings of each Legislative Assembly shall be open to the public provided that in exceptional circumstances on the request of the Government or of a majority of its members strangers may be excluded.

42. Bills may be introduced either by the Government of each Federated States or by any representative in the Legislative Assembly, and shall be passed by a simple majority.

43 (1) A motion of no confidence passed by a simple majority, or a vote of censure passed by an absolute majority shall oblige the Prime Minister to Place his resignation in the hands of the President of the Federal Republic or be declared to have forfeited his office; and the President may then dissolve the Legislative Assembly.

(2) President discord between the Government and the Legislative Assembly shall enable the President of the Federal Republic to dissolve the latter of his own accord or on the proposal of the Prime Minister.

(3) New elections shall be held within two months of dissolution

AMENDMENT OF THE CONSTITUTION – TRANSITION AND SPECIAL

(4) Until investiture of a new Prime Minister the outgoing Government shall be responsible for the dispatch of current business

44. (1) The Speaker of each Federated State shall within twenty-one days forward bills passed for the President of the Federal Republic, who shall within a further fifteen days promulgate them.

(2) Within the said period the President of the Federal Republic may either request a second reading by the Legislative Assembly or act under Article 14.

(3) At the expiry of such period the Speaker of the Legislative Assembly in question may record the President's failure to promulgate and do so himself.

45. In so far as they do not conflict with the provisions of this constitution the existing laws of theFederated States shall remain in force.

PART X
AMENDMENT OF THE CONSTITUTION

46. (1) No bill to amend the constitution may be introduced if it tend to impair the unity and integrity of the Federation.

(2) Bills to amend the Constitution may be introduced either by the President of the Federal Republic after consultation with the PrimeMinisters of the Federated States, or by any member of the FederalAssembly

Provided that any bill introduced by a member of the Assembly shall bear the signature of at least one third of its membership

(2) The amendment may be passed by a simple majority of the membership of the Federal Assembly

Provided that such majority include a majority of the membership elected from each Federated States

(3) The President of the Federal Republic may request a second reading of a bill to amend the constitution as of any other federal bill and in like manner.

## PART XI TRANSITION AND SPECIAL

47. The jurisdiction defined in Article 5 shall pass without more to the federal authorities as soon as they are set up

48. The Government of each Federated State shall forward to the Federal Government all papers and records necessary for the performance of its task, and shall place at the disposal of the Federal Government the service destined to exercise federal jurisdiction under the authority of the latter.

49. Notwithstanding anything in this Constitution, the President of the Federal Republic shall have power, within the six months beginning from the 1st October 1961, to legislate by way of Ordinance having the force of law for the setting up of constitution organs, and pending their setting up for governmental procedure and the carrying on of the federal government.

## TRANSTION AND SPECIAL

50. The President of the Republic of Cameroon shall be for the duration of his existing term the President of the Federal Republic

51. For the duration of the term of the first President of theFederal Republic; and the disqualifications prescribed by Article 9 for the Vice President of the Federal Republic shall during that period be inapplicable

52. With effect from the 1st October 1961 the National Assembly of the Republic of Cameroon and the House of Assembly of the Southern Cameroon shall become the first Legislative Assembly of East Cameroon and of West Cameroon respectively

53. Until the 1st April 1964 the Federal Assembly shall be composed of members elected from among themselves by the Legislative Assemblies of the Federated States according to the population of each State in the proportion of one member to every eighty thousands of the population

54 notwithstanding the provisions of Article 11 and until the election of a Federal Assembly under Article 16 the offices of Federal Minister and Deputy Minister may be held together with parliamentary office in either Federated State

55. Government of the Republic of Cameroon and the Government of the Southern Cameroons under British trusteeship respectively shall become on the 1st October 1961 the Governments of the two Federated States

56. Pending the setting up of the Federal Economic and Social Council, the Economic and Social Council of the Republic of Cameroon shall be preserved.

57. Pending approval of a definitive federal budget a provisional federal budget shall be drawn up an shall be financed by contributions from each Federated State to be settled after agreement with the Government of each such state

58. This Constitution shall replace the Constitution of the Republic approved on the 21st February 1960 by the people of Cameroon ; shall come into force on the 1st October 1961; and shall be public in its new form in French and in English, the French text being authentic

59. (1) For the purposes of this Constitution the population of each Federated State shall on the Faith of statistics of the United Nations Organization, be taken to be as follows

East Cameroon    3 200,000
West Cameroon    800 000

2) Such figures may be amended by a federal law in the light of significant variation established by census

**Yaoundé, the 1st September, 1961 Ahmadou Ahidjo**

# Appendix IV

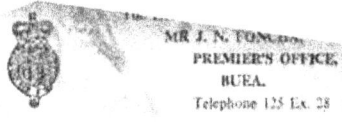

MR J. N. FON...
PREMIER'S OFFICE,
BUEA.
Telephone 125 Ex. 28

24th June, 1960.

Mr. A. Ahidjo,
President of the Republic of Cameroun,
YAUNDE.

My dear Mr. President,

I am to understand that you have now had a successful sitting of the first meeting of the first Parliament of the Republic of Cameroun. We over this way have understood how much difficulties you have in managing a revolutionary Section of a peaceful people. However great your difficulties, we hope you will now give part of your time to the study of reunification question.

You know how much we are hard pressed now by Nigerian stooges. You are aware that the Opposition have amassed much money from Nigeria and are trying to capture the Government hook or crook. You are aware that they have successfully won over one elected Member to equalise us, but how legally we can still run the Government. They have tried to win over one other Assembly-man from the K.N.D.P., but failing to do so by using money, they used threats of arms and still failed. They have now instituted a case of libel in the sum of £25,000 or about 20,000,000 frs and have got six lawyers from Nigeria to stand for them.

We now ask you to come to our aid in a big way. We know your Government is poor because of the terrorist activities, but you now stand the chance to borrow from the Countries of the World. We think this is the time you can help us in any way you can have the money. We must use money to hire lawyers, pay field secretaries, send people to the United Nations and organise the K.N.D.P. as the only striking force for reunification now left in the Southern and Northern British Cameroons. We were looking forwards to getting a messenger from there to bring us any all you have, but not finding any, we have now decided to send two people, Mrs. N.B. Martins the daughter of the late Chief John Manga Williams who died on active Service for reunification and Mr. Lifie Carr the Publicity Secretary of the K.N.D.P. We hope to get them back as soon as possible with your needed donation to help us keep up the fight.

I am happy to have been given to understand that you will be in the Southern Cameroons as from the second week in July. We are anxious to get you hear at that time. We shall be grateful if you make this a firm arrangement so that we may put out a programme for your reception. It has been suggested that you should pay a Courtesy visit to Lagos before coming to the Southern Cameroons, but we have stoutly refused to have it that way. We are not a part of Nigeria, and any move to bring you to Lagos before Buea would mean surrendering our authority to Nigeria. We hope you will resist any suggestions made to you by the British Consul.

God bless you all.

Yours sincerely,

# Bibliography

Achebe, Chinua. *Things Fall Apart.* London: Heinemann, 1958.

Ahidjo, Ahmadou. *Contribution to National Construction.* Paris: Presence Africaine, 1996.

Ajayi, J. F. Ade & Michael Crowder (eds.). *History of West Africa. Vol II.* London: Longman, 1974.

Anyangwe, Carlson. *Betrayal of Too Trusting A People: The UN, The UK and the Trust Territory of Southern Cameroons.* Bamenda: Langaa Research and Publishing CIG, 2009

Ardener, Edwin. *Coastal Bantu of the Cameroons.* London: International African Institute, 1956.

─────── *Historical Notes on the Scheduled Monuments of West Cameroon.* Buea: Government Printer, 1965.

Atang, Lucas. *My Struggle in the Catholic Priesthood.* n.d. 2003.

Atem, George. *How United is the Republic of Cameroon.* ANUCAM, 2012.

Benjamin, Jacques. *West Cameroonians- The Minority in a Bi- Cultural State.* Canada: Montreal, 1998.

Boh, Herbert, and Ntemfac Ofege. *The Story of Cameroon Calling Prison Graduate.* Nigeria :Calabar, 1991.

Cardinier, David E. *United Nations Challenge to French Policy.* London: Oxford University Press, 1963.

Carr, E.H. *What is History?* London: Palgrave, 2001.

Chilver, E.M.*Ministry of Primary and Social Welfare and West Cameroon Antiquities Commission.* Buea: Government Printer, 1966.

Mukong, Albert ed. *The Case for Southern Cameroons.* Enugu: CAMFECO, 1990.

Elango, Lovett Z. *The Anglo- French Condominium in Cameroon 1914-1916, nd. History of a Misunderstanding.* Limbe: Navi Publications 1987.

Epale, Simon J. *Plantations and Development in Western Cameroon: 1885 - 1975: A Study in Agrarian Capitalism.* New York: Vantage Press, 1985.

Eyongetah, Tambi and Brain, Robert. *A History of Cameroon.* London: Longman, 1965(?).

Fonlon, Bernard, *A Simple Story Simply Told or The Rise of Dr. Pavel Verkovsky, First Archbishop of Bamenda*. Yaoundé: CEPER, 1983.

Forde, Daryll (ed.). *Coastal Bantu of the Cameroons*. London: Part XI, International African Institute, 1956.

Gardinier, David. *Cameroon: United Nations Challenge to French Policy*. London: Institute of Race Relations, 1963.

──────*Global Conflicts and International Relations. The Uncertain Future*. Bamenda: Global Press, 2011.

Gros, Jean –Germain (ed.). Cameroon: *Politics and Society in Critical Perspectives*. America Maryland: University Press, 2003.

Joseph, A Richard. *Radical Nationalism in Cameroon Social Origins of UPC Rebellion*. Oxford: Clarendon Press, 1977.

Joseph, Richard (ed.). *Gaullist Africa: Cameroon under Ahmadou Ahidjo*. Fourth Dimension Publishers, 1976.

Joseph, Richard. *Radical Nationalism in Cameroun*. Oxford: Clarendon Press, 1977.

Kale, Paul M. *Political Evolution in the Cameroons*. Buea: Government Printers, 1967.

Killingray, David and Rathbone, Richard eds. *Africa and The Second World War*.MacMillan Press Ltd, 1986.

Kwast, Llyod E. *The Disciplining of West Cameroon: A Study in Baptist Growth*. Michigan: William Eerdmans Publishing Coy, 1976.

Lantum, Daniel N.*Tribute to Dr. John Ngu Foncha*. Yaoundé: nd. 1999?.

LeVine, Victor T. *The Cameroons from Mandate to Independence*. Los Angeles: University ofCalifornia, 1964.

Loh, Choves. *Ugly Journalism*. Bamenda: n.d.2013.

Lugard, Lord. *The Dual Mandate in British Tropical Africa*. London: Frank Cass & Co. Ltd. 1965.

M'carthy, Frank. *The Wanderings of an APF Organizer*. 1994.

Malcolm, Milne.*No Telephone to Heaven From Apex To Nadir - Colonial Service in Nigeria, Aden, The Cameroons and The Gold Coast 1938-1961*.Meon Hill Press, 1999.

Marwick, Arthur. The Nature of History. London: Macmillan Publishers Ltd., 1985.

Mbile, Nerius N. *Cameroon Political Story-Memories of an Authentic Eyewitness*. Limbe: Presbyterian Printing Press, 1999.

# INDEX

## A

Abdoh, Djalal Dr., - 116
Acha, FonofBatibo, - 52, 53
Achiribi II, Fon of Bafut, - 115
Adametz, Captain, - 51
Administrative Law, - 149
Africa in miniature, - 25
Africa, Central, - 41
African National Congress (ANC), - 111
African Trusteeship Territories, - 90
Afrikaners (Great Trek), - 44
Ahidjo, Ahmadou, - 241 Factor, - 10; Regime, - 73,98, 146, 21, 29; Solid Steps towards a Federal Constitution, - 142; President, - 6, 14,21, 34, 56, 61, 70 – 73, 82, 97, 139-143, 145, 147, 149, 152, 153, 157, 159
Ajaga, Nji, Professor, - 84, 86, 91
Aka Emmanuel, - nothing
All Anglophone Conference (AACI), - 53, 55
Ambo Village, - 53
America, - 88, 90
Anglo-Cameroonian Friendship, - 177
Anglophone, - 16; Cameroon, - 16;
delegates - 16; 57, 67; land mark,
53; and Francophone Regions, - 77; problem - 61-62; at Mount Mary, Buea - 58, 60, 75, 77 sector, 76 ; 135
Anglo-Saxon, legacies, - 3; Minority Needs Protection, - 10
Anlu,- 132
Annexation, - 7, 73, 77, 83, 97, 100, 143, 144, 178
Anyangwe, Carlson, Professor, - 68,81
Ardener, Edwin, - 31
Assale, Charles , - 70, 72, 74
Painful Truth and Arrogance
assimilation, 7
Awolowo, Chief Obafemi,122

Aymerich, Joseph, - 83
Ayuk, Rev. Pastor, - 59
Azikiwe, Benjamin Nnamdi,- 89, 118

**B**

bad faith, - 7, 152, 175, 176, 178, 184
Baforchu, - 52, 54, 55
Bakweri, - 151, 162
Balewa, Abubakar Tafawa , - 62, 63
Bali - German Hegemony and Brutality, - 51
Bali Nyonga, - 52, 54-56, Empire, - 50, 55, Ngyenmbo neighbours, - 54; Chamba, 54
Bamboko, - 45, 104
Bamenda – Grasslanders,- 49; Congress Hall, 1; All Party Conference, - 54; Ecclesiastical Province (BAPEC),- 77, Grasslands, - 19, 41, 44, 48; Station, - 53
Bamileke , - 46, 103, 104
Bamoun, - 103, 104
Bangwa country, - 49
Bantu, Coastal, - 45
Banyo, - 53
Baptist Boys' High School, Abeokuta, - 113
Baptist College, Ndu, - 97, Baptist Missionary, - 97
Based Mission Church, - 55
Bavaria and Prussia, - 67
Beckley, George P, - 99
Belgian Congo, - 79
Belgium, - 78 79, 81
Bile, William Chief (King ) of Bimbia, - 98. Bimbia, - 96
Bismarck, Otto von, - 67, 100
Boys' High School, Abeokuta, - 113
Brigade Mobile Mixte (BMM), - 158
British, Administration, - 17, 20, 38, 73, 128, 159; Southern Cameroons, - 3, 5, 6, 15, 17; Ambassador to Yaoundé, - 14; and French Cameroons, - 87, 94, 160, Colonial Administration, - 4, 17, 20, 31; Colonial Policy – 7, 13, 15, 17, 20, 31, 117, 122; Northern

Cameroons, 3-5, 83, 87, 88, 145, 154, 202, 213, 217; secret papers, - 1, 4, 13, 14, 20, 176, 193; Double Standards, - (nothing came up)
   Brook Mount Mission House, - 102
   Buea Mountain, - 101, 102, 173, 177
   Burnley, Stephen, - 99
   Bush, George - 61, 192

## C

Cameroon, Anglophone Movement (CAM), - 7; Baptist Convention (CBC), - 77; Mountain 89; National Federation (CNF), - 155, 168, 174; National Union (CNU),156; Protestant College Bali, 100;

Radio and Television Corporation, - 70; United Congress (CUC), - 166, 186; Welfare Union (CWU), - 68, 84, 89, 95; West of the Mungo,- 16, 88; Republic of, - 2,6, 8, 10,67, 157, 170; Youth

   League (CYL), - 89. Cameroonisation, - 133, 134, 136; Policy, - 122
   Cameroons and British Northern Cameroons, - 3
   Canada, - 88, 90, 104; cannibals, - 18
   Casement, Roger, - 102
   Central African Region, - 29, 44
   Central Peoples, - 103
   Chacon, Don Carlos , - 98
   Chilver, EM, - 44
   Clifford Constitution, - 89
   Colonial, Government Treasury, - 46;
   Office, - 13, 40, 106, 110, 129, 133, 199, 201, 213, 223
   Communist Russia, - 192
   Congo Brazzaville, - 82, 111
   Conrau, Gustav, - 49, 50
   Conspiracy Theories, - 13, 192
   CPNC opposition, - 107, 109

## D

Declassified British secret papers, - 1, 4, 13, 14, 20, 176, 193
Democates Camerounais (DC), - 154
Deputy Commissioner of Southern Cameroons, - 14- 15, 20
Dibongue, RJK, - 26, 39, 62, 95, 150
Dinga, A, - 132
Dobell, - 83
Down Beach Victoria (Limbe), - 102
Dual Mandate, - 117


# E
Eden Xtra Magazine, - 12
Efange, Peter M, - 147
Egbe, Emmanuel Tabi, - 150, 176, 178
Ekotie-Eboh, Chief Festus , - 20, 35, 68, 70, 71, 77, 120, 142-149, 152, 163, 167, 179, 198, 200, 207, 217, 228
Elad, Ekontang , - 10, 186;
Elder Dempster, - 10, 23
ELF SEREPCA, - 10, 143
Emens Textiles, - 95, 96, 98, 102
Emergency Laws, - 13, 16
Endeley, EML as Leader of Government Business - 1
Evolved Political Culture, - 95, 103, 123


# F
Fanso, Verkijika G., - 175
Federal Inspectorates, - 160
Federal Constitution, - 21, 34, 62-64, 162.
Federal Republic of Cameroon (FRC), - 1, 10, 14, 91, 143
Federal Republic of Nigeria, - 10
Federation of Nigeria, - 111
Fernando Po (Malabo), - 85, 87-88
Field, Johnson O, - 14, 38, 116, 128
Fiftieth Anniversary Celebrations, - 1
Fokum, Tita , - 51
Fomuso, John, - 55, 56

Fonlon, Bernard, - 12, 136, 164

Fonyonga II of Bali, - 52

Foumban Constitutional Conference,- 16, 20, 60, 71, 120, 126, 144, 145, 147, 160, 178, 179, 207

France Overseas, - 91, 93

Francophone, - 28, 34, 35, 42, 57, 69, 73, 74, 77, 85, 122, 175, 210, Members of

Parliament, - 73; politicians, - 67

French, Cameroon, - 6, 18, 42, 45, 68, 70, 81, 83, 84, 87, 88, 90, 93-95, 111, 114, 139, 169, 179, 203, 211, Welfare Union (FCWU) - 88; colonial policy, - 92, 94; Overseas Community, - 68; Policy of Assimilation - 91; Union – 91, 94, 144

Frenchy people, - 18

Functional History, - 191

Futa Jalon Mountains, - 44

# G

Gabon , - 82

Galega I, Fon of Bali Nyonga, - 33, 48, 117, 206

Gauteng Legislature, - 111

GCE Board, - 28, 59

German, Basel Mission, - 103; colonial plantation, - 63; colonial policy, - 46, 54; flag, - 82, 97, 100; Government, - 47, 48, 100; Kamerun, - 3, 80, 82, 83, 97, 187; legacy: Quest for Robust "Native Labour" - 46; plantation interest, - 47; plantation labour policy, - 46, 65; plantations, - 43, 46, 209

Germany, - 65, 67, 81-84, 87, 178

Glauning, Captain Hans, - 52, 53

God's Little Devotional Book for Graduates, - 181

Gold Coast, (Ghana), - 20, 46, 94

Golden Age, - 28, 105, 137

Golden Age of Southern –West Cameroon, - 137; Golden Jubilee, - 1, 2, 146

Grand Camarade, - 139, 157, 158

Grass, Fields, - 45, 47; Landers – 32, 44, 54, 57, 63; lands, - 19, 31, 34, 40, 41, 44, 48, 54, 56

Grassland and Forest, - 32
Great Britain, - 3, 9, 10, 78, 81, 90, 97, 100
Greater France, - 91
Green Tree Accord, - 77
Gwan-"Fogbe" "Mesia", - 56


**H**
Halle , Lawyer Nico, - 35
Hewett, Edward Hyde, Her Majesty's Consul, - 99, 100
Hippocratic Oath, - 14
Historical Panorama, - 1; historiography, - 2, 189, 190
Hope Waddell Institute Calabar, Nigeria, - 113
House of Assembly, Federal, - 73, 175
House, of Assembly,- 9, 21; of Chiefs, - 9, 20, 73, 94, 148, 175, 235
Houses of Assembly, East and West Cameroon, - 73
Hutter, Captain Franz, - 52


**I**
Ibadan, Government College, - 112. Indirect Rule, - 84, 90, 93, 117, 128, 129
Ivory Coast, - 61, 109, 127


**J**
Jamaican Mission, - 96
Johnson, Thomas H, - 99
Johnson, Willard. – 32, 44, 103, 162; Johnson, William, - 99
Johnston, Harry, - 102
Joseph, Michael, - 99
Jua, Augustine Ngom, - 112, 203


**K**
Kale, Paul M, - 89, 112, 121, 242

Kamerun Idea, - 5, 45, 104, 179; National Congress (KNC), - 5, 26, 89; National Democratic Party (KNDP), - 13; People's Party, - 90; United National Congress, (KUNC), - 88, 89

Kemcha , Peter M., - 121, 144, 223

King, CE, the British Ambassador to Yaoundé, - 14.

King, Leopold II, - 79; William, - 96, 98, Bell and Akwa, - 97, 100

Kingue , Abel, - 124, 125

Klerk, Frederic W. de, - 61

KNC/KPP alliance, - 40, 41, 62, 110, 116, 119, 131

KNDP opponents, - 40, 107

Kobinyang, - 54

Kpe-Mboko Group, - 45

## L

Lagos, - 39, 41, 46, 62, 89, 113, 221

laissez passer, - 84

Le Temoin', Le Patriote , - 70

League of Nations Mandate, - 3

Legislative Assembly, - 9, 235-238

Littoral and Western Regions, - 37

London Baptist Missionary Society, - 99, 103; long pens (crayons), - 111

Lower Ashong, - 53

Loyalty to Endeley, - 38

## M

Macpherson Constitution, - 89, 118

Malawi, - 44, 79

Malcolm Milne, - 13, 15-21, 38, 69, 104-108, 112, 118, 126, 129-132, 137, 171, 177, 178, 223, 242

Malcolm Milne, Glowing Tribute, - 131

Man O'war Bay, - 96

Mandela, Nelson, - 61

Mankon, - 17, 26, 31, 54, 56, 108, 119, 120, 149, 185

Maquizzards, Rebels, Nationalists, Freedom Fighters, - 122, 127

Marcelina Sylvester, 99; marginalization, - 7, 67
Marketing Board, - 42, 97
Mazrui, Ali, - 110
Mbene, GJ, - 89
Mbida, Andre Marie, - 103, 114, 139, 154
Mbile, Nerius Namaso, - 112, 113
Mbinglo, Fon of Nso, - 117
McCormac, Fr. Arthur, - 76
Members of Parliament, - 9, 73, 143, 161
Men – of – War ships, - 98
Merrick, Joseph, - 96, 97
Mfecane (or Shaka Wars), - 44
Minister of Arts and Culture, - 1
Minor Seminary at Akono, - 114
Mobutu Sassa Seko Wazabanga, - 128
Moghamo, - 46, 52-55
Mokam, David - 110
Mondoleh Island, - 102
Moor Plantation, Ibadan, - 113
Motomby Ndembo Woleta , - 112, 113
Moumie, Roland Felix, - 114, 123-125
Mount Mary, Buea, - 58, 60, 75, 77
Moussa Yaya, - 156, 161, 165, 166, 168, 171, 172, 179, 204
Mozambique, - 44
Mukong, Albert Womah, - 117, 119, 127, 147, 176, 185, 241
Muna, Solomon Tandeng , - 112
Munzu, Simon, - 68
Murdock, - 32

# N
Nachtigal, Gustav Dr, - 97, 100
Nachtigal, Eugen Dr, 89
Namme, NN, - 89
National Order- in-Council, - 134

National, Assembly of la Republique du Cameroun, - 71, 72; Congress of British West Africa (NCBWA) - 94;Council of Nigeria and Cameroons (NCNC), - 89, 94

Native, Administration (NA), - 117, 129; Authorities, - 90, 91, 118

Ndi, Anthony, - 57, 182-186, 188

Neu Kamerun – 80, 82

New Zealand, - 88

Ngoh, Jean Claude, - 150, 151

Ngoh, Victor Julius, Professor, - 1, 12, 182, 195-197

Ngu, John Foncha, - 155

Nigeria, - 3, 39; and British Cameroonian nationalists - 94; Federal Elections - 5, political party, 80; Youth League, (NYL), - 89

Nji, Ajaga, - 84, 86, 91

Nkomfe Mandla, 99

Nkrumah, Kwame, - 94

Nkwenti , Wilfred, - 26, 151, 161, 170

North and South West Provinces, - 10

Northern Cameroons, - 3-5, 83, 87, 88, 145, 154, 202, 213, 214, 217

Northern Elements Progressive Union, - 4

Northern Kamerun Democratic Party" (NKDP), - 4;

Northern People's Congress (NPC), - 4

Northwest hegemony, - 37

Nyobe, Reuben Um, - 114, 122, 125

Nzoh-Ekhah Nghaky, - 165

## O

O'Neil, Bob, (Robert) - 46, 47, 53, 54

Obama, Barrack, US President, - 61

Okala, Charles, - 179

Old Moghamo Trade Friends, - 223

One Party system (Partie Unifie), - 52

Operation cale cale, - 119, 139, 161, 168, 172

Organisation of African Unity (OAU), - 149

Ottawa, - 31

Ouandie, Ernest, - 104

## P

Partie Unifie, - 138, 153, 155, 163
Partition of German Kamerun, - 83
Peaceful, Harmonious Transfer of Power in 1959, - 116; Percival, John, - 16-18, 34, 107, 108
Phillipson, Sir Sydney, - 22
Policies: Socio-Economic and Political, - 93
Political Leaders, High Calibre, - 118
Political Maturity, - 105, 107
Presbyterian Church in Cameroon (PCC), - 77
Presidential Decision, - 35 press-ganged, - 43
Prestation, - 84, 92
Printania, - 97
Priso, Soppo, - 61, 197, 202
Privy Councillors, - 56
Pseudo-History, - 192
Public, Apologies, - 58, 61; Service Commission, - 9, 133

## Q

Qaddaffi, Muammar, - 127, 129
Quan, Eric D., - 132, 162
Quasi, Federal State, - 94; status, 8
Quebec, - 104
Queen of England, - 98

## R

Ramsay, Captain, - 50. Raw Deal, - 25, 118, 195-197, 206
Referendum, - 6, 11, 35, 71, 73, 94, 226
Refused Independence, - 9
Regional Symposium, - 1
Republic of Cameroon, - 108
Reunification, - 6
Revolution, - 6, 11, 81, 152, 160, 168
Richard's Constitution, - 89, 117, 118
Rio del Rey, - 96, 99

Rogozinski, (Pole), - 102, 103
Roman Catholic Mission (RCM), - 111
Ronan, Williams, Canterbury Archbishop, - 61

## S

Sacred trust, - 128
Safari, - 44
Saker, Alfred, - 97, 99, 101
Saker's Hinterland Vision, - 101
Salvation Army School, Lagos, - 89, 113
Second Option, - 126
Sekou Touré, Mohammed, - 94
Sengat-Kuo, François, - 169
Senior Divisional Officer, (SDO), - 128
Slavery, - 53, 55, 93
South West Region, - 8, 32, 37, 45
South West, Conference of Chiefs, - 37
Elite Association (SWELA), - 37
South- Westerners, - 7, 36, 57
Southern Cameroons 3, 4, 5, 10, 13, 15-18, 21, 35, 65
Soviet Socialist Republics (USSR), - 79
St. Charles' TTC Onitsha, - 113
St. Francis' Teachers' Training College, Fiango, Kumba, - 111
St. Joseph's College Sasse, - 76, 111
St. Peter's Teachers Training College, Bambui, 111
Standard Six Certificate, - 106, 111
Summit Magazine interview 1-2

www.ingramcontent.com/pod-product-compliance
Lightning Source LLC
Chambersburg PA
CBHW051353290426
44108CB00015B/1988